FINDING FREEDOM

THE ROSE CITY SERIES
BOOK TWO

VALENTINA BURNS

Editing by: Jacqui Nelson

Proofreading by: Erin Delude and Jacqueline Wedick

Cover design by: Books and Moods Graphic Design

ISBN electronic book: 978-1-7389724-9-4

ISBN print book: 978-1-7389724-8-7

For the silent—and the not so silent—majority

*And for everyone who's ever been made to feel like they don't
deserve a happy ending.
You do. I promise you, you do.*

AUTHOR'S NOTE

Finding Freedom is a story about life after sexual assault. While the sexual assault happens off page, there are vivid memories, depictions, nightmares, and discussion of what happened. I am very aware that sexual assault is something that has affected most women in one way or another. This story is not meant to be a reflection of every woman's experience. This is very much Ivy's story. This entire series is based on my own personal experiences, the experiences of those very close to me, and are the stories I needed to tell.

What I hoped to achieve in this book, and in this entire series, is to show the ripple effect of sexual assault. To show that this is something that alters the life of many people. If you aren't an Ivy, you are a Hope, or a Sean, or a Joel. We all know someone who has been impacted by sexual assault, even if we think we don't. As a society, it is all of our responsibility to try to change the course of the future, so that no one ever has to be afraid to go to a party, or walk to their car at night, or wear a certain outfit, or the many other things many women are afraid to do because they have been conditioned to anticipate the consequence before it even happens. It should not be a consequence anyone should have to anticipate.

Finding Freedom is about Ivy's freedom from the chain that has tied her to the assault she suffered for too long. But it is also a story of hope that we can live in a future free of sexual assault and fear.

This is not a book that everyone might be ready to read. Please note and consider the following content warnings:

- Sexual assault that has happened three years in the past (off page)
- Memories, nightmares, and conversations around the assault (on page)
- Main character being triggered by certain reactions and movements

Additional trigger warnings:

- Death of a parent from cancer (off page in the past)
- Sibling who has been in prison
- Graphic, consensual, sexual content
- Side character who is trying to conceive

CHAPTER ONE

In order to maintain her sanity, Ivy Harrington always started her run forty minutes before sunrise. A practice she'd started almost three years ago, during her final semester of college.

What had begun as an experiment to overcome her fear of the dark quickly became habit, with the side benefit of clearing the fog from her mind after her typically restless nights so she could face the day. Since she'd never been one for long conversations or counseling sessions, her pre-dawn run also became her preferred form of therapy.

Lifting her face to the sky, she concentrated on the moment. The hushed rhythm of her feet on the pavement. The rush of air moving in and out of her lungs. The fresh smell of early autumn trees heightened by the water. The caress of the cool air on her sweat-slicked skin.

As per her ritual, she completed her routine as the sun broke across the Willamette River, illuminating Portland's West Coast magnificence in a fiery burst of color.

The sight filled her with a rare sense of hope, and though it passed as quickly as the daybreak—vibrant and alive for an instant—that brief time was always worth it. Because when those first tendrils of orange, red, and yellow crawled into the sky, Ivy allowed herself to believe that maybe there was a light at the end of her tunnel. And not an oncoming train.

She never understood why people slept through these precious few minutes of the day.

All in all, this was the best part of her day, and by the time she arrived back at her building, she'd slowed to a walk, feeling like she'd shed a layer of dead skin. As light infiltrated the city, she clung to the last of the silence, knowing that when she next came outside, her world would be raucous with the hustle of Portlanders tackling their Monday morning.

Stopping outside her building, she did a quick shoulder check to see who was around her before she faced the wall. Using it as resistance, she pressed her foot against the stone, feeling the gratifying stretch run up her calf. Ivy loved this building; it stood on the corner of a popular intersection in the Pearl District and had been renovated a decade or so ago. The beautiful brick facade set it apart from the surrounding buildings. Its uniqueness drew notice constantly, but that wasn't the only thing that had people flocking. The bar on the street level, Bowie's, was very popular with the locals, and it always brought in a good crowd, especially on weekends.

She'd been lucky to rent one of the two apartments above the bar and had no plan to move anytime soon. Oddly, the bar's noise and crowds didn't bother her. In fact, like the dark, she enjoyed it. Living in the city's heartbeat allowed her to fade in and out of her surroundings without anyone paying much attention. It wasn't that she didn't like being around people. Like most, she had a social bucket that needed topping up, but overall, she preferred being alone. She'd grown up a lone wolf and had gotten used to it.

Unlocking the building's front door, she took a final glance over her shoulder before she jogged up the stairs to her apartment. Out of habit, she peeked at the door across from hers and it stared back, the silence mocking her. The opposite of last midnight when female laughter had echoed in this same hallway, waking Ivy from an unusually deep sleep.

At the time, she'd tiptoed to her own door and stared through the peephole, taking in the scene of a drop-dead gorgeous woman wrapping herself around an equally stunning man, drawing out an obviously reluctant goodbye. Reluctant on the woman's behalf. Ivy happened to know that the man was probably trying to get her out of his place as quickly as possible. He had a kickboxing class to teach at six the next morning, and he wasn't one to arrive sleep deprived or anything less than on top of his game.

Ivy knew this because she knew him well. Sean Thompson. Friend, business partner, neighbor, and hottest man she knew in the flesh. Ivy had watched through her peephole, as Sean carefully disentangled the curvy brunette's arms from his broad shoulders and escorted her toward the stairs down to the front exit. Her flirtatious giggles ringing in their wake.

It shouldn't have bothered her. But last night's rendezvous had caught her off guard because, regardless of the many women who flirted with Sean, she'd seen no evidence of them since he'd moved in across the hall—five months ago after his best friend, Gabe Walsh, left the apartment to live in a house with her best friend, Hope Morgan.

At the gym, and at Bowie's it was a free-for-all, with women eyeing Sean as brazenly as Ivy eyed barbecue chips in the grocery store's snack aisle. But here at their apartments, she'd never seen or heard a woman come or go from his place. Not until last night. And now that it had happened, she realized she didn't like it. She couldn't place the feeling that had settled in the pit of her stomach since she'd seen the woman with her flawless hair and musical laugh, wrapped around Sean like a pretzel; but whatever it was, it sucked.

As she took a quick post-run shower, she reminded herself that she had absolutely no reason to be anything but friends with Sean. But she couldn't fight the wave of inexplicable irritability that rose within her. So much for her centering pre-dawn run.

When she'd first arrived in Portland, fresh out of college, Sean had given her a chance and rented her the space in his gym for her physiotherapy clinic. Despite his lean, mean, fight-ready physique, he'd been friendly, sweet, and completely non-aggressive from the moment they'd met. Combined with his dominant persona and protective nature, being around him had soothed her like aloe on a burn.

During their time working closely together in the gym, often discussing the needs of clients, they'd developed an unexpected friendship. Unexpected because Ivy wasn't good at building relationships of any kind.

And when he'd begun training her in kickboxing, their friendship had turned into a bond, and despite herself, she'd started to trust him. Which was an even bigger deal than making a friend because she could count on one hand the number of people she trusted. Eventually, they'd started hanging out outside of work, and their relationship fell into a natural flow. Somewhere along the line, it had started to feel like Sean was hers.

He was hotter than sin and a genuinely nice guy. Basically, the rarest of all species, so of course the ladies flocked to him. But he didn't flaunt them, and for the most part Ivy could pretend they weren't there.

They'd blissfully meandered along in their comfortable but platonic friendship, because she couldn't offer him more than that. Not that he'd ever so much as hinted he wanted more.

And she was okay with that. More than okay.

Then last night had happened, and now it looked like the tide was finally turning, and her happy, safe, platonic thing was ending. Which made her grumpy. By the time she pulled up to the gym in her hatchback, the zen buzz from her run had completely worn off, and the two cups of coffee she'd downed hadn't taken the edge off. She pushed through Thompson Kickboxing's main entrance and strode past the reception desk without making eye contact with the woman behind it.

"Hey girl!" Erica's voice floated jovially through the air, landing in Ivy's vicinity.

She grunted in acknowledgement and kept walking. She turned left and headed to her physio clinic, scanning the gym on autopilot for Sean, even though she knew he was in the back studio teaching a class.

Walking through the clinic, she entered the small room off to the side that served as her office, she dumped her duffle bag and folders onto her cluttered desk, then plopped down behind her desk and switched on the computer.

She'd skimmed half the morning's emails when she registered a movement at the door in front of her. Lifting her head at the same time as the smell of coffee hit her nostrils, she let out a breath, allowing the stiffness to release from her shoulders.

"You're crankier than usual this morning." It was Erica

again. She was one of the trainers at the gym who sometimes moonlighted as the receptionist. She was sweet and pleasant at the front desk, but a major ass-kicker in class.

Ivy took Erica's kickboxing classes when Sean's were full. Or when she was in the mood for a drill sergeant. Essentially, they saw each other every day, and Erica had come to know Ivy's nuances well. She handed Ivy a steaming mug of coffee.

"Am not," Ivy grumbled before taking a long sip of coffee, then rolling her eyes in ecstasy. "God, what is it about this stuff that's so satisfying? It heals all that ails."

"See," Erica said. "Something ails you. Spill." She cocked her hip against Ivy's desk and crossed her arms, looking every inch the knockout she was. Erica belonged on the cover of an elite women's sportswear magazine. She was tall and toned, with a wild crown of black curls and smooth skin that looked perpetually glowing.

For the most part, Ivy didn't bother envying other women's looks, mostly because no good ever came from the comparison game. But Erica had a stop-dead-in-your-tracks-and-stare-shamelessly beauty, with a radiant confidence to match, and it was hard not to want that. Especially the confidence. If Erica wasn't so damn nice and cool to boot, Ivy might even resent her for it, but she didn't. Erica was too genuine, like Sean. As if altruism was their natural state of being. And the fact that they were both insanely good looking was simply coincidental.

With her cranky attitude and hard shell, Ivy was the odd one out in this gym by a landslide. And even though she didn't deserve them, she was grateful both Erica and Sean were in her life. Especially Sean. If she was the darkness, he shone the light.

Would he be seeing the late-night bombshell again tonight?

"Earth to Ivy Harrington." Erica nudged Ivy's chair with her leg. "What's up with you today, girl?"

"Nothing," Ivy mumbled. What could she say? That Sean might have a new girlfriend, and she was jealous? Right, that would go over well. Especially since she most definitely was not jealous. Not even close.

"Have you seen Sean today?" she asked without thinking.

Erica paused, staring down at her with big brown eyes. Then a slow smile broke out over her full lips and her nose crinkled endearingly, showing off the sprinkle of freckles that lay there. "Oh, I see."

Ivy shifted her attention back to her computer. "You see nothing. There's nothing to see. It was just a question. I have a client coming in at nine who trained with Sean pre-injury. I wanted to know if he was here so I could touch base."

"Uh huh."

"What, uh huh? There's no 'uh huh' okay."

"Girl, you've had it as bad for that man as he's had it for you since you walked into this place. And now that he's moved in beside you, the tension is only getting stronger. I mean, I can practically feel it."

Ivy shoved back in her chair and looked up. "What tension? There's no tension. Sean is a friend. That's it."

Erica opened her mouth to say something but was interrupted by a tap on the door. Both Ivy and Erica swiveled their heads to see who it was, and Ivy's jaw hit the floor.

"Excuse me," said none other than the hallway bombshell from the night before. "I'm looking for Sean." When neither Ivy or Erica answered, she added, "Sean Thompson."

Ivy blinked, as Hallway Bombshell stepped forward in the awkward silence, looking totally out of place in a gym wearing a sexy wrap-around dress that showed off her cleavage and holding a plate of what looked to be fresh homemade cookies.

"Um..." The woman glanced over her shoulder as if looking for something they might be gawking at. "I waited at reception, but no one was there, so I came a bit further and saw this office. I don't think I'm in the wrong place. I mean, his name is on the gym, after all." She laughed, and the familiar musical sound hit Ivy like a punch to the throat.

Erica recovered first. "I am so sorry. It's my day at reception. I brought Ivy coffee, and we got carried away talking." She offered a brilliant smile. "We didn't mean to be rude, it's only that Sean doesn't often have his girlfriends bring him cookies to the gym."

Hallway Bombshell threw back her glorious head of thick hair, and laughed. "Oh no, I'm not his girlfriend. I mean, I wish. He's a work of God that man is. Finest I've ever seen. But I'm only here with a peace offering." She lifted the plate of cookies higher. "I think I may have accidentally crossed some lines last night, and I didn't want to come across as disrespectful."

The beautiful mystery woman's dark eyes shifted to Ivy. "You're Ivy?" she asked sweetly.

Ivy searched for a sign of bitchiness in her tone, but there was only genuine kindness dripping off the woman. She was bloody perfect.

Ivy nodded stiffly, wondering why in the hell this woman appeared to recognize her name. Hallway Bombshell's head bobbed sagely as she offered a low "mmhmm" that purred sexily from her throat, which only confused Ivy more, before the woman thrust her plate of cookies into Erica's hands.

"Well, can you tell Sean that these are from Tina?" She turned to leave, but paused to add, "Tell him he can keep the plate." Then she winked and sashayed her perfect apple bottom right out Ivy's clinic.

Erica angled her whole body toward Ivy in one slow motion. "Okay. What was that?"

Ivy, who was still reeling from the fact that the woman from last night had appeared in her office with a plate of baked goods, knowing her name, shrugged.

Erica stared at her for another beat before she burst into laughter. "Holy cow! I mean, she was a ten! No, more like an eleven." Erica snagged a cookie off the plate and shoved half into her mouth. "I definitely need to hear this story," she said through a full mouth as she walked to the office door. "I'm gonna find Sean and get the deets. I'll fill you in over lunch, k?" And with that, she departed, leaving Ivy alone and baffled.

Questions rolled through her head at rapid speed along with an odd feeling of relief mixed with dread. If Hallway Bombshell wasn't Sean's girlfriend, why had she brought him homemade cookies? As a peace offering? For what? Being a knockout? Keep the plate? Was she kidding? Would he really not want to see her again? And most importantly —why did the woman know her name?

She definitely needed deets, and it couldn't wait until lunch.

CHAPTER TWO

"One more set, bro. You got this," Sean said encouragingly to Jason, one of the guys he trained regularly.

It was strength training day, and Sean had him on the bench press. They had upped the weight, so Jason was sweating bullets and grunting like a pig. Sean hoped he'd get through the set without dropping the bar on his neck, but he stood braced and ready behind him at the bench, just in case.

Eight strained and shaky reps later, Sean helped Jason return the bar to its cradle. "Good job. You'll feel it tomorrow, but it's progress."

From the bench, Jason groaned. Sean chuckled. Most people thought six-packs came easy. One of his greatest pleasures was setting up a training program that proved them wrong while delivering results. In Sean's experience, the best things took the most work to attain, and it was good to be reminded of that from time to time.

"Okay, water break. I'll meet you in the ring in five." He lifted his gaze from the sweaty, exhausted male flopped across the bench to lock eyes with the most piercing blue he'd ever seen.

Every time he saw them was like a sucker punch to the gut. That perfect ice blue, so light they were nearly white, set under dark brows, and against soft pale skin, framed with thick, dark lashes. He'd never get used to the effect it had on him. Or the woman strutting up to him with a confidence that belied her guarded nature.

He gave himself a mental shake. *Get your head out of the gutter man, she's not interested.*

Understatement of the year. As far as he knew, Ivy wasn't interested in anyone romantically. Ever. And he'd added it to the list of the many things he worried about when it came to her. Her fear of men, her chronic angst, the way she was constantly on guard, her lack of sleep, her relentless pursuit of physical strength. Her aversion to cheese. His list was a mile long. The only thing that counterbalanced his worry was his attraction to her. And since the incident at Bowie's five months earlier when she and Hope had been accosted by some slimy blast from the past, coupled with Sean now living right across from her, both his worry and his attraction had amplified. He needed to find a happy medium, and he needed to find it fast.

"Thompson," she said to him by way of acknowledgment, stopping in front of him.

Ivy had the smoke and mirror effect down better than anyone he knew. On the outside, she came across as fierce, tough, and mildly bad-tempered, but on the inside was an uncertainty and mistrust that left her deeply vulnerable. Too vulnerable, and he hated not knowing what caused it. Because if he didn't know, he couldn't fix it.

One thing he did know was, he had to tread carefully. Pushing her for information about her past—or anything—

would only make her run. Or fight. If she wasn't running, she was fighting.

And with that in mind, Sean braced himself and said, "Hey, what's up?"

Her gaze darted everywhere but him. When she glanced over her shoulder, he scanned the people behind her, as he was prone to do whenever she did these frequent shoulder checks, to see what she might consider a threat to her.

There was no one as far as he could tell. So why did she appear nervous? And not the scared kind of nervous but the hesitant kind, which was weird because while she was many things around him, nervous wasn't often one of them.

A few more awkward seconds passed before she said, "So, um, I've got Smith coming in at nine."

Dylan Smith was an amateur fighter who'd trained with Sean for the last few years. He'd received a nasty concussion a couple months back during a fight and since then had been rehabbing with Ivy. They frequently discussed Smith's therapy, so bringing him up wasn't unusual. But Sean knew that Smith wasn't what this was about. Call it his Ivy intuition.

"Oh yeah?" Sean said. "He's still making good progress?"

She twisted her hands. Something was definitely up, and it wasn't the concussed welterweight.

"Yeah, he should be ready to return to the ring soon." She shuffled her feet.

Interesting.

"You okay, Ivy?" he finally asked.

Her eyes immediately shot up to his, defensiveness written all over them. Now this was more like the Ivy he knew.

"Of course, I'm okay," she shot back.

His mouth quirked in a smile, relieved to see her acting herself again.

"You smell like cookies." She sniffed, tilting her head to the side, nose up.

Ah, so that's what this was about. He'd wondered if she'd met Tina when she'd visited earlier today. Erica had been too busy mocking him when she'd delivered the plate of chocolate-chip cookies to mention anyone else being present.

Sean sighed inwardly. Here was the complicated thing between him and Ivy. She appeared to avoid having, or wanting, any kind of a romantic relationship. Yet, she seemed to hate the idea of him having women in his life. Her frosty attitude made that clear anytime anyone made the faintest pass at him.

He reacted the same way whenever he witnessed another dude flirt with her. Like Greg-Fucking-Lewis, who was the biggest flirt in his gym. But luckily for him, Ivy was more than capable of putting off unwanted male attention. Unlucky for him, he was uncertain how much of his or any male attention she might actually be interested in.

Which left them suspended in this non-relationship where they were closer than typical friends, but hadn't yet crossed the boundary into the territory of real intimacy. That was pretty much the point where Ivy's walls went up— and stayed up.

So, over the last couple of years, they'd fallen into a comfortable, non-sexual, but not quite platonic (at least not in his fantasies), emotionally complicated, pseudo-relationship that he'd come to accept and embrace because one thing he wasn't willing to do was give her up.

"You met Tina," he deduced, smirking in satisfaction

because, hell, he couldn't help it. Every once in a while, he liked to see Ivy squirm.

She shrug dramatically. "She seems nice." Then her gaze darted around again. "I heard her last night. Um, in the hall." Her gorgeous crystal-blues dropped to the floor. "Sounds like you two had a great time."

Shit. Guilt tugged at his heart. Fun was over. He nudged her chin up with his finger until she met his gaze. "Tina is an old friend. I ran into her in the bar last night, we had a couple beers, talked for a bit, then I ordered her an Uber when things wound down. She followed me up to my apartment, where I let her wait—in the hallway—until the car arrived to pick her up." Fuck, he'd never needed to explain himself to a woman the way he did to Ivy.

She held eye contact as if she was reading him for honesty. Then she blinked, and all of her apprehension vanished.

She smiled, a bit shyly. "They were good cookies. I grabbed one off the plate in your office."

Sean smiled, relieved that she trusted him so freely now, because he knew it didn't come easily for her. He'd worked years to earn that trust. If it was all he'd ever get from her, it was worth it.

"They were pretty damn good. Might call her a ride more often." This earned him a hard shove in his shoulder. He rolled with it, chuckling.

"Hey, you want to come over tonight for takeout and True Detective?" She asked.

Monday night crime shows were their weekly tradition. He brought the pizza. She got the tub of ice cream and two spoons. He was about to say yes—*wanted* to say yes, had the word on the tip of his tongue—when he remembered he had a date. A real, official date. One he'd been hoping to avoid telling her about because it was meaningless, but he'd gotten himself roped into it regardless. It was a blind date. He couldn't remember the last time he'd been on one of those, if ever. But he'd be on one tonight.

He was taking out the sister of one of his master coaches, and honestly, he still couldn't fucking believe how it happened—out of his best intentions.

Donovan Saunders was one of his best trainers, but in the last couple of months he'd been slacking on his own training. Not quite lazy, but not pushing himself as hard as Sean expected from his elite staff. When Donovan had asked him one afternoon if Sean would take his sister out, Sean had thought that it might be the motivation Donovan needed to push his ass a little harder. So he'd laughed and said, "Sure, if you knock me down I will."

He'd hoped it would spur Donovan on, motivate him to put in the effort it took to take on someone like Sean in the ring. He hadn't expected the bastard to take him down in the third round.

Donovan had promised it would be a one-night thing saying, "She never gets out, man. It's not healthy. You don't need to put a ring on it, just get her out of the house. That's all." And Sean had given his word, so he was going to follow through on it.

He'd set the date for tonight, figuring a Monday would be less pressure on everyone. And he'd convinced himself that there was no reason he shouldn't date. It might even be good for him. Get him out of this weird thing that he'd gotten himself into with Ivy.

Looking at her now, thinking about how nice an evening with her on the couch eating takeout and watching bad TV would be, he regretted the whole thing all over again.

"I can't," he finally managed. "I've got—" Shit, why was

this hard? He wasn't being a dick because he and Ivy weren't a thing. He took a breath and went for it. "I made other plans for tonight."

"Plans? Like a date?" Her eyes narrowed slightly. Vaguely accusing.

A surge of defensiveness filled him. Did she think he'd always be ready and available? That he didn't have a life of his own? Damn, is this what it had come to? He scrubbed a hand over his head and down the back of his neck. Maybe this date was the best thing for both of them.

"Yeah." He nodded. "A date."

Disappointment swamped her eyes. As quickly as it came, it was gone.

"Of course. No problem." She made a show of looking at her wristwatch. "Well, I've gotta go. Dylan will be here any second. I'll see you around." She turned on her heel and strode back to her physio clinic.

Sean dropped his head between his shoulders. This was so fucked up. He couldn't keep going down this road. He needed to stop the game they were playing. Either he had to come clean with his feelings for her, consequences and high likelihood of being rejected, be damned. Or he needed to live his life, put himself out there, find a healthy relationship, and forget this mind-boggling adoration and lust he had for Ivy Harrington.

Obviously, there was really only one choice.

CHAPTER THREE

It was almost eight in the evening. Half empty boxes of Asian noodles were littered around her, and a bottle of Pinot Grigio sat on the coffee table. Her best girlfriend, Hope Morgan, was sunk into the cushions of the couch beside her as they watched the newest season of *The Bachelorette*. Despite all this goodness in her current radius, Ivy still couldn't drag herself out of the doldrums.

She sat cross-legged on the couch in her favorite leggings and oversized sweater, staring at the TV, same as she had for the last forty-five minutes, and she couldn't have answered a single question about the episode. Her mind was in another world. A world where Sean's 'other plans' included a beautiful, sexy, confident woman who had her shit together—and could give him everything he wanted and deserved. Like fun, adventure, and orgasms. Probably lots and lots of orgasms.

"Okay, that is the third time in the last half hour you've moaned and hit your head against the sofa," Hope said. "Are you going to tell me what's wrong, or do I have to guess?"

Hope and Ivy had been friends since their college roommate days. They'd been through the best and worst of it together, and Ivy knew she could count on Hope for anything. She had proven herself time and time again—always being there for Ivy and keeping her secrets, even when it almost cost Hope a chance at her own happiness.

Ivy didn't want to bother her with her pathetic insecurities now. Hope was a newlywed, a new stepmother, had a whole life that demanded her attention. It wasn't fair that Ivy emo dump all over Hope anymore.

"It's nothing," Ivy mumbled, stuffing cold noodles into her mouth.

"Right," drawled Hope, grabbing the TV remote and turning down the volume by several notches. "Look, I love fake boy drama as much as the next girl, but I think I speak for women everywhere when I say I prefer *real* boy drama more."

Ivy sent Hope a side-eye. "What makes you think I have boy drama?" she asked through a mouth full of noodles. "Do you know me at all?"

"Yes. I do know you, Ivy. In fact, I wager that I know you better than anyone. So, I think I'm spot on when I say that something is bugging you, and that something is a man."

"More like lack of man," Ivy muttered, tossing the empty takeout carton onto the coffee table and reaching for the wine. She gestured to Hope's glass with the bottle in offering.

Hope glanced at her empty wineglass, then at the bottle, then back at her wineglass. Finally, she shrugged. "What the hell. After another negative test this morning, I might as well enjoy a glass or two."

A sharp sting of guilt filled Ivy, followed by an even more needling pity. Here she was feeling sorry for herself, as usual, when her friend was dealing with her own heartache.

"I'm sorry, Hope," she said sympathetically, as she poured golden liquid into her glass.

Hope and Gabe had married over the summer in a small ceremony along the Oregon coast. Gabe was a widower with an adorable daughter, Ruby, but Hope and Gabe were eager to expand their family. They'd been trying since the spring, but with no success.

Hope blew out a frustrated sigh. "It's so funny, you know. I spent most of my sexually active life doing everything possible not to get pregnant. I assumed..." she gestured haphazardly toward the TV where a dozen men were vying for the attention of the one woman—dressed in red silk— who sat among them, "that we're all one Fantasy Suite away from an unplanned pregnancy. But then when you actually want it to happen..." She shrugged helplessly. "It never occurred to me that it would be hard, you know?"

Ivy didn't know. The possibility of having children was so far off her radar, she'd never thought about it. She was on the pill, but beyond that she didn't even think about pregnancy, preventing it or otherwise, and since sex wasn't on her radar either, it was currently one worry she didn't have. Which was all part of her bigger problem, she knew. But for now, she placed a comforting hand on Hope's shoulder, rubbing gently. Her problems could wait. Her sympathy needed to be with her best friend.

"Look, I can't pretend to know anything about what you're going through. But I'm here to listen. Maybe these things take time?" She had no idea if that was the right thing to say. No idea what the right thing was, but Hope sniffed a little and offered a small smile.

"You're right. That's what Gabe says too. That it takes time sometimes, that there's no rush. And I know that. We have Ruby, and she's such a gift to us. I need to focus on the good stuff. A baby will come when it's ready. Or not." She shrugged, as if it didn't matter, even though it was obvious that it mattered a whole lot.

"It will." She wished she could guarantee that Hope would get everything she wanted in life. More than anyone else that Ivy knew, Hope deserved happiness the most.

Hope nodded, but a big tear escaped and rolled down her cheek, so Ivy pulled her into a hug.

"I'm sorry," Hope cried into Ivy's shoulder so that the words were muffled. "I know other couples have struggled much longer and have things much harder. I don't know why it's getting to me this much."

Ivy rubbed her friend's back soothingly. "Because you want it that much, Hope. Sure, everyone has a different experience, but this one is yours, and right now it's scary and it sucks. It's okay to feel all the feels on this one."

After a minute, Hope pulled back and swiped the tears from her face with her palm. "Okay, pity party over. Thanks for that. It feels good to let it out once in a while." She used a napkin to mop up the rest of her wayward tears. "But back to you now. You were saying something about lack of men?"

Somehow, it didn't seem right to be discussing the frivolities of her romantic life, or lack thereof, when her friend was dealing with a heartache of her own. "I wasn't really saying anything. I want to talk about you more," she said, mostly because Hope deserved the time and space to talk about the things that bothered her, but also, selfishly, so that Ivy didn't have to talk about the things that bothered *her*.

Hope shook her head adamantly, her eyes dry and clear. "Nope, I'm done. I got it out. It's frustration more than anything right now. It'll happen eventually. In the meantime, Gabe and I will have fun trying." She winked on a smile. Ivy's glass-half-full best friend was back on the saddle. "So, you want a man, Ivy?" Hope asked with a suggestive eyebrow waggle.

"No," came the automatic response. A cop-out more than anything, and she knew it. She also knew that if she wanted anything in her life to change, she'd have to stop with the cop-outs. "Maybe," she added begrudgingly.

"Any man, or one man in particular?" Hope asked, and Ivy knew immediately to whom she was referring.

She wasn't ready to go there, so instead she answered with another truth. "Maybe it's not so much that I want a man. Maybe it's more that I'm tired of being afraid to go for it."

Hope was silent, listening serenely as she sipped her wine. The silence allowed Ivy's train of thought to flow out of her.

"I thought I had it all behind me. I thought that if I made myself strong and learned how to defend myself, then I wouldn't be afraid, but what I didn't count on were all the other things I would still be afraid of that have nothing to do with being attacked."

There were a handful of people who knew that Ivy had been sexually assaulted in college. Hope was one of them. She'd been there the night it happened, and in the aftermath, and for every moment since.

She was as much a part of this journey as Ivy, so Ivy knew Hope spoke with deep understanding when she gently said, "You mean like trust. Intimacy." She set her glass on the coffee table. "Sex."

Ivy dropped her gaze to her lap and nodded. "Yeah," she whispered. "It's not like I don't ever want to have sex again. Heck, I'm just as horny as most twenty-somethings. I see someone I like, and I want to jump on them like any other hot-blooded person." Namely, she wanted to jump on a certain six-foot-five, amazingly muscled but gentle-hearted, specimen of a man who'd been the only one in recent history who got her juices going. "It's been a long while, and the last time was, well, against my will and, you know, ugly, so it's scary to think about going there again. Even if I want to."

"Of course it is," Hope acknowledged. "So maybe it's time you took a leap of faith and worked toward overcoming those fears."

Ivy looked at her dubiously. "Overcome my fear of sex?" She wasn't sure it was possible. How was she ever supposed to go there again with a man and not have it tainted by the horribleness of the past?

Hope nodded. "Yes, and your fear of intimacy. Build on your ability to trust." She spoke so calmly and assuredly that it sounded almost easy. "Take back your sexuality, Ivy."

"How am I supposed to do that? I can't walk up to someone and say 'Hey, you're hot and you seem like a nice guy too. Wanna do it?'"

Hope let out a laugh. "No, not exactly, but maybe find someone you trust and let him help you rediscover your sexuality in a safe, meaningful way. Pick someone you care about and who cares about you and will be gentle with you and go at your pace."

Ivy snorted. "Oh yeah, like that guy actually exists."

Hope raised her eyebrows knowingly, because they both knew that guy actually did exist. And he lived across the hallway.

"I couldn't ask Sean to do that," Ivy murmured, taking a sip of wine to take the edge off the butterflies that had erupted in her stomach at the prospect of rediscovering her sexuality with Sean. She thought of his strong arms around her, hoisting her up his long body so she could wrap her legs around his waist, and took another gulp of wine to ease her suddenly dry throat.

"Ivy, everyone knows Sean has been interested in you for eons."

"He is not." To emphasize her point, she flicked her hand toward the door. "He's out on a date as we speak. With someone who is not me."

"Maybe because you shot him down every time he made any kind of pass at you."

"Sean has not made a pass at me," Ivy declared. She got an incredulous stare in response. "Has he?" she demanded, her mind backtracking through all the moments she and Sean had shared, and there were many.

Hours spent together in the gym, training or consulting on clients. Friday evenings in Bowie's, sharing a drink and talking about the week. After he moved in across the hall, there'd been many nights watching Netflix, eating popcorn, and making bad jokes about the equally bad TV they were consuming. Since she'd come to Portland, she had countless memories that featured Sean. None of them included him making a pass at her. She wasn't that oblivious. Was she?

"Plenty of times. Enough that it's obvious to everyone but you that, yeah, he's just that into you." Hope looked at her meaningfully, arching one of her perfectly groomed eyebrows. "Ivy, he moved in beside you. He didn't have to leave his old place. There was nothing wrong with it. It was closer to the gym than this apartment. But he moved in as soon as Gabe and Ruby moved out. Why do you think that was?"

Ivy hadn't ever thought about it. When she'd heard Sean was moving in she'd been giddy with excitement. She hadn't really questioned why. "It's a two-bedroom?"

Hope rolled her eyes then reached for her wineglass and

downed the contents. She got up and gathered the empty takeout boxes. "Look, I have to go. I told the sitter I'd be back by 9:30, but for the record, I think this is a good plan."

"Plan? Asking Sean to be my fuck buddy is not a plan, Hope." *It's a fantasy.*

Hope pursed her lips, making a face that reminded Ivy she was every inch the aristocrat she'd been raised as. "Don't be crude, Ivy. Not a fuck buddy, more like a friend, who you trust, who is the perfect person to help you reclaim your confidence as a sexually healthy and vibrant young woman." She headed toward the kitchen, pausing only to toss a casual look over her shoulder. "And if anything happens to grow from there, well, then that's a happy consequence, right?"

Right. As if.

Assuming that she actually went ahead with this, and further assuming Sean actually agreed to this ridiculous plan, there was little to no chance that after he saw how insecure and uptight she was when it came to sex, that he'd actually want her. The idea was ludicrous. She knew he cared about her, but a man like him was used to women like Tina. Confident, sensual, warm, open to anything. Ivy, on the other hand, was disgusted at even the thought of having a man kiss her, never mind lie on top of her.

Unless she imagined Sean's lips on her, then she was the opposite of disgusted. The thought of having those firm lips work their way across hers sent heat ricocheting through her body and she got up from the couch to distract herself from the sensation. He'd make it good. She would bet the bank on it, but—there were so many buts. Starting with she most certainly did not know how to make it good for him and ending with he could never know why she had major hang ups in the bedroom.

Ivy shuddered at the notion of Sean finding out what had happened to her. It would change everything, and not in a good way.

A familiar chill replaced the heat as that night three years ago hovered closer to the edges of her memory. She shoved it back. It had been the singular most horrific moment of her entire life, and over the last few years she'd found she did her best when she didn't relive it. When she thought of how her body had betrayed her that day, freezing on her, not even attempting to fight back. When she remembered what had been done to her, it made her skin crawl. Like a horde of ants skittering over her body, leaving a trail of ickiness behind. The sensation always left her with a strong urge to shower, or go for a run until she could shake it off.

Inhaling deeply, she focused on the task of helping Hope put the leftovers in the fridge. She centered her full attention on closing lids and setting glasses in the sink. Slowly, she brought herself back to the present.

No, Sean could never know. She couldn't even imagine how she would tell him. She'd told so few people in her life.

Other than the counselor she saw right after the incident, and Hope's brother who'd been involved in the complicated aftermath of the assault when Hope had nearly been kicked out of college, and Gabe, no one else knew. No one. And the very last person she could face with the truth was Sean. He was too important. She didn't want him to see her ugly side. Her weaknesses were revolting, even to herself.

Which made overcoming them so much more important. Could she really ask Sean to help her get comfortable sexually? And overcome this one massive dread that still lingered inside her? He was her friend. Her *best* male friend.

She trusted him. He'd be gentle and patient with her. A man like Sean Thompson would die before he hurt any woman. She knew that much.

The solution seemed perfect. With Sean's help, she could rediscover the joy of sex. Her sexual experiences didn't have to be haunted by the sole one that had been violent and out of her control. She didn't have to be afraid. Sean could help her get there.

The wheels started turning in her head so loudly Hope must have heard them, because suddenly she was standing in front of Ivy, her jacket already pulled on, purse slung over her shoulder. Her look was knowing.

"Ivy, you deserve to be happy, fully content, and at peace with your body. You deserve to uncover all the delicious pleasure your body is capable of. Living paralyzed by what happened isn't what you deserve. Go for this. Go for him." With the resolute statement, Hope pulled her in for a fierce hug. "I love you," she whispered into Ivy's ear.

Ivy hugged her back, but said nothing. She loved Hope, like a sister, but she'd never told her. She hadn't told anyone. It seemed too—intimate.

"So," Hope drawled as she opened the apartment door. "It's going to be a week. I am volunteering at Ruby's school, and I have the guy coming to reno the basement into a rec room, but—" She broke off when she saw something beyond Ivy's line of sight.

Sometimes it sucked being the short one. Ivy boosted herself up on her tiptoes to see over Hope's shoulder. Past her doorway, across the spacious hallway, Sean was shoving his key into his lock. In slow motion, Hope turned her head to face Ivy, slightly closing the door behind her. Her mouth formed a small "o" shape, her eyes went wide.

This was not good. Ivy knew this look. Hope was formulating an idea that was either poorly timed, ridiculous, or downright bad.

Hope turned fully toward Ivy. "This is perfect. He's home." She pulled out her phone and checked the time. "And it's not even ten. Which means the date sucked."

"That's ridiculous. It's Monday night, so of course the date ended early. He teaches at 6:30 a.m. tomorrow. He's not going to stay out for all hours."

"If it was a good date, he would have," Hope whispered. "Ivy, this is your chance!" Hope's eyes were nearly bugging out of her head with excitement.

"My chance to what?" Ivy asked, because there was no way her friend could actually be thinking what she thought she was thinking.

"To ask him," Hope hissed.

"No," Ivy said matter-of-factly. No way, no how. She needed to formulate a plan first. She couldn't simply go up to Sean without a script and ask him to—

"Ask me what?" came the delicious baritone that Ivy could pick out from a room of a thousand voices. It was coming from right over Hope's shoulder.

Oh shit.

Hope jerked to full height and turned abruptly to face him. Oh dear God, he was right there. Only Hope's tall, willowy body separated Ivy from total humiliation.

CHAPTER FOUR

There was no doubt that Hope was a striking woman. Especially when she was standing directly in front of a man with a smile spread across her perfectly tinted lips in a manner that suggested he was exactly the person she wanted to see. But Sean wasn't interested in Hope, never had been, and not because his best friend had put a ring on it not so long ago. Sean wasn't interested in Hope, or any other woman, including sweet Callie from this evening's date, because he was only interested in the fiery, deeply complex pixie of a woman with haunted blue eyes.

Eyes that were looking up at him from over Hope's shoulder this very minute. And they looked worried. Maybe even a little panicked.

Interesting.

"Ask me what?" he repeated when neither woman made a move to respond.

They continued to stare at him like two deer caught in headlights.

Hope came to first, fully opening the door as she stepped into the hallway to join him. "Oh, you know." She waved her hand flippantly. "We were discussing things and your name came up. Nothing important, really." She cleared her throat and amped up her smile another watt or two. "Well, I should go." She moved to pass Sean, and he retreated a step to let her. "I'm going to pop down to the bar and see if I can sneak a goodnight kiss from my husband before I head home." She looked from Sean to Ivy, then back to Sean. "You two enjoy the rest of your night."

Sean thought he saw her shoot a glare in Ivy's direction before heading to the door at the end of the hallway that led down to Bowie's.

He turned to Ivy, jerking a thumb over his shoulder in the direction Hope had disappeared. "What's up with her?"

Leaning against the door to keep it open, Ivy lifted her free shoulder. "Oh, the usual. Meddling. Interfering. Dictating." She seemed to have recovered from her earlier discomfort. "So, how was your date?"

Sean shrugged. It'd been okay. Donovan's sister, Callie, was a nice girl. She was a bit reserved at first, but once he got her going on a topic she was excited about—her love for nineties horror movies—he found her to be quite chatty. She had been cute, too, with a sprinkle of freckles across her nose and round hips that swayed when she walked. They'd shared a meal, then gone for a stroll along the river. The night had even ended with a pleasant hug and a friendly kiss on the cheek. Overall, a fine date. But he and Callie had both communicated in one way or the other that there wouldn't be another one. She had emphasized that she was busy with work projects, and he simply hadn't offered to call her sometime. He was confident they both knew where they stood.

To Sean's mind, if the feeling wasn't there—the spark,

the chemistry, the interest, whatever you want to call it—then there was no point dragging out another date.

He wasn't opposed to the occasional casual fling with a willing woman, but at thirty-two years of age, he wasn't interested in a relationship he knew from the get-go wasn't going anywhere, it wasn't worth it. And luckily, Callie had come to the same conclusion.

"That shrug doesn't tell me much." A hint of irritation flared in Ivy's eyes. She stepped forward, letting the door shut behind her. Coming almost toe to toe.

"I don't kiss and tell," he returned. Sometimes, pushing her buttons was too irresistible and riling her was too damn easy. He'd expected an eyeroll, maybe even a shove in the shoulder, or some sort of verbal insult. What he hadn't expected was her piercing look of hurt.

"You kissed her?" she whispered, taking a step back so that her spine was against the closed door. For a moment, she looked utterly betrayed, although the twist of her lips told him, she was clearly fighting to hide it. Ivy was not the kind of woman who let her weaknesses show often. Or ever.

Unable to help himself, he sighed. He couldn't figure her out, and he was getting so tired of trying. He wanted clarity, for both of their sakes.

"Ivy, what is going on?" When she stared up at him silently, he added, "With us." He took a tentative step toward her.

She eyed him warily, so he stopped his approach. Still, he was close enough that the heat coming off her body warmed him, close enough that the scent of her invaded his air space.

"This." He waggled a finger between them. "This thing that we have going on. What is it? Are we just friends? Are we working toward something more? Tell me, Ivy, because it's messing with me, not knowing where we stand and what you want."

He didn't know what she'd say to that, was pretty damned shocked he'd even said it. It was the first time either of them had acknowledged the elephant in the room. As the silence stretched between them, his heart hammered in his chest. Would she play it off and pretend she didn't hear him? Turn around and slam the door in his face?

She didn't do any of those things. Instead, she stunned him stupid by stepping so close that their bodies touched, raising herself up on her tiptoes, and pressing her lips against his in a lightning-quick, featherlight kiss. She retreated instantly and plastered herself back against her apartment door, leaving Sean reeling.

Had Ivy Harrington kissed him? There was still the wet tingling where her mouth had touched his. But then again... It had happened so quickly maybe he'd imagined it.

Ivy stared at him with wide, luminous eyes. Like a trapped doe. She had. She'd kissed him.

Move! His body screamed.

Careful, this is important. His brain cautioned.

This was Ivy. He had to think.

While he stood thinking, Ivy grabbed the doorknob behind her, twisted it open, and took a step backward into her apartment—moving away.

No!

He stopped thinking and let his body react in time with his heart. He reached for her, held her arms lightly, and when he didn't feel any resistance in her, he dipped his head and pressed his lips against hers. He kissed her fully, the way he'd always fantasied about, licking his tongue across the seam of her mouth until it opened for him.

He'd dreamed of this so many times, and it was a thousand times sweeter than he'd ever imagined. Ivy didn't show one hint of the hesitation he was half expecting from her. Instead, she looped her arms around his neck and opened her mouth so he could access more of her. They clung together, tongues dancing, seeking, exploring.

God, she tasted so sweet. He wanted to devour her.

Careful.

From a distant part of his brain that was still functioning, he heard the warning. If he feasted on her the way he wanted to, he'd scare her.

Needing to get a hold of his self-control, he grabbed the last tiny thread of sanity that remained and clung to it.

One more second.

His body had never been this desperate. Her mouth against his unleashed months of yearning inside him, years even. And it took everything to pull back from her.

When he did, her limp body slid down his. She was breathing hard and looked more than a little dazed. Several seconds ticked by before she tilted her face up to his, her crystalline eyes darkened by lust and desire. The dredges of his control wavered.

"That's what you want, Ivy?" His voice was hoarse with need. *Please say yes, please say yes*, he silently begged her.

Sean's heart burst wide open when she offered up a small nod. But after years of doing this dance with her, he needed more than a nod.

"Say it." His voice sounded rough with the intensity of everything he was feeling, but his world had shifted dramatically, and he couldn't keep the emotion out of it.

Ivy straightened, her shoulders squaring as she regained some of her composure. "I want this." Her voice was clear and determined. Her eyes had refocused, and she moved away from him. Not a full step, but enough that there was space between their bodies. "But only this."

The romantic music playing in his brain came to a screeching halt.

Say what? All the elation and hope that had been building and spinning inside him stopped dead.

"This?" he repeated numbly.

"This," she replied adamantly, with a brisk, business-like nod. "Sex. With you."

"Sex?" He knew he sounded like a parrot, but none of this was making sense. Why did he suddenly feel like he was in some fucked up business negotiation?

But Ivy nodded again, sharply. "Yes. Sex. Just sex."

Oh hell no. He was not hearing what he was hearing.

"You want me to be your fuck buddy?" he asked bluntly, needing to be clear that this was actually happening.

Ivy rolled the gorgeous blue eyes that had slayed him more than once over the years. "Don't be crude," she said, her voice haughty, almost disdainful. It sounded foreign.

He didn't even recognize it. Or her. Or anything.

"More like…" She tilted her head as if thinking it over, then met his gaze again with a satisfied look. "Friends with benefits."

This could not be fucking happening to him. Once upon a time hearing this offer might have been right up there with courtside tickets to a Bulls' game. Right up there with Grandma's warm apple pie. But hearing it from Ivy—the one and only woman he actually wanted to be more than fucking friends with benefits with—it was like a knife twisting in his gut.

~

As time stretched on without Sean saying anything, Ivy started panicking. He stood in front of her, stock-still, expressionless, as though completely unmoved by her words. She'd just offered him the most vulnerable part of herself, and he wasn't even acknowledging it. Not how she saw this going. Especially not after their kiss.

Oh God, their kiss. When she initiated, her lips trembled as she awkwardly pressed them to his. She'd imagined a soft, teasing, lips only kiss that hinted at more. Something sultry and inviting. Instead she'd given him a hard peck on the mouth, lacking totally in any kind of finesse. So, when Sean had pulled her back and taken her mouth in a hot, wet, delicious ride that made her heart spasm and her body clench with need, she'd been amazed. The way he'd invaded her mouth, taking over all of her senses, she could no longer deny that he'd wanted her. It seemed too good to be true.

A single kiss had rocked her whole world off its axis. But he acted like it hadn't moved him one iota. How could he kiss like that and not want sex? She was offering him something most men would beg for. That others took without even asking.

He wouldn't say no. He couldn't say no.

"No." His lips barely moved as the word came through.

Ivy blinked. The rest of her body was too numb to do anything else, and even though she'd only need to reach out to touch him, in that moment, he was as far away from her as he'd ever been.

The sting of humiliation and rejection heated her cheeks.

"I don't want to be your friend with benefits, Ivy." Each of his harshly spoken words lashed her heart. "The last thing I want is to fuck you like it—"

"Okay," she interrupted loudly. She'd heard enough. She wasn't an idiot.

Sean didn't want her that way.

Got it.

Check.

No need to go over all the reasons why. She was aware of her shortcomings. She didn't need to hear about them from Sean Thompson. Likely he'd kissed her back a second time to see if they had any chemistry? Which he obviously thought they did not.

Exhaustion swamped her. Maybe it was best if she and Sean weren't friends with benefits. Maybe it was best if they weren't even friends. Things between them had become too —complicated. And if Ivy wanted to execute her plan, she needed for things to not be complicated. She needed simple. Clear. Defined.

"Forget I said anything. I don't know why I asked you. Momentary lapse in judgment. I'll find someone else to meet my needs." She pushed open her door and took a definitive step inside, putting a good three feet between them.

He responded by taking a step forward. "Ivy, wait. What do you mean *someone else*? Fuck, can we talk about this before—?"

"Look," she interrupted, desperate to stop this train wreck of a conversation. It was too much. Humiliation filled her entire body. She avoided making eye contact. She didn't want to see what lay in his gaze. Horror, disgust, pity. It would all be bad. The last thing she wanted to do was backpedal and explain her impromptu fuck-buddy experiment. "It's been a long night. I'm going to bed. I'll see you at the gym tomorrow."

"Good night, Sean," she said quietly before closing the

door in his face and sagging against the hard planes of the wood.

So much for regaining her sexual confidence. Not only had she failed epically seducing Sean into going for her plan, but she'd humiliated herself and probably ruined their friendship. Ivy clunked her head against the door. There was nothing she could do now but let the shame wash over her. She'd figure out how to face him again in the morning.

CHAPTER FIVE

The next morning, Ivy ran harder and longer than she had in a long time. She ran until she doubled over and had to fight to keep down the contents of her stomach. Luckily, at six-thirty, there hadn't been much in it.

Her run didn't reduce her anxiety, clear her mind, or keep her in the moment. It failed her completely. Her conversation with Sean stayed on continuous replay in her brain. As did their kiss.

A kiss that had blown her socks off and left her craving more. So much more. More than she ever thought she could ever want again.

By the time she reached Thompson Kickboxing at 7:30, the knots in her belly had tightened into one hard stone. Sean was in there. Ivy knew she couldn't avoid him forever, although she was damned well going to try.

As she approached the gym's glass double doors, she spotted three women inside. They were poised behind the large oval reception desk, like beautiful, hyper-fit mannequins. All three were in the same pose, elbows propped on the countertop, chins on palms, staring expectantly at the door.

Their images were slightly blurred behind the glass but she recognized them instantly since a gym specializing in martial arts and combat sports didn't draw nearly as many women as men. Sean was working hard to change that, but these women had been with the facility since the beginning and were powerful representatives of Thompson Kickboxing.

Ivy had grown to admire all three and considered them very close acquaintances, since she didn't really do the whole friend thing. Except, of course, for Hope. And Sean. And maybe Gabe. And Joel was more honorary big brother than friend. Anyway, the whole friend thing was still outside her wheelhouse, but she'd allowed these gals to crack her shell, because she really, really liked them. And, more importantly, each of them had taught Ivy something about strength, resilience, and grit over the last few years, which had also earned them her respect.

The tall, toned, and gorgeous Erica was first in the lineup. She was probably Ivy's closest co-worker. Up until last night, that title had gone to Sean, but since the kiss debacle, Erica had quickly been upgraded to gym bestie.

Wendy, who was standing beside Erica, was one of the gym's Brazilian jiu-jitsu instructors—and the only resident fashionista. Her ebony ponytail gleamed like silk falling over her shoulder to her waist. She looked ready to grace the cover of a fitness magazine, not kick ass in a class in half an hour.

At the tail end, there was Christine, the only woman Ivy knew in real life who had an eight pack. She was the vegan who could lift twice Ivy's body weight without breaking a sweat, and Ivy's spotter of choice when bench-pressing.

As Ivy pushed open the door, all three women raised their chins slightly off their palms, three sets of eyes widened hopefully as they looked beyond her, then drooped in unison when Ivy emerged through the entrance, alone. Disappointment was palpable.

She slowed her stride as she approached the desk.

"Am I missing something, ladies?" She glanced over her shoulder at the door she'd walked through, because clearly something better than she had been expected.

"It's Tuesday," Erica offered by way of explanation.

This meant nothing to Ivy, so she responded by nodding slowly. "Yes, and tacos are two dollars at the Taqueria today. Lunch is on me. Why the puppy dog faces?"

"It's training day. And they'll be here any minute, so if you'll just—" Wendy made a shooing motion with her hand, waving Ivy away from the door she was blocking.

"This is a gym. Every day is training day." Instead of walking by the desk and down the hallway to her PT clinic, Ivy ducked under the liftable flap top and joined the ladies behind the counter.

"Oh my God! I think they're here!" Christine shrieked.

All three women threw themselves closer to the desk and the door on the other side like a bunch of hyped-up boy band superfans straining against a red-carpet partition gate. All they needed were hand-painted 'Kiss Me!' signs.

Moments later, five tall, buff, and good-looking men sauntered through the doors. One had the Portland Fire & Rescue logo on his dark-blue t-shirt. Another had it on the duffle bag slung over his shoulder.

"Hey ladies," one of the hulks drawled as they strode by the reception desk.

A couple of the others winked at them.

"Good morning, fellas," Erica purred in her rich, raspy voice.

Wendy squeaked in what probably was meant to be some sort of greeting, and Christine leaned against the counter, her biceps snug against either side of her chest, making her firm breasts appear more supple and prominent in her workout top.

Ivy curled her lip. "*Huh?*"

Erica, Wendy, and Christine were highly trained, extremely capable, intelligent women whom she considered mentors, advocates, and fellow feminists. They worked hard to build a reputation and a name for themselves in a male dominated sporting arena. They kicked asses and took names later. She'd seen them all take down men twice their size. Erica had a girlfriend at home for chrissake, and yet all three were shamelessly gawking at the firefighters.

Their gazes followed the men as they weaved through the equipment toward the training ring at the back.

Wendy sighed. "Jason winked at me."

"Luke looks so hot when his hair is curling out from under his backward baseball cap. I mean, God, I could eat him for breakfast," was Christine's assessment.

"Tightest asses I've ever seen," Erica observed.

"Are you guys kidding me?" Ivy announced loudly, drawing the attention away from said tight asses. "You're undoing at least a decade's worth of women's lib with that disgusting display of male adoration."

Wendy looked at her like she had grown a second head, potentially even a third. "Ivy, just because I can flatten any one of them in under a minute, doesn't mean I can't appreciate a fine ass when I see one."

Erica nodded. "I'm still gonna stick it to the patriarchy.

But I can also enjoy the early morning eye candy while I do it."

Ivy's jaw dropped open. "What would Anna say?" she asked of Erica's long term, live-in girlfriend.

Erica shrugged casually. "She'd agree that them boys have some firm asses."

Ivy groaned. "I can't believe this. You three were my heroes."

Wendy pushed past her, lifting the desk flap and leaving the reception—on a beeline toward the back of the gym. "Well, this hero is going to watch the first few minutes of their training. The best part is when they work up a good sweat and the shirts have to come off. Who's with me?"

Christine and Erica followed with no hesitation, while the world as Ivy knew it came crashing down around her. She followed out of sheer bewilderment and utter desolation.

Their foursome headed past the punching bags and training mats toward a large training ring that dominated the back of the gym.

Walking through the sleek multi-purpose fitness center, a surge of pride swelled in her heart. Thompson Kickboxing had everything needed to compete with any elite martial arts and combat training gym in the country. Considering it had started as an old, run down warehouse, Sean had done an amazing job building the gym to be one of the most modern, quality facilities in the city.

She knew Sean had a rough childhood growing up in one of Chicago's decaying suburbs. One night during a typical Pacific Northwest rainstorm, they'd been sitting on his couch sharing a Hawaiian pizza, and he'd told her about when his father had died in a workplace accident when he was ten, followed by his mother getting sick with cancer when he was sixteen and dying a couple of years later. She'd struggled to swallow the pizza around the lump in her throat, but it had been a precious moment of trust between them.

He had a brother, but he rarely spoke of him. And, as far as Ivy knew, he had been alone when he came to Portland over a decade ago.

Knowing this made his current accomplishments all the more impressive. He'd broken free of a difficult past and rebuilt.

Last night, she'd hoped he might help her do the same. But that wasn't going to happen the way she planned. And now she had to live in the awkward world she'd built.

As they approached the ring, the three women beside her inhaled a collective sigh of appreciation as the firemen stripped down to their fight shorts and climbed between the ropes into the ring. But Ivy barely registered their glistening pecs and bunching muscles. No, she was too busy fixating on their giant, perfectly built, deeply focused instructor. A wave of awareness moved through her from fingers to toes as she took him in.

Since she had this harebrained idea of overcoming her sexual inhibitions with Sean riding shotgun, she had a permanent image of him looking exactly like this in the back of her mind. Ripped, focused, intense.

He said no. He turned you down. He doesn't want you. Not like that. Her heart squeezed painfully at the memory. Despite everything, she'd thought he might say yes. Watching him now, his hard abs flexing as he led the trainees through their warmup exercises, his broad shoulders bunching, the muscles in his biceps contracting with every movement, was like torture. Self-inflicted torture.

Walk away, her brain told her body. Her body didn't

move a single inch. Besides, he hadn't noticed her, so her humiliation wasn't complete. She could risk another minute of ogling. As long as no one drew attention to her, she was safe.

"Hey Ivy." The loud, familiar voice came the same second a solid arm looped around her shoulders.

When Ivy glanced up at the gym regular, Greg Lewis, she relaxed the tension that had instinctively knotted in her shoulders.

Greg's Ken doll face had somehow managed to escape any permanent damage from his time spent fighting in the ring. He was climbing quickly up the amateur fighter ranks and was feared by most of his competitors, but here at Thompson Kickboxing, he was best known for his chronic flirting.

When she'd first met him she'd immediately disliked him. The smooth, confident, boyishly good-looking types tended to rub her the wrong way. And maybe it was unfair to lump everyone who looked, walked and talked a similar way into the same category, but sue her, she'd done it. On day one, she'd decided she wasn't going to like Greg Lewis.

Time passed though, and Greg had grown on her. She'd seen him be helpful and respectful to his fellow peers at the gym. Gabe didn't hate him, which she counted as a big plus. Then she'd spent some time with him over the summer when they'd taken the same weeklong intensive training camp, where she'd seen his more serious side. They'd shared good conversations over lunch with some of the other participants, and it had been refreshing to see him through another lens. They'd become...friendly acquaintances.

"They're getting there aren't they," he rumbled in his typically confident, sex on a stick voice, referring to the firefighters who, over the months, had gotten significantly faster, stronger, and more agile.

The Fighting Five, as the firefighters had been dubbed, had been coming to the gym regularly for months, though obviously she hadn't paid them the same attention as others had, she mused glancing over at the doe-eyed gym sharks beside her.

While Ivy didn't go gaga over their looks, she did admire their determination. They were pouring every spare minute they had between shifts at the firehall into training for the annual "Fight for the Cure" fundraising gala. No one could say they weren't dedicated to their cause.

"Fight for the Cure" was the annual, high-profile, red-carpet, black-tie charity event held at one of downtown Portland's most elegant hotels. First responders from around the county signed up to train for this amateur boxing event to raise money for local cancer treatment and support initiatives. Most took it very seriously, training for months so they were fight ready on the big day, which was coming up in early November.

Each registered fighter had to work with a sanctioned certified trainer. This year Sean had agreed to take on the Fighting Five, and by the looks of it, he'd done a good job. All five of them appeared ready to kick some serious ass in the ring in one month's time.

"Yeah," Ivy agreed. "Sean will have them ready for the gala."

Greg snorted. "They better win a few rounds, can't have anything tarnish Thompson's spotless reputation."

Ivy frowned at the sarcasm. "Of course they'll win. Sean's one of the best trainers in the city, if not the best."

Another snort. "We'll see," Greg said, but left it at that.

No one could seriously question Sean Thompson's abilities as a trainer, a fighter, or a mentor. He *was* the best. Period.

Still, nobody could say there was any love lost between Greg and Sean. They were two titans in the kickboxing scene. They had egos to protect and reputations to uphold. Ivy had come to realize that razzing each other was part of the deal. A stupid, ridiculous male part of the deal if anyone asked her.

Nevertheless, they were standing in Sean's gym, and ultimately Greg bowed to his master. He never veered beyond razzing into the realm of disrespectful, so they maintained a distant but amicable rivalry.

The arm around her shoulders tightened affably. "So, when are you gonna let me take you out for a drink and a night on the town?" he asked, changing the topic.

Ivy rolled her eyes, like she always did when he asked. She'd turned him down every time he asked. They both knew her answer would never change.

And why not? Her brain demanded out of nowhere. She hadn't ever considered him seriously, but now that the thought had been planted, she couldn't ignore it. Sean clearly didn't want anything to do with her fuck friends scheme, whereas, as far as she could tell, Greg only did the fuck friends thing.

Despite his annoying playboy ways, he'd always been decent to her. Greg wasn't a bad guy. A little lost maybe, definitely a whole lot horny. But not bad. Maybe one day the right woman would set him on the straight and narrow.

She was definitely not that woman, but then again, she didn't want him on the straight and narrow. She wanted him in her bed, helping her erase her bad memories.

To say he was sexually experienced would be an understatement. He'd show her all she needed to know—and then some. He'd be gentle and kind. He'd respect her boundaries.

She could trust a man like Greg in the bedroom. Her gut told her so. And she'd bet her last dollar that he'd make it good too.

So why not Greg? Maybe it was time to accept his offer.

Turning so Greg's arm around her shoulders moved with her, drawing her in so they probably appeared like they were in an embrace, she looked up and met his laughing blue eyes.

"How about Friday?" she asked casually, enjoying the way his carefree face morphed into nearly comical shock.

"Are you fucking with me, Ivy?" A frown marred his handsome features.

She almost laughed. Oh, if he only knew.

"I don't fuck with anybody." *Literally.* That was the point of this entire escapade.

He watched her for another couple of seconds, most likely trying to use his shit-o-meter to gauge how serious she was. His shit-o-meter must have registered low, because a goofy grin split his face and his eyes resumed their flirtatious sparkle. Ivy wished those eyes could move her, that his smile could cause a tingle in her belly, but they didn't. The most she could muster was an appreciation for his friendly nature.

It would have to do. He'd be as good a teacher as any.

Was it a foolproof plan? Absolutely not. Maybe it was the worst idea she'd had yet, but she'd reached the end of her rope and she needed to try something different. Anything to make this gnawing, aching feeling in her soul go away.

After three years of living like this, she'd finally hit her wall. She was emotionally drained. Tired of living with the memories of violent, alcohol induced brute strength and pain. Tired of feeling like that's all she'd ever equate sex with.

Therapy had helped her overcome her initial fears and trauma—in finding a way to get out of bed in the morning without hating or blaming herself. After she'd moved to Portland and started her PT clinic, she realized that maybe she didn't want her sex life to end. That maybe she wanted to replace the ugly memories with new ones. Ones that led to sexual satisfaction instead of sexual disgust.

She understood that healing was not a linear process. Her counselor had hammered that one home. There was no checklist to follow that would cure her trauma, no set date where she had to be 'over it.' But if she wanted to move forward, she would need to try. And Greg, well, he wasn't her first choice, but he wasn't a bad choice either.

Embracing her utopian fantasy where she had a shot at a normal sex life, Ivy let herself fall into the moment with Greg, appreciating the warm weight of his arm around her, the brilliant white of his teeth, and the fall of his golden hair across his brow. She tried to work up a sense of anticipation. Really, she tried, but she couldn't ignore the incessant tugging sensation that distracted her heart and mind. It was like an invisible string connected her brain to her soul's desire, pulling her attention to the man who'd built this gym from nothing, like he called to her without using words.

Sean stood in the corner of the ring closest to her, muscles tensed, fists clenched at his sides, eyes thin slits as he watched her. Powerful. Dangerous. And for some highly inexplicable reason, that filled her with satisfaction. He wasn't totally unaffected, and it soothed the wound that his rejection had caused.

Greg seemed oblivious to the giant in the ring who

looked ready to jump over the ropes and rip his throat out. He chuckled amiably, rubbing his hand up and down her arm, drawing her closer. Ivy could swear she heard a low, murderous growl come from the ring.

"Guess my patience paid off, huh?" Greg's fingers played with the ends of her short ponytail.

She shrugged. "I'm going through a dry spell. Need to break the cycle before I shrivel up for good." She didn't want him thinking she desired anything more than a quick fix that might turn into something longer.

Greg laughed. "Trust me babe, with me, you'll be anything but dry."

"Ew." Ivy curled her lip. "Don't make me regret this decision, please."

Greg shrugged. "I appreciate a woman who knows what she wants and says it, but I've got manners. I'll wine and dine you first. What time shall I pick you up at your place?"

The invisible thread in her brain tugged violently. This time, she refused to look at Sean. "Seven."

Greg nodded. "I'll be there." He flashed her another smile, one that had likely dropped many a panty, and moved toward the punching bags.

Ivy inhaled a deep breath. That wasn't so bad. Except the thread in her brain was now yanking so hard it was starting to cause a headache.

"Um, Ivy," Erica's voice came near her ear.

Ivy rubbed her temple and glanced at her friend, who was still standing close by.

Erica's eyes were wide as she stared straight ahead. "I think you poked the bear, and he's not happy."

Ivy turned to look at the ring. Sean stood, feet planted, fists flexing at his sides, nostrils flared. His eyes bore into hers, burning a path to her very soul. Why he appeared angry she couldn't guess, since less than twenty-four hours ago he'd not so gently refused her offer.

So, she figured he must be annoyed to see her cozy up with Greg in the middle of his gym. Gym flirtation was Sean's pet peeve, and he always reiterated that a gym was a place to train and sweat, not an opportunity to speed date.

Well, if that was what was bothering him, then he could go sit on his thumb as far as she was concerned, because this was her life, and she was ready to live it.

Ivy narrowed her eyes and gave him a challenging glare of her own. Then she spun on her heel and stalked off to her clinic.

The rest of the day went by in a blur of clients, writing up charts, and catching up on admin work. Mostly Ivy specialized in sports injuries, rehabbing cases that ranged from sprains to concussions to knee and shoulder damage and beyond. Her clients came from Thompson Kickboxing or from referrals from orthopedic surgeons, family doctors, or trainers at other gyms. Lately, she'd acquired a few new clients from word of mouth, and it pleased her that she was building a reputation in Portland. She'd worked hard to get here. It was satisfying to see it paying off.

By five-thirty she was helping her last client of the day. Chase Richards was an amateur kickboxer with an MCL injury she'd been rehabbing—on the referral of his trainer —for the last few weeks. "Don't push it, Chase," she warned as she observed a tremor run down his body as he lowered himself into a one-legged squat on the air cushion she'd asked him to balance on.

"I'm fine," he replied in a strained voice.

When a sheen of sweat beaded his brow, she wondered if he was downplaying his discomfort. The young, testosterone fueled athletes often put up a tough front, pretending nothing was wrong and overworking themselves, thinking that would get them back into fighting shape faster.

To Ivy it was common sense that pushing too hard, too fast only set you back, but clearly it wasn't as common as she thought, so she always had to remind them to slow down, breathe deep, and focus on the immediate exercise, not the end goal. The smallest movements often went the longest way in recovery.

Chase did another five one-legged squats before she told him to stop. It might not physically be hurting him so much right now, but she could tell by the way his body was reacting that he was overdoing it, and if he continued, his knee would swell again.

"You're done for the day." Then, even though he was almost a foot taller than her, and the same age, she reassuringly patted him on the shoulder like a parent might a child. "You did good. You'll get there."

Chase ran a frustrated hand through his hair, his face tight with exertion and irritation. "I need to get there soon. I can't fall behind on training or I'll lose my shot at making the championships this year."

"Look at it this way, Chase. If you push too hard now, then you really will set yourself back and fall behind."

His narrowed eyes didn't look so sure.

"Do what I say, when I say, how I say, and you'll be back in the ring before Christmas. But you need to be honest with me. If it hurts, you have to tell me."

Getting these big alpha males to admit when it hurt was one of the most challenging parts of her job. Then again, she didn't admit when it hurt either, so on that level she got it. Showing where it hurt meant showing weakness. And when weakness is exposed, someone could take advantage of it. In the ring and out.

She was listing the daily exercises she wanted Chase to do between now and their next appointment when she heard booming footsteps coming down the hallway from the reception area. She knew who it was even before he tossed open the glass door to her clinic.

Instantly, Sean's body consumed the space. Chase was six-foot-two and solid muscle, but he appeared stunted next to Sean, especially a pissed Sean. She rarely saw Sean like this. Actually, she couldn't remember seeing him more than mildly annoyed, but he certainly was now, and somehow it made his muscles bulge even more than they usually did.

Chase looked from Sean to Ivy, back to Sean, then to Ivy again. "Uh, everything okay?"

Bless him, the poor kid had no idea. And only God knew what it must look like to him. But the fact was, a thrill shot through her when Sean appeared in her doorway. A complicated mix between anticipation and relief. If he wanted to have it out, she was ready.

She maternally patted Chase again on the shoulder. From the corner of her eye, she saw Sean following the movement with a steely glare.

"Everything is perfect." She handed the daily-exercise sheet to Chase. "Three times a day, each. Stop if it hurts." She made direct and focused eye contact with him. "Don't push it," she repeated in a firm tone. "Got it?"

Chase grinned, probably amused that such a tiny person was giving him orders, but she fisted her hands on her hips and stared him down until he said, "Got it."

Then he headed out the door, but not without giving

Sean a pretty impressive stare down of his own. Ivy mentally upgraded Chase to her new favorite client.

When they were alone, she turned to Sean and crossed her arms. He watched the young kickboxer strut away from them. Was she mistaken or did she spy some respect in Sean's expression?

Since she was still hurt and embarrassed by his rejection the day before and confused by his sudden anger with her today, she opted to be blunt and harsh. "What the hell do you want?" Being defensive and as standoffish as possible was one of her ways of dealing with emotions she'd rather avoid.

And apparently, Sean was on the same page.

"Are you gonna tell me why you let Greg-Fucking-Lewis put his hands all over you this morning?" he growled as he slowly faced her.

Ivy snorted a laugh. "Why would you possibly care?"

His brown eyes softened marginally, and she thought she saw the briefest hint of hurt pass over them. But it was gone so fast she likely imagined it.

"It's my gym. I care about everything that happens here."

"Well, you don't have to care about this. My thing with Greg is not your business," she said indignantly.

"You shouldn't tangle with him."

Ivy unfolded her arms, and propped her hands on her hips. "Are you kidding me, Sean? I shouldn't tangle with *him*? And why the hell not? He's nice, he's hot, he's into me, oh, and also, I happen to be a free goddamn woman, so please tell me why I can't tangle with him?"

Sean's eyes hardened, and he straightened himself to full height, making the room shrink further around him. "Because I don't like it," he said in a deep *Mr. Serious* voice.

Most people would cower at the sheer dominance emanating from him.

Ivy responded with a snort of laughter. "Oh, that's rich coming from you. Besides," she sniffed, assessing her nails as if she had a lovely manicure to admire instead of half bitten stubs. "You're too late. We're going on a date."

"Like hell you are!" His voice boomed so loudly that they could probably hear him at the reception desk.

Ivy recoiled, jerking backward until she nearly stumbled. Luckily, she caught herself before she made a total ass of herself and fell.

With a low growl, Sean reached out to help steady her. This time, she resisted the urge to flinch, barely. As if he sensed her knee-jerk fear, Sean took a massive step backward, and closed his eyes, pinching the bridge of his nose. After about ten seconds, he opened his eyes, looking more in control, though not necessarily calmer.

He assessed her for a moment, then he scrubbed a rough hand over his head and down the back of his neck. He inhaled fiercely through his nose before he exhaled loudly. Crossing to a chair by her desk, he fell into it. Immediately, the tension in the air lessened.

"What's going on with you, Ivy?" he asked in his usual gentler tone.

Ivy moved behind her desk and started tidying the folders and reports from the day. *Lie, don't look at him.* "I don't know what you mean."

"Yes, you do." Sean's voice was a rumble. "Look at me."

The intensity of his tone gave her no choice. Like a moth to a flame, she raised her gaze to his, and the invisible thread that constantly pulled her in his direction eased.

"First last night. Now with Lewis. Something's up. You're

not yourself." He leaned forward, bracing his elbows against his knees. "Talk to me. You always tell me everything."

Not everything. Not even close.

Guilt clawed at her. In so many ways, Sean was closer to her than anyone, even Hope. Hope knew Ivy's every secret, but with Sean—it was like he knew her soul.

From the beginning, when she showed up at his gym inquiring about kickboxing classes, it was as though he saw right through her. He could read her nuances flawlessly, knowing when to push her and when to let her retreat. He understood, without having to ask, when she needed to be held close and protected, and when she needed to stand on her own and feel strong and capable. She never had to tell him. Their connection was intuitive. Their friendship had been effortless.

Until she'd screwed it up by throwing the curveball of all curveballs and kissed him, then demanded he be her friend with benefits. Of course he was confused by her behavior. It was night and day from what he was used to. Night and day from what *she* was used to.

It would be so much easier if he knew where her sudden demand for casual sex had come from, and it wasn't like she hadn't thought about telling him a thousand times. But each time she thought about it, the result was the same. She was convinced her history would change the way he thought about her, and Ivy couldn't risk that. She didn't want Sean to see her as broken, or worse, damaged. She didn't want to see the look of worry in his eyes that she often saw in Hope's— and now Gabe's, too.

Sean was always gentle with her, but he never handled her with kid gloves. He expected her to live up to her full potential, no excuses. If he knew that she'd been violated so traumatically, he'd wrap the tragedy around her like a blanket. He'd treat her like a fragile, cracked piece of glass. She knew that about him. His protective instincts ran deep, and if he knew the truth, he'd never treat her the same.

All she wanted was to move on. To feel normal. To be touched and not have a panic attack. To have sex, like a normal person, and not constantly be trapped in her head. If Sean knew about the assault, he'd never treat her like a normal, healthy woman. And he probably wouldn't want to have sex with her. Make that definitely, since he hadn't wanted to have sex with her yesterday and he knew nothing.

"There's not much to tell. Greg's been asking me out for months. You know that."

Sean grunted in disapproval.

A surge of frustration shot up Ivy's torso. "What's wrong with Greg? He's handsome. He's a decent guy. He's persistent. And most of all, he wants to go out with me."

She let the insinuation hang there. *Unlike you.*

"He wants to fuck you, Ivy. There's a difference." Sean shot out of his seat and paced the room at a lion's pace. "He doesn't care about you. You'll just be another notch on his belt. A trophy for his case. Another victory he can claim. He doesn't actually *care* about you!"

"Like you do?" she fired back.

"Yes! Like *I* do," he barked. "I care about you, and I'm trying to fucking understand where all this is coming from when a week ago we were fine sitting on your couch eating pizza and watching bad TV."

And there it was. Sean was happy in the friend zone. He cared about her, took care of her, made her feel safe, but she'd never be more than his friend. With no benefits. Their explosive kiss was a one off, not a premonition of the future.

She sighed loudly. "*True Detective* is not bad TV."

His hard gaze didn't waver.

"And maybe I'm not happy with that anymore. Maybe I don't want the rest of my life to be yoga pants, dry shampoo, and takeout with a friend. Maybe I want to know what it's like to have passion in my life. To finally put my hormones to good use. Did you ever think that maybe I had needs that went beyond knowing if the husband actually got a contract killer to take out his wife?"

By the end of her tirade, Sean's jaw was pure granite, and she took pity on him. Her change of heart must have seemed out of the blue for him. She'd never once let on she'd wanted more in her life from a man than friendship. Up until recently, she'd been too timid, too afraid. But she was tired of that.

"Look, I know Greg. He's a playboy," she conceded. "And he doesn't try to hide that which, to be honest, I appreciate about him. It makes things between us clear. No games. No emotional entanglements."

She held Sean's gaze wanting her underlying message to be clear. What she planned with Greg would be straightforward. She wouldn't have to guess as to his intentions or spend restless nights lying in bed wondering how much he expected from her. It would be casual sex. Exactly what she needed right now. With all the anxiety she had around sex, she didn't need any compounding complicated emotions making it worse.

"So, you want a fling with some random dude you hardly know?" Sean asked.

Ivy didn't bother to remind him that Greg hadn't been her first choice, that she had asked him first and been rejected.

"I want uncomplicated, Sean," she explained. "I can't handle anything else right now."

I can't handle you.

The second the thought materialized in her head, she knew it was true. And the truth hit her like a smack to the forehead. How naive she'd been.

Sean knew her too well. Their past was too complicated. Being with him could never be casual, no-strings. Nothing between them had ever been that way. They'd always been too close, too connected. Embarrassed that she hadn't accepted it sooner, she conceded he'd been right to turn her down. They had no chance.

"So, Lewis," Sean said, looking defeated, like he'd just tapped out on the biggest fight of his life.

"I know where I stand with him," Ivy replied smoothly.

Sean came to a stop in front of her. So close. So far away. He lifted his hand and ran his fingertip down her nose. The featherlight touch sent a shiver through her. Then he dropped his hand and stepped back. The loss of his warmth made her wrap her arms around herself to keep the familiar chill away.

"I hope you find what you're looking for, Ivy." His eyes softened as they held hers, then he headed toward the door.

"Sean," she called after him.

The thread between them was strained, stretching taut. When he stopped but didn't turn to face her, a throb of pain flared behind her breastbone.

"We're okay, right?" she asked.

He didn't speak, and Ivy was left clinging to herself as she watched his back—strong, silent, still. She held her breath waiting for his reassurance. He'd never let her down. Not once. Not ever.

At the side of his hip one hand flexed. It was the only perceivable movement on his entire body. Finally, he responded in a tight, forced voice. "Always."

And without a backward glance he was gone.

Ivy hugged herself tighter—afraid she'd just lost her soulmate.

CHAPTER SIX

F uck. Fuck, fuck, fuck, fuck.

Sean punched the heavy bag hanging in his living room over and over in rhythm with the expletive pounding in his head like a drumbeat. Every time his fist hit the bag's vinyl casing, he imagined Greg Lewis' face.

It was Friday night and that meant Ivy was out with Greg-Fucking-Lewis. After a long week of avoiding both Lewis and Ivy at the gym, Sean had more pent-up fury than a bull chasing a red flag. He wasn't a violent man, or at least he hadn't been in a long time, but the image of Lewis with his arm draped around Ivy, the thought of them getting cozy on Ivy's couch where he should be sitting watching crime dramas with her, and the dread that Lewis might soon have his playboy mouth on Ivy's sweet, innocent body—was making him feel like he was losing his fucking mind.

Wham. Wham. Wham. He slugged the bag, waiting for the pressure in his chest to subside. He'd been at it for an hour, and so far hadn't noticed a difference.

Their kisses. They plagued him night and day. She'd kissed him first, and it had been sweet, shy, and rushed.

Their second kiss had been a scorching, soul-deep connection. Then she'd said he didn't want her. Had she not noticed how much he wanted her in that kiss? How could he make it any clearer?

The air made a hissing sound as his fist whizzed through it and slugged the bag. Frustrated did not even begin to cover how he felt. If she weren't so dead set on keeping things casual, he'd be the one with her right now. He'd be the one sharing a fancy dinner with her and opening car doors for her. He'd be the one bringing her home and taking care of her needs. Fuck. She'd told him she had needs. Well, he had fucking needs, too. Except, on his end, there was nothing casual about them.

And goddammit, he knew there was nothing casual about hers. He couldn't put his finger on the exact kind of game she was playing, but he knew she'd come to him first for a reason. She wasn't out to use him. She'd asked him first because she trusted him. And he would have given her what she wanted if he could have gotten on board with her nonchalant agenda. But he couldn't.

And now she was out with Greg-Fucking-Lewis.

Christ. He wanted to hit something other than this bag. Preferably Lewis. He couldn't remember being this worked up over anything in his life. Of all his friends and acquaintances, he was the one with the level head. And it wasn't an accident. He'd seen first-hand what losing your cool and making rash decisions could do. Over the years, he worked hard to build his diplomatic nature and bank of wise, philosophical quotes. He earned his reputation, and normally nothing phased him.

Nothing except Ivy going on a date with someone who wasn't him.

Twenty minutes later, dripping sweat, muscles aching,

Sean finally forced himself away from the bag. He glanced at the clock, noting that it was almost 9 p.m. Dinnertime was over. He slumped onto one of his kitchen bar stools and wondered where Lewis had taken Ivy.

Would they go to Lewis' place or Ivy's after they finished whatever they were doing? Would she let Lewis touch her? Sean couldn't let his mind go there. Not when the only hands he'd ever considered on her body were his.

He needed a drink and a distraction. Bowie's could provide him with both. He jumped to his feet with enough force to almost tip the stool over and headed toward the shower.

Yanking his sweat-soaked shirt over his head, he tried to be logical. Ivy wouldn't seriously let a guy like Lewis put his paws on her. Not only did she have more sense than that, but for as long as he'd known her, he'd never seen her let any man get that close to her. And he knew why.

Something dark had happened to Ivy before she'd come to Portland. That much had been obvious from the moment she'd showed up at his gym to sign-up for kickboxing classes. Pale, hollow, and quiet, she'd barely looked at him. She'd avoided eye contact, dressed in dark baggy clothes, and spent most of her time hugging herself as though she might splinter apart if she let go.

Growing up the way he had, in the neighborhood he had, having seen the things he had, it hadn't taken much for him to put two and two together. In his youth, he'd known plenty of survivors of violence—not to mention the ones who didn't survive. His parents tried their best to protect him and his brother, but it was always there, in the periphery of their lives. And later, after his dad passed, a lot closer than any child should have had to live with.

He'd been helpless and afraid. It was why he'd become

so disciplined with his training, regimented and obsessive until he'd perfected the craft of martial arts, so he could control how he used it to defend himself and others. But he left Chicago, without protecting anyone. And that failure had followed him like a ghost all the way to Portland—where it haunted him day in and day out.

Until he met Ivy. He had considered her his redemption. His chance to leave the world a better place than when he found it. In those early months, he poured all his energy into training her, because if he could prevent her soul from succumbing to brutality, then maybe he'd make up for the soul he'd sacrificed.

The joke was on him, though, which was something he'd quickly gotten comfortable with where Ivy was concerned, because she wasn't his redemption. She was pure vengeance. Whatever she'd been out to get, whatever ghost she was fighting, she acted hellbent on getting the better of it. She pushed herself harder than anyone he'd ever met. She took the drills he gave her and ran them over and over, never once complaining, pushing the limit until he thought there was no way she could take anymore. But she had. She never quit, and she'd morphed into the powerful, resilient person she was today.

He couldn't take any credit for her transformation. It had been her fortitude, her grit, her tunnel vision when it came to her training.

But knowing that it all came from a place of darkness—fuck, that had triggered a protectiveness in him to the point where he considered himself her personal bodyguard.

So no, Ivy wasn't his redemption. She was the single most precious thing in his life. He had to protect her. This compulsion had become as involuntary as breathing. A reflex that kicked in without thinking. Like it had a few months ago, when Ivy had fully panicked at Bowie's when a drunken blast from her past had shown up. After Hope had her go at the asshole, Sean had taken his turn, in the more private location of the alley behind the bar. He'd made sure the lowlife got the message never to come near either woman again.

Lewis was different. Sean didn't lump him into the scum-of-the-earth category. But he was still the biggest player Sean knew. And even though Ivy had given him a big speech about her newfound desire for a friend with benefits, something about her spiel didn't sit right. Nothing about it sounded logical to him, and it was driving him mad.

He needed to rein himself in. He needed to get out of his apartment.

After his shower, he donned a pair of jeans and rooted through his clean laundry pile for a shirt. He'd pulled it half way over his head when every muscle in his body tensed with awareness as the sound of rumbling male laughter filtered through his front door.

Do not go to the door. Do not go to the door.

Ivy's unmistakable giggle filtered through next.

Stay out of it. Stay out of it. Stay out of it.

Jesus. Why were these doors so fucking flimsy? He was going to have to talk Gabe into installing some weatherstripping, if this was going to be his new normal. *Sonofabitch.* This could *not* be his new normal. He'd go crazy.

There was more gruff, male rumbling. Then the sound of keys jangling. And, Christ have mercy on his soul, he was at his apartment door in a flash, ears tuned in, his eyeball on the peephole.

Was he invading Ivy's privacy? Maybe. But he figured he was being less Peeping Tom and more Personal Security Service.

He was simply going to make sure that Lewis respect-fully dropped her off, and that he didn't make any unwanted advances. That was all.

So far, it all looked innocent enough. They weren't touching. Lewis was saying something in a low tone Sean couldn't quite make out, and Ivy was smiling up at him. A surge of satisfaction shot through Sean. He knew that smile. It was her polite but not interested smile. Yeah, her night was done.

Sean exhaled a satisfied breath and was about to step away, when Lewis braced his arm against the wall next to Ivy's head, boxing her in. When he reached his free hand to stroke her beautiful, dark hair, every muscle in Sean's body tensed. But it wasn't until the meathead dipped his face toward hers that Sean grabbed the doorknob with a falcon's grip. Ivy turned her face, trying to avoid the oncoming kiss, and he caught a clear view of her panic-stricken look. As she fumbled to open her door, he ripped his own ajar so hard it slammed loudly against the other side. Maybe he should have cared more about his intrusion, but when he saw the relief in Ivy's wide eyes as Lewis jerked away from her, he could not muster up a single fuck.

"Keep your hands off of her, Lewis!" he growled, as he strode into the hallway.

Lewis spun to face Sean, then relaxed. His chuckle filled the hall. "Or what, Thompson?"

Sean clenched his fists at his sides. He stopped short of baring his teeth. His body was shaking with the effort of not ripping the smart-ass' throat out. "Or I'll fucking break them off. That's what."

Had he just said that? Yes, he had. Was Ivy going to give him shit? Yes, she was. How many fucks did he give? Zero. Because he'd read her fear. He'd been reading it since he first locked eyes with her three years ago. Her relief when Lewis had jerked away from her wasn't something Sean had made up. She'd been panicked, and knowingly or unknowingly, Lewis had stirred that panic in Ivy. So he had to pay the price—by leaving. Now.

Sean had a couple inches on the guy—and was broader, more muscled. But Lewis was well-known for his skills in the ring, and Sean never underestimated any opponent. Not that he wasn't looking for a fight. He just wanted to ensure Ivy was safe and unafraid. That was all he ever wanted.

"Date night's over." He clenched his fists at his sides to keep them from doing anything stupid. "Leave."

Annoyingly, Lewis didn't move, didn't even look all that threatened. Much to Sean's immense irritation, he looked somewhat amused, the corners of his mouth lifting ever so slightly.

"You got an issue with me kissing Ivy goodnight, Thompson?"

Fuck this prick. He was goading him—or trying to.

In response, Sean stepped so far into Lewis' space he made sure the cheeky bastard had to look up at him to meet his gaze. "Doesn't look to me like she wants your lips on hers, is all." He was grinding his molars so hard he could barely get the words out. "So, I'm gonna tell you one more time. *Leave.*"

Lewis, who had more grit than Sean had given him credit for, squared his shoulders and cocked his head to the side. "I'll leave when she tells me to leave."

A rough, growling noise escaped from deep within Sean's throat as he inched even closer. Forget not looking for a fight. If this little shit wouldn't leave on his own two feet, he'd send him—airborne.

"You're kidding right?" Through the red haze, Ivy's voice

boomed from directly below his left ear, threatening to bust a drum. "Sean, back the hell off right now. You're being ridiculous."

He did not move an inch. His eyes bore into Lewis', whose baby blues sparkled back with amusement. The little fucker was enjoying this.

"What part of *now* don't you understand?" Ivy demanded.

Sean's jaw flexed as he clenched his teeth even harder. He knew that tone. She used it when she was reaming out the Bachelor contestants during a group date episode or scolding a naive character in a horror movie who was about to meet her maker and should have seen it coming four scenes ago. He'd even heard her use it with clients who hadn't done what she'd told them to do and consequently re-injured themselves. Where he'd never heard it was used on him. Until now.

With one last hard look, he took a step back.

Lewis chuckled and smoothed down the front of his shirt and jacket as if he'd even been touched. "Dude, you need to chill. Ivy's a big girl, you know. She doesn't need you breathing down her neck every second of the day. Right, darlin'?"

Sean frowned at the endearment but—not wanting to piss Ivy off any more than she already was—he kept his mouth shut. The heat of her wrath was already scorching him, and he was fine with that. He'd take her rage over the possibility that she might have let Lewis manhandle her tonight.

"What I don't need," she bit out, her tone hard, "is two man-children acting like Neanderthals. For God's sake, all you need are wooden clubs, and you'd look the part you're acting. Which, by the way, is not a turn-on in the least."

Sighing loudly, Ivy turned to Lewis and said, "I'm sorry. I had a really nice night, but I think it's probably best if we say goodnight."

To his credit, Lewis didn't argue. He nodded before walking up to her and brushing a chaste kiss across her temple. It was innocent, but Sean still had the urge to smack those lips off her forehead.

"Goodnight, darlin'," he murmured to Ivy. "I'll catch you at the gym later." Then with a wink he added, "We'll nail down a date for our next dinner then."

With that, he sauntered toward the staircase down to the main door of the building. Neither Ivy nor Sean spoke a word as they listened to the door open, then click closed. They stood for one last beat of silence before Ivy rounded on Sean, her eyes fierce with anger.

"What the hell was that?" she demanded.

Knowing there was absolutely no correct answer to that question, Sean opted for a casual shrug. "Looks like he had to go."

Ivy shoved him hard with both hands. Sean hardly moved. "You are such an asshole. You purposely drove him away by picking a fight."

Sean narrowed his eyes. "I stepped in because I know he's not what you want or you wouldn't have looked so panicked when he tried to make a move on you."

"And how would you have seen that? Were you spying on me?"

Well, damn. Caught red handed. He crossed his arms tightly over his chest refusing to feel regret for what he'd done. "You're the one who told him to go."

"Because I didn't want you to pulverize him and get blood on the carpet! Do you know how much Gabe would charge for that?"

"Hope is looking for any excuse to change these carpets. She'd have thanked me."

Ivy blew out a breath, anger flushing her pale skin. So pretty, even when her ice-blue eyes were flashing daggers at him.

"Are you going to see him again?" Where had that come from? He didn't want to know the answer to that, and yet the words had left his mouth.

It was Ivy's turn to cross her arms. They stood toe-to-toe in their defensive positions.

"That," she huffed, "is none of your business. "And so what if I do? What do you care? You're the one who said you weren't interested in being with me."

"I said I wasn't interested in being a friend with bene-fits," he returned evenly, gauging her reaction.

Her eyes widened in surprise, then narrowed with doubt, before finally shuttering, a visible wall going up against the truth he was trying to tell her. His frustration flickered back to life.

"Well, friends with benefits is all I can give right now," she offered shakily. "And Greg is a willing participant in that, so I'd appreciate it if you didn't threaten to manhandle him next time I have an actual chance of having a decent guy wanting to spend the night with me."

Sean kept his expression fixed. This wasn't the time to tell her he thought her little fuck-buddy plan was a total crock of shit. She was already mad as it was. But hell, a woman like Ivy deserved to be worshipped. It was criminal that she'd consider settling for less.

"Is that what you want, then? A meaningless fling with an over-sexed gym shark?"

Ivy shrugged. "Maybe I just want to feel normal. Desir-able." Her voice was hushed, and for a second, she reminded him of the vulnerable, broken woman who'd come to his gym three years ago.

"Ivy." Her name came out of him softly, like a breath of air. He hated when she said shit like that. How could she not feel desirable when she was the most gorgeous thing he'd ever seen, not to mention the most determined person he'd ever met. Everything about her called to him, and he'd spent every year they'd shared fighting his feelings because even though he didn't know exactly what had happened to her, he knew something bad had, and he didn't want to overstep her boundaries. He cared about her too much.

But those boundaries had blurred lately. There wasn't a label for what they were to each other. He only knew their connection was precious, and he didn't want to destroy it.

Her out-of-the-blue determination to take on a casual lover had blindsided him. A hit out of left field, which at first he hadn't understood, but now he saw the truth in her shattered eyes.

She was terrified, and this ludicrous plan of hers was a misguided attempt at finding something before she lost it completely.

Sean stroked the sides of her arms, certain that the shiver that ran along her skin wherever he touched was similar to the one that was racking his own flesh, sending heat to every part of his body.

Christ, how could this stunning woman not think she was desirable? People stared at her wherever she went. He was constantly noticing when someone checked her out. How could she not?

Slowly, he ran his hands up and over the curve of her shoulders and neck, until he cradled her face in his palms, tilting her chin up so her gaze met his. For a moment, all he could do was look at her, holding eye contact long enough that it should have been uncomfortable, but knowing it never would be with her.

Everything. Her eyes were everything to him. As long as he could look into them, he could stay anchored—while everything that had come before, and everything that might come after, was a blur around them.

Sean watched closely as Ivy's pupils dilated until they almost obscured her ice-blue irises. Her mouth parted slightly, and she drew in a breath like she wanted to say something, but nothing came out. When her tongue darted out to run along her upper lip, he gave in to the pull that constantly tugged between them and brought his head down to hers.

CHAPTER SEVEN

Heat exploded through Ivy the second Sean's lips touched hers. How she could be so mad and so turned on at the same time? She had no idea, but it was happening.

When Sean had barreled out of his apartment like an overprotective alpha, she'd been furious. Her evening with Greg had been pleasant. He'd been sweet, and funny, and casual with a *no expectations* vibe. Exactly the kind of thing she'd been after. She'd been fully prepared to invite him in —and then he'd leaned down to kiss her, and immediately the recognizable chill of panic had crawled up her spine and taken hold. For long seconds, she stood frozen, her brain knowing exactly what it should do, and her body betraying her by doing absolutely nothing. A horrifically familiar scenario.

Then Sean had appeared, killing her fear instantaneously and replacing it with the equally familiar burn of fury.

The man had some nerve standing off with Greg, especially after he'd explicitly turned her down not that long ago. He had no right to scare away her dates—even if his timing had been impeccable. He'd saved her from embarrassing herself by having a full panic attack in front of Greg.

But where was hesitation now? With Sean's lips pressed possessively against hers, she only felt need, and a surge of heat that pooled low in her belly.

The way his lips worked their way mercilessly against hers made her feel desirable. Which in turn made her feel strong. Like she was the reason this beast of a man was moaning against her mouth, like he was losing himself in the mere taste of her.

Unable to stop herself, Ivy ran her hands up the rippled length of his torso and wrapped them around his neck, opening her mouth to deepen the kiss. Inviting him in.

On a sexy growl of approval, Sean picked her up so she could wrap her legs around his waist. With their height difference, this new position made it easier for them to kiss. It brought her level with him. Equal.

"Keys," he murmured against her lips as he carried her toward her apartment door. Not wanting to lose contact with his lips, Ivy blindly dug her hand inside her purse. When the cool metal touched her palm, she yanked her keys out and pushed them into his hand.

With one arm anchored under her bottom, his free hand worked the key in the keyhole, his mouth never leaving hers. He pressed her against the door, his tongue exploring the depth of her mouth, his one hand firmly squeezing both cheeks of her ass until, finally, the click of the lock gave way, and he walked them over the threshold of her apartment.

Running her hands over his hair, she inhaled his kisses and rubbed her lower body against the hard ridge under his jeans. She heard Sean kick the door closed behind them at the same moment a curse ripped from his mouth.

"Jesus, Ivy. You're killing me. Fucking killing me."

Ivy couldn't relate, since she'd never been this alive in her life. Had never imagined she could after—everything. But every part of her body was hot with desire and pulsing with need.

"Couch," she panted. Locking her arms tighter around his neck as she brought his lips back to hers. She relished in the masculine noises emanating from deep in his throat.

And then she was being lowered onto the soft cushions. One warm, firm hand found its way under her shirt and caressed her stomach, moving up to her chest. The other slid down her thigh, bending her leg at the knee and pulling it tight against his hard, muscled leg. The touches, the grinding, the kissing, it was primal. Everything she had been seeking. A desperate, mutual, sexual encounter to counteract the darkness inside her.

And then the weight of his body fell over her, and she was catapulted back to another night. A night where another body had fallen over her, heavy and unwanted. She'd been pinned so that she couldn't move, not even enough for her hands to get between them so she could push back. She'd been crushed so she couldn't breathe, her screams trapped in her throat as a rough hand clamped over her mouth. Tears blurred her vision, and the heaviness totally and completely swallowed her. It had been like a drowning.

As Ivy once again let herself go under rather than suffer the weight of suffocation, the heaviness vanished. The pressure released, replaced with a cold weightlessness that left her startled and gasping. But it was the curse, low and vicious, that brought her back to reality.

Blinking her way out of the haze, Ivy shoved herself up to her elbows as she tried to focus on the space around her.

Her couch, her apartment. Sean stood a few feet away, scrubbing his palms over his face roughly as he cursed again.

And realization hit her. The worst had happened. The flashbacks had taken over right when she was supposed to be losing herself in the pleasure of Sean's strong, safe arms. Drawing her knees tight against her chest, Ivy huddled into the far corner of the couch and hugged herself. In that moment, she knew—she'd never erase the memory of what happened. It was doomed to live inside her. Forever.

"I-I'm sorry," she stuttered, not even wanting to think about what a broken mess Sean must think she was.

But he dropped his hands from his face and stared at her. His features a hard, unreadable mask. In two long strides, he was in front of her, dropping to his knees. "Not your fault," he ground out in a strangled voice. Tentatively, he lifted his hand toward her. "Can I?"

When she nodded, he brushed her hair off her cheek where it had been stuck to her skin by tears she hadn't realized she'd cried. His gaze locked with hers, searching, and a moment passed between them wherein Ivy would have sworn he'd glimpsed every reel of her past like a slideshow.

Abruptly, he pushed off of his knees and away from her again. "Fuck!" he roared, pacing the length of her living room, fingers interlocked behind his neck, biceps flexing hard, like he was struggling against the urge to lash out.

No wonder he'd declined her friends-with-benefits request. He couldn't deal with her baggage any more than she could. She'd ruined whatever friendship had been left between them.

After a few tense moments where neither of them spoke, and the only thing that could be heard in the whole apartment was the harsh sounds of Sean's breathing, he finally spun to face her and said, "Get your running clothes on."

Ivy blinked up at him, trying to follow his train of thought. "What?" she croaked, her voice still thick with the emotional agony of her flashback.

Sean's eyes hardened at the sound. "We're going for a run," he bit out. "Together." He held out his hand to her, which she stared at for several seconds before she gave him hers. Gently, he tugged her to her feet. "I need to burn off some of this energy, and you do as well, and I am not leaving you alone right now. So, get changed and come with me. Please," he added, more softly.

"Oh." Of course, he would know exactly what would work for her. She needed to reset, get back into the moment, breathe in the fresh air off the river, and purge the ugliness of the memories that refused to loosen their grip on her.

"Unless you want to..." he said slowly, almost reluctantly. "You know, be left alone."

Ivy shook her head vigorously. Hell no, she did not want to be left alone right now. Not when her flashbacks could turn into a surge of restless nightmares in no time. She scrambled to her feet, and if she wasn't mistaken, she saw a flash of relief cross Sean's face. "Give me a second."

By the time she dressed and exited her apartment, Sean was stretching in the hallway. She took in the sight of his tall, extremely fit body covered in shorts and a long-sleeved athletic top that hugged every tight ridge of his abdominals, and cursed herself again for being so damaged. If she was normal, she'd be wrapped around that hard body right now, naked, and probably screaming his name until her voice was hoarse. Heat flooded her body simply thinking about it. How could she respond so quickly to the mere thought of him, but shut down at his touch?

God, why was she so *broken*?

"Ready?" he asked, his gaze trailing down her body. He wasn't looking at her in any way that might be deemed sexual. If anything, it was more like he was searching her for injuries. Little did he know they were all on the inside.

Still, every part of her warmed under his appraisal. Then his head snapped up, and he had his gonna-kick-your-ass fitness trainer look in his eyes.

"Ready," she affirmed.

"Let's do this then." He turned toward the staircase, and Ivy followed where he led.

He ran her mercilessly, almost as if he'd forgotten she was beside him struggling to keep up not only with his pace, but his six-foot-five gait. Anytime Ivy looked over at Sean, his face was an unreadable mask. He stared straight ahead, breathing hard through his nose until finally he deemed they'd run far enough to turn back.

Ivy considered herself a strong runner. She had stamina and kept a decent pace. For the last three years, she'd trained her body relentlessly so she could outrun anyone. So she'd never be caught and held down again. But this run, with Sean, nearly killed her.

By the time they arrived back at their apartments, she was dripping sweat and her legs shook like wet noodles. She clung to the handle of her door, mostly because it was the only thing keeping her upright.

Taking her keys from her shaky fingers, Sean took the liberty of opening the door for her, and for a moment, she had a flashback to not so long ago when he'd done the same thing. A flashback that included her legs wrapped around him and his tongue in her mouth. Except this time when he nudged the door open, he ushered her through, his expression was undecipherable.

"Shower and bed, Ivy." His voice was low as he gazed down at her with eyes so dark they were nearly black.

The heat from his body poured over her, stilling the shiver that had started to wrack her limbs as sweat cooled on her skin. Her internal Sean magnet tugged from deep within, dragging her a step closer to his heat.

His name fell from her lips, a whisper so quiet she wasn't sure it came out as a word or a breath. What she did know was that she didn't want him to leave. She didn't want to be alone. Their eyes held for another impenetrable moment, and Sean's lips parted slightly, as if he wanted to say something too. But whatever he might have said died when he shut his mouth, took her by the shoulders, and gently but firmly maneuvered her farther into her apartment.

"Shower, bed." He stepped away, into the hallway. "Lock the door behind me. I'll wait until I hear it." He then shut the door to her own apartment in her face.

After she flipped the lock, she immediately plastered herself to the peephole, and her heart plummeted as she watched him enter his own apartment without a backward glance.

Turning her back to the door, she slid down it, hugged her knees to her chest, and dropped her face onto them as she tried to breathe her way through the moment. The moment where Sean had abandoned her to her memories, heartache, and past.

CHAPTER EIGHT

The next morning, Sean's fist hit the tight leather of the punching bag with a force that reverberated through his knuckles and straight up his forearms. He followed up with a powerful side kick and let a grunt escape through his clenched teeth. He'd arrived early that morning, more than an hour before the gym opened, but had since lost track of time. Eventually, he heard the sounds of the gym coming to life around him. A speed bag being pummeled, the clang of weights, the whir of spin cycles, the grunts and smacks of fists hitting flesh in the ring.

At some point during his vendetta with the bag, the gym had officially opened, but to him it was all background noise. Turned out, the run he'd forced Ivy to go on last night hadn't done much to cool his jets or ease the knot sitting low in his gut. Added to that, memories of last night kept repeating in his head, like a scratched record stuck playing a song he fucking hated.

He didn't regret sending Greg Lewis off the way he had. He was a player who had no business putting his hands on Ivy, and Sean was going to make sure date night didn't happen again. He didn't care if that put him in the Neanderthal category. It was what it was.

Sean was lost in the abyss of regretting everything that happened after that. He never should have kissed her, should have exercised more self-control. But he had kissed her, and as soon as his lips touched hers, he'd gone up in flames. His blood still burned with the knowledge that he'd been ready to take her right then and there if she hadn't frozen under him like a trapped animal freezes under its predator.

He'd lost her in that moment. He'd been so adrift in the frenzy of his own lust and desire, he'd missed all her cues, until she'd turned to stone under him. It was his worst nightmare come true. And apparently hers as well.

Goddammit.

His fist connected with the bag as the expletive rang through his head. He'd known it, hadn't he? All these years, he'd known something had happened to her. He hadn't needed her to tell him. He'd told himself he didn't have to hear her say it, but if he had any uncertainty before, he sure as hell didn't have any now. Ivy had been hurt. Christ only knew how bad, but the thought that Sean had made her relive even a second of it had self-loathing coursing through his veins with a ferocity that burned him from the inside out.

Leaving her in her apartment after their run, when all he wanted to do was hover close by to make sure she was alright, had been harder than he could have ever predicted. He'd forced himself back to his apartment, showered, then lay in bed staring at the ceiling, every possible scenario of what might have happened to her spinning in his head until the dawn's light started to seep through his window blinds.

He'd grown up around all kinds of violence. His parents

had tried to make life as normal as possible for his brother and him, but there were things they simply couldn't protect their children from while trying to raise a family in a low-income neighborhood in inner city Chicago. When his dad had been alive, they'd lived in a small, rented house in an area that had been decent during the daytime, but sketchy enough after dark that his parents hadn't let him and his brother out. After his dad died, everything changed. They'd had to move to a rougher part of town, where rent was cheaper. His mother had worked two jobs to make ends meet. If his father had thought their first neighborhood was a shithole, he would have rolled in his grave at the one they ended up in.

The sounds of sirens, glass shattering, people screaming and cursing, and the not infrequent pops of gunfire were the soundtrack of his youth. Though he grew up in a peaceful home, violence had surrounded his upbringing. It existed, like a living, breathing thing, circling him. And as such, he was always braced for it. He never looked for a fight, but he was always ready for one.

And Lord knew he'd tried to avoid it. For years he avoided the needless street fights, running from the gangs, engaging with people who tried to goad him into a fight over petty shit. But when his mom had gotten sick, the rug had been pulled out, and for a brief moment he'd found himself wrapped up in a world his parents had tried so hard to protect him from.

Mostly, he'd trained himself not to think about that time. He'd rebuilt himself, and now, instead of watching people be destroyed by violence, he'd made it his mission to show them how to use that strength and power to build themselves back up or never get beaten down in the first place.

How to fight with control, purpose, discipline, and not rage, desperation, or power trips.

Nothing good came from that kind of violence. All it left was a trail of devastation. He'd seen too many hollow eyes and haunted faces back in Chicago. Seen it in his brother's eyes countless times, as well as in Ivy's the first day they met.

Supporting her training, helping her become strong and resilient, watching the hollowness recede bit by bit, he wanted to believe he'd been a positive part of her journey. But last night his own lack of self-control had put that look back into her eyes, and he hated himself for that.

Then, as if his past had caught wind of last night, he'd received a text from his brother that morning, reminding him that his self-loathing had layers.

He punched the bag again, and this time, two hands caught it on the other side, stilling the back swing. His best friend's face appeared around the side of the bag, his brow furrowed with concern.

Sean dropped his arms to his sides, breathing heavily. "What the fuck do you want?" he demanded, knowing he had no reason to sound so harsh, but needing an outlet for all the rage that was still swirling inside him.

Gabe cocked an eyebrow. "I'm supposed to be the grumpy one, remember?" He pointed to himself. "I'm the asshole," he said slowly, as if he were teaching a lesson. Then he pointed at Sean and said, "You're the chill one."

Sean grunted a humorless laugh. "Not today, I guess."

"You wanna go a round in the ring?" Gabe asked casually, which Sean guessed was about as close as he'd get to outright asking what was wrong.

Gabe knew him well. They'd been friends almost from the week Sean arrived in Portland. Sean had wandered into the bar looking for a cold drink and a distraction from his stress, and he'd found a friend instead. He'd been there when Gabe's first wife died in a car crash seven years ago, and through all the messy stuff that came after. And Gabe had been there for him as he struggled to get his gym up and running, backing him financially when he would have had to fold otherwise, and kicking his ass when Sean was low on optimism. Since then, Sean had paid back both the money and the ass-kickings. Civilized ones, of course.

But there was still a lot his friend didn't know. Shit about Ivy. How could he possibly explain what happened last night? Gabe knew Sean had a brother serving time back in Chicago, but he didn't know what had landed Jordan in jail in the first place.

Guilt poked at him for keeping this secret from his friend, but sitting down with Gabe and telling him about all of his many shortcomings wasn't anywhere near the top of his list of things he should have a chat about.

He'd rather do a round in the ring. Lifting a shoulder, he said, "Sure."

They made their way across the gym and slipped between the ropes. They started off dancing around each other, tossing the odd jab to test the waters. Sean was by far more skilled in any and every kind of martial art than Gabe. He'd had years of training and practice that Gabe couldn't compete with. But Gabe had spent a lot of time in the ring with Sean, so he was well versed in his fighting style, and had learned how to stay on his feet. Plus, Gabe was no wimp, his muscles had muscles, and he was well over six-feet. Because of that, Sean never doubted it was a fair fight. And it wasn't like Gabe ever got pulverized.

They lay into each other for a couple of minutes, landing a few solid punches each. Releasing his frustration in this calculated, disciplined fashion was what had attracted him to martial arts in the first place. It was all mastery and restraint. Biding your time and being strategic, as opposed to losing control and lashing out. At the same time, it provided an outlet. A safe place for him to let out his emotions, which happened to be a hell of a lot of frustration today.

His father had started both him and Jordan in lessons when they were quite young, believing it wouldn't hurt for his boys to build street smarts and self-defense knowledge from an early age.

Fond memories from those days long ago flickered through Sean's mind like an old movie. His dad sitting on an old wooden chair in the dojo, observing his boys as they received their training from the instructor who seemed at least a hundred years old. Repeating movements over and over with his brother beside him. The scent of bleach, stale sweat, and old wooden floors thick in the air. The single floor fan whirling in the corner by the chair where his dad sat.

It had been a crumby place, the cheapest option, but Sean had fallen in love with it right away, along with the sport. And as his dad had hoped, he'd pursued his training with a passion that, ultimately, kept him too busy to get wrapped up with the other extracurricular activities that many young men, his brother included, ended up getting involved in. Gangs, violence, and crime being the top three of those activities.

Barely dodging an uppercut from Gabe, Sean gave his head a quick shake. He needed to get his mind together before he gave his friend bragging rights for life. Shit, with his brother and Ivy occupying every inch of real estate in his brain, he was losing his hard-earned focus.

He counter attacked Gabe with a quick double jab and a straight right punch to the body getting himself back in the fight.

Jordan. The text from this morning had been on his mind all day. Jordan had always been the fucking renegade. Never could follow a single goddamn rule to save his sorry ass. The martial arts had tempered his defiant nature somewhat, but after their father had died, and they had moved to an even worse part of town, he'd amped it up again. Not coming home until all hours, sometimes not at all. Stints in juvenile detention for getting wrapped up in low-level crimes. It had broken their mother's heart seeing her oldest son spiral down that path.

So, Sean had done everything he could to make up for his brother's lack of direction. He stayed focused in school, got a part-time job to pay for his continued training, and helped his mom in any way he could. When he'd been halfway through high school, his mother had started talking about him attending college, even though he knew they could never afford it. But in the end, it hadn't even mattered, because she'd gotten sick, and every spare penny had gone into paying for her medical treatment.

Who knew it would take a terminal diagnosis to bring his wayward brother home?

When Sean went in for a knee strike, Gabe caught him around the waist in a clinch and almost brought them to the ground. Jesus, he was more zoned out than he thought because he hadn't even realized when their friendly spar had crossed the line into the fight zone.

Focus. If Gabe knocked him down, he'd never hear the end of it. Striking out with a hard left foot jab, he put some distance between them and regained his footing.

Fucking memories. He threw out another jab, harder

than the last one. Every time the past bubbled to the surface, a renewed regret swamped him. He'd made so many mistakes in his life, so many things he wished he could take back. And he'd been pretty good at pushing the guilt down. The outrage and self-disgust. But lately, it was getting harder to keep all of the monsters at bay.

The crack had emerged when his brother had started reaching out to him again, a sliver of an opening that let his suppressed feelings about his past slip through. Then Ivy had come up with her hair brained idea, pushing against the crack until it burst wide open, and now feelings he'd worked so hard to clamp down over the years were reawakening.

All at the same fucking time.

Anger, frustration, grief, despair, not to mention the fear that he was going to make another wrong move and lose yet another precious thing in his life. They were all working together to chip away at his hard won, easy-going persona, revealing the true Sean Thompson that lived beneath. And it was becoming abundantly clear that there was nothing easy-going about him at all.

Vaguely, as though from a great distance, he heard a pained grunt coming from Gabe followed by the sharp cry that sounded terrifyingly like Ivy. Emerging out of the past, he grappled to regain control. But it must have been worse than he realized, because when he turned his head towards where he'd heard Ivy call his name, he found her trying to crawl through the ropes and into the ring.

What the fuck was she doing? Sean attempted to reach for her, but like he was moving through sludge, his limbs wouldn't cooperate. His brain remained trapped somewhere between the past and the present. The two not reconciling in time with his body.

That's when two horrifying things happened. Greg Lewis grabbed Ivy around the waist, trying to pull her out of the ring. She resisted him, gripping the rope, but slipped and her cheek smacked the canvas hard at the exact same time he heard the crack of a glove against his jaw.

And then all the lights went out.

CHAPTER NINE

Ivy stood in front of the bathroom mirror and pressed an ice pack to her cheek, trying to work through what had just happened. Never in all the time she'd known Sean had she seen him like that before. Unfocused. Disengaged. Like he wasn't even there.

When she approached him in the ring, she knew he'd lost control of the fight. To anybody else, it might have appeared like he was taking it easy on Gabe, who was an amateur fighter. But Ivy knew Sean too well, and had seen the shift almost the moment it happened. A blankness had entered his eyes that told her he was somewhere else entirely.

Greg had been standing by her, so she'd voiced her concern, but he'd laughed it off. "Thompson doesn't lose control. His focus is like granite, un-fucking-breakable. And believe me, I've tried."

But that hadn't sat right with her. Something was wrong, very wrong. And when things quickly spiraled she reacted instinctively by trying to jump into the ring yelling and screaming. Truthfully, she hadn't even been thinking. She'd simply reacted. Like jumping into churning waters to save someone from drowning, without even considering whether you could keep yourself afloat first.

Not that she even got close, because Greg had pulled her down before she could, and Sean received the knock-out punch.

Poor Gabe. The expression on his face might have been comical—an absurd mix of victory, shock, horror, and confusion—if the gym hadn't erupted into chaos immediately after. Their fearless leader lying motionless on the floor had been panic inducing.

The seconds that had passed felt like freaking years to Ivy. Her heart lodged in her throat, air trapped in her lungs, until the moment Sean's eyes blinked open and he heaved himself into a sitting position. He'd immediately sought her out, trying to get up to come to her. But by then Donovan had arrived at the scene, and since he was probably the only person in the gym strong enough to force Sean to stay seated while he got checked over, Sean hadn't gotten very far.

While Donovan crouched in front of Sean, blocking her from his view, Ivy had fled to the private bathroom in her clinic where she now stood icing her cheek and trying to rein in her reeling thoughts.

In the three years she'd known Sean, she'd never once seen him lose control of a fight or a spar or—anything. It had scared her, but more than that it made her wonder what had been going on in his head to pull him so far away. The incident had been so unlike him. But then again, there had been many incidents recently that were so unlike him. Glimpses of a Sean Thompson she wasn't sure she recognized at all.

A few weeks ago, she'd been convinced that all they were

to each other was friends. Good friends, close friends, but still just friends. But now... Now she was starting to wonder if maybe there was more.

She let the idea of Sean as *more than a friend* curl up and settle in her heart. It rested there comfortably for a second. And a second was about as long as the thought lasted before her fear of relationships and insecurity around connection rushed in and crushed it.

Seriously, what outcome could there possibly be if Sean wanted more than friendship and she couldn't make it through a single romp in the sack? She couldn't even fathom the amount of intentional intimacy it would take to form a romantic relationship. She'd have to tell him everything, and the thought of him knowing the truth made her stomach drop. Disclosing the assault wasn't the only thing that worried her...how did she begin to explain that her own parents hadn't even thought she was worth enough to bother sticking around for?

She trusted him enough to be her first positive sexual experience, but could she trust herself enough to let it be more than that? She hadn't the foggiest, but she wasn't optimistic.

The squeak of the door opening snapped her out of her contemplation, and she let out a surprised yelp, her hand fluttering to her chest. When Sean's immensely powerful body appeared in her bathroom, her heart sighed in relief and settled. There he was, whole, safe, solid.

He stood there, unmoving, as he scanned her face, eventually landing on the spot where she'd smacked it against the floor. His eyes darkened, then almost immediately melted, regret and pity softening his features. Unable to stomach him looking at her like that, she lowered her gaze to the floor.

"No."

Ivy heard the door click shut behind him, then the thump of his steps as he crossed the floor toward her.

"Don't ever lower your eyes to me." His voice, deep and commanding, filled the room like his presence, dominating it, and she lifted her face to meet his gaze.

His eyes burned into hers, and the invisible thread that connected them pulsed to life. With a jerk of his chin, the thread tugged, and she lifted her face to the side, fully exposing the place where she'd been hurt.

A sharp inhale hissed through his clenched teeth. "What happened—?"

She couldn't let him finish. She spun to face the mirror and held the ice pack to her cheek again, covering the red spot. "That's my question, Sean." Her voice surprised her by coming out strong and clear. "What happened out there?" Then quieter, she asked, "Are you okay?"

Their gazes met in the mirror.

"I'm fine, Ivy." His soft baritone did what it always did to her. It sent a shiver down her spine to her core. "I sparred with Gabe, and I let him get one on me when I got distracted by you climbing through the fucking ropes. What the hell do you think you were doing?"

Okay, that pissed her off. She dropped the ice pack and whirled on him. "I was trying to get to you! And don't pull that crap on me, like it's my fault you got knocked out. You were already gone, Sean, like you were having an out-of-body experience or something. And nobody seemed to notice! So, I—I wanted to help you."

"Help me? Ivy, you don't have to help me. Or worry about Gabe. His fists are softer than a three-year-old's."

"Yeah, well," Ivy sniffed, facing the mirror again. "The

bruise on your face says otherwise." A heavy sigh filled the air beside her, and she realized he stepped closer.

"I hate this," he murmured, as he reached over her shoulder for the ice pack sitting on the counter.

She winced when he placed it gently against her cheek.

"I hate seeing you hurt. I hate fighting with you. I hate what we're becoming."

Turning to him was as natural as taking her next breath. The welcoming warmth of his chest was her safety net. "Then let's stop, Sean. Can't we go back? To before?" *Before I ruined everything.*

"Ivy." His lips came down and pressed against the crown of her head.

Her hands went around his waist, drawing him closer, fingers barely dipping into the waistband of his shorts, smooth skin against soft fingertips. His scent in her lungs. Her mind reassured against his lips.

For a while, they simply stood, locked together.

"Mmmm." A sigh of comfort and satisfaction left her. "This is why I wanted it to be with you."

"Want what to be with me?" The question brushed against her hair, while his palm rubbed up and down her back, lulling her into a familiar sense of security.

"My trust fall."

This brought his head up, and he tipped hers back with a nudge of his finger. Deep, searching eyes met hers, as if he was trying to read the meaning behind her words. She swayed closer, seeking his solid warmth, waiting for his next words. But if he was going to respond, he never had a chance, because the door to the bathroom swung open again.

"Well," Erica's raspy voice interrupted the loaded pause that followed. "This is unexpected."

Against her body, Sean's giant chest heaved in a sigh. Slowly, he untangled from her, but kept eye contact, his dark irises communicating a dozen things she couldn't translate. Or was too afraid to.

"Sooo," Erica continued. "Is this, like, a thing?"

From the outside, Ivy could only guess what it must have looked like. Her and Sean locked together. Ivy's fingertips digging into the back of his shorts. Sean's head inclined toward Ivy's. From the back, they probably looked like they were making out. Which was a rumor she didn't want spreading around Thompson Kickboxing.

"No," Ivy managed, her body still missing the warmth of Sean's. "We were having a discussion about safety in the ring."

"Ri-ight. 'Cause that's exactly what that looked like, right there. A discussion between friends."

And maybe it was the way Sean's gaze burned into hers, or maybe it was the way her heart was suddenly galloping in her chest at the word *friends*, because everything about the last few minutes had been decidedly more intimate than anything friends would share. Or maybe it was simply that he was her friend, and she didn't want to lose that because the thought of disappointing him by trying to be anything more was more terrifying than losing him completely. But whatever it was, she heard herself responding, "Yep, that's exactly what it was. A discussion between friends."

Sean's eyes leveled with hers, narrowed. Then hardened. Finally, he nodded. "Friends," he uttered straight at her, followed curtly by, "Don't ever pull a stunt like that again when someone is sparring in the ring. Ever."

Then he was gone, the door swinging shut in his wake.

She glanced at Erica, who was looking at her with a palpable sympathy.

"Don't," Ivy said, holding up her hand. "Please don't say anything."

Erica's mouth curved into a sad smile, but she stayed silent, and Ivy loved her all the more for it. Exhaustion swamped her, weighing down her body and aching in her bones. The last thing she needed was slap-stick banter about what Erica had walked in on.

But there was no banter forthcoming. There was only silence as Erica wrapped Ivy in a big embrace, holding her together so she didn't fall completely apart.

CHAPTER TEN

I t was finally Friday. Thank fuck. Sean walked into Bowie's not knowing exactly how he'd made it through the week in one piece, only that he somehow had. And now he needed a beer. Badly.

It was 7 p.m. and Bowie's was already packed. It was one of the most popular local hangouts in the city, and Sean always thought a huge part of the allure was that Gabe kept things simple. The decor didn't have a particular theme or ostentatious design that might attract some and isolate others. It was a classic space with bar stools and tables set up around the edges, the main bar dominating the back of the room, and a space in the center for a dance floor. Local art, including pieces painted by Gabe's wife, hung in strategic locations. There was an alcove off to the side for private conversation or a game of pool or darts, if that's what customers were looking for. Which Sean sometimes was. But not tonight.

Tonight, he was looking for a drink, so he headed straight to the bar and claimed one of the stools. His ass had barely touched the seat when a beer was shoved under his nose. When he glanced up, Gabe nodded at him in greeting from his usual place behind the bar.

He was wearing the classic black Bowie's t-shirt that all his staff wore and had a black bar cloth slung over one shoulder.

"Thanks," Sean muttered, then lifted the cold glass to his lip and drank deeply.

"Face looks better." Gabe made himself busy wiping down the bar, but Sean knew his friend still felt bad about what happened. "Look, man, I know I've apologized like a hundred times, but I'm so fucking mad at myself. I wasn't in my head when I took that last shot at you." He took his time drying off a glass, watching it intently as he dragged the cloth over it. "I guess I just had my mind stuck in the future, worrying about shit I have no control over and not focusing on what was in front of me."

Sean knew his friend was talking as much about his real life as he was about the fight. Just like he knew Gabe and Hope's trouble conceiving a baby was weighing on them both, and those worries had ultimately distracted Gabe in the ring.

"Yeah well, if your head was stuck in the future, mind was stuck in the past. I took a few shots I shouldn't have too, so forget it dude. It's in the rearview." Sean cracked a smile. "Besides, it's gonna take more than one punch from your soft hands to mess this beauty up." Sean stroked his knuckles over his cheek while fluttering his eyelashes.

Gabe laughed, and his shoulders relaxed. "You're such an ass."

Sean chuckled, grateful for the ease of communication between the male species.

Communication with women seemed to be a thousand times more complicated. He hadn't talked to Ivy since the incident, though he watched her like a hawk whenever he'd seen her in the gym. It seemed she was avoiding him because she hardly came out of her PT clinic except to train or take a class. Not that she'd taken any of his classes lately. He hadn't sought her out either. What was there to say? Things between them were so...lost.

But it drove him crazy—needing the distance, but wanting her close.

"Why is it that men can have an entire conversation without saying much at all?" Hope came up beside her husband, kissed him on the cheek, then grabbed a bottle of whisky off the shelf. She was wearing the Bowie's staff shirt, which told Sean she was pulling a shift behind the bar tonight. She did this from time to time, joking that it was about as close to a date night as she could get with her husband these days.

Gabe never found the joke funny, but Sean knew Hope didn't mind the work. She was good at it and understood that the bar was Gabe's passion. She never resented the time Gabe had to pour into it, rather she embraced it as an extension of their family. Which was part of what made her perfect for Gabe.

Envy twisted like a knife in his gut. He wasn't sure he'd ever have what his friend had—the perfect wife, a great kid, a house that was a home with a yard big enough for a dog. He wasn't even sure it was what he really wanted. But Hope and Gabe made settling down look pretty damn tempting.

"That's because we don't need to hash over every little detail of every little thing." Gabe looked at his wife affectionately. "There's something to be said for not overthinking every damn thing."

"I'm the queen of overthinking," Hope countered as she

poured two shots of whisky into a glass, then reached for the bitters. "You've never complained before."

"Yeah, that's because you're my Queen too. And because I'd like to keep my balls where they are."

Hope grabbed the bar towel off his shoulder and smacked him with it. Gabe chuckled and ducked his head to steal a kiss.

"Should I call Carter so you two can get a room?" Sean quipped, then realized something. "Where is he anyway?" It was a rare thing not to see Gabe's right-hand serving liquor behind the bar.

Gabe stared at the drink he was mixing. "Night off," he murmured.

Sean glanced at Hope as her worried gaze darted toward the dance floor. Sean turned in his seat to follow her line of vision.

Carter was on the dance floor. With Ivy. Dancing like nobody was watching.

His first thought when he saw them wiggle their way around the floor was *Jesus-Fucking-Christ, not another one.*

Honestly, he'd never met a person more hellbent on putting him into an early grave than Ivy Harrington. And she was going to do it by flaunting every rat bastard in front of him until he lost his ever-loving mind.

Except Carter wasn't a rat bastard. He was outrageously outgoing, too good looking for his own good, and attracted nearly everyone who came his way. And there were many, from all different backgrounds, genders, colors, and personalities who came his way. But he was a decent guy. Upstanding, loyal, protective. And if Sean had to handpick a guy for Ivy, it would probably have been Carter.

The night in the bar, a few months ago, when that dick had approached Ivy and she froze, Carter had taken her away, kept her safe and cared for her while Sean, Gabe, and mostly Hope had handled the situation. Sean trusted Carter with Ivy, and if he had any say in who she was going to pick for this damned plan of hers, which he was under no illusion he did, he'd have given Carter a pass. Carter had *fuck buddy extraordinaire* written all over him.

And yet, watching them together, Sean couldn't stop the tick in his jaw from working its way up to his brain.

"I'd say," Hope said, interrupting his aneurysm. "It's better she dances with Carter than the beefcake in the corner who's been eyeing her all night."

Sean's head swiveled to where Hope had nodded. There on the bar stool sat a ripped Adonis type with so many muscles they covered most of his neck, leaving only his giant head bulging out from his crisp white shirt. Staring over the rim of a Martini glass, of all fucking things, Beefcake watched Ivy and Carter dance with an intensity that would melt her clothes with his eyes alone.

Shit. He should have stayed home. Sean chugged the rest of his beer before banging the glass down with slightly more force than necessary.

"Why does she have to be so motherfucking persistent with everything?" he asked to no one in particular.

Hope took his beer glass and replaced it with a soda water. She knew his routine and his one beer limit.

Taking a sip, he watched Ivy and had to admit, he liked seeing her like this. Carefree. Not giving a flying fuck what anyone thought. Losing herself in the music. Happy.

She deserved it.

Hope leaned forward, resting her chin in her palm, following Sean's line of sight. "You know, Sean, I've always thought there was something between you and Ivy. Maybe—"

"You thought wrong." His tone sounded unintentionally harsh. Being more than Ivy's friend was a dream, and the more she pursued this ridiculous friends-with-benefits sex scheme, the more Sean was starting to think a dream was all it would ever be.

Even so, Hope looked at him like he was the wrong one and she was about to tell him so, but a customer came up to the bar with an order before she could open her mouth to speak.

One song shifted into another and the tempo changed slightly. Out of the corner of his eye, Sean noticed Beefcake rise from his seat and head toward the dancing duo.

Fuck's sake. His life was starting to feel like one big déjà vu. Before he could give it any more thought, he stalked over to where Ivy and Carter were laughing like lunatics on the dance floor.

"Can I cut in? We need to talk," he said, taking her by the elbow and leading her away from Carter—and Beefcake making his way toward them.

"About what?" Her eyes flashed as she glared at his hand holding her arm.

He released her immediately.

Feeling a familiar, but still pathetic, sense of desperation clawing its way up his spine, Sean bent until he was at her eye level. "Please?"

Ivy reeled back, her face indignant, hurt swimming in her eyes. Hurt he'd put there.

"Why are you doing this?"

"Ivy—" He needed to set the record straight on a few things here, but a movement behind her caught his attention, and he panicked as Beefcake rapidly approached.

Ivy followed his gaze, then jerked her head back, aghast. "Are you kidding me, Sean? Tell me you aren't coming to pull me over here because you think that hunk of muscle is headed my way?" She pushed her fists onto her hips and stared up at him. "Tell me."

Looking at her straight on was always his greatest exercise of control. Her body sizzled in a tight little skirt and a loose, flirty top. Layers of hair falling around her chin, accentuating her soft jawline and high cheekbones. Her eyes, like always, were incandescent, stunningly beautiful. She was his friend, but whenever he so much as glanced at her, he saw his whole future.

He wasn't exactly sure when his life became unimaginable without her. Everything with Ivy had happened so gradually, like a wave in the middle of an ocean starting as little more than a movement, but landing hours later on the shore with a crash.

What killed him was that, within the span of a few weeks, a distance had grown between them. Like she was being pulled away by a tide of fear and anger. His fear, her anger. And he had no fucking clue how to stop it.

They wanted different things. She wanted a friend with benefits. He wanted everything. Every piece, the cracked and the chipped, the whole and the parts in progress. He wanted it all. He wanted the benefit of their friendship to be love.

She was ripping him a new one, yelling at him about being a jerk, but his thoughts were louder. Her hands curled into tight fists around his shirt as she pushed his chest. And all he could think about was how much he wanted her, and how fucking hard it was to stand this close to her and not have her. In his heart, in his life, and in his bed.

And suddenly his hands were on her, gently enveloping her face, threading his fingers through her hair. Time slowed, music dulled, Ivy's lips stopped moving. Her eyes grew wide, like twin moons. So bright they were almost a silvery-blue, and in them he saw it—the need that mirrored the one firing through him.

He rubbed his thumb across her bottom lip. "Can I kiss you?" He wasn't sure he'd spoken out loud or if he simply projected the words into her mind, but he saw her nod. One small movement of her head while her eyes held his, signaling consent, and he was pulling her in, crushing his lips against hers.

The music blurred with the hard beat of Sean's heart. People faded along with the bar. All that remained was the heat of her lips against his, the mist of breath, and their passion waging a battle to surrender between them.

He lifted his mouth off hers and clamped it down on the soft flesh right below her earlobe. His grip on her tightening when he heard her low moan. Maybe he could kiss some sense into her. Maybe if his lips never left her body, she'd allow herself to admit it. They were so much more than friends.

It was that thought that shocked him into stopping. Never in his life had he used sex to manipulate a woman, and he wasn't starting now. Especially not with Ivy. If she was going to let him in, he wanted her to do it freely and wholeheartedly. He *needed* her to do it freely. Especially since he was pretty damn sure that freedom had been taken away from her before.

Fuck.

The heat in him was doused like a bucket of cold water had been dumped on it. He lifted his head, watching as her eyes slowly opened, a little bit dazed, a little bit reluctant. The blue was darkened with lust. She wanted him. But not the way he wanted her to want him. And that wasn't her fault. He'd leave her be and lick his wounds in private.

"Sean, you can't keep kissing me, and then tell me you can't give me what I want."

"I know. Jesus, I know."

"I need to do this my way."

"I know," he repeated, solemn now because he did. However she chose to deal with it, he needed to accept it. This wasn't his battle to fight. But dammit...

"I'll never not worry about you, Ivy." Obviously, she deserved more of a statement than that, but right now, with his heart thundering in his chest, and his mouth still wet from her kiss, it was all he had. When he straightened and looked past her shoulder, a defeated sigh escaped him. "Although it looks like my concern was misplaced this time."

"It's always misplaced," she retorted, turning her head to follow his gaze.

Beefcake was leaning against a bar table, chatting up Carter.

Ivy snorted. "Sometimes I envy him."

"How so?" Sean asked, watching Carter laugh at something Beefcake said.

"It's like he doesn't have a single insecurity. He's so effortlessly confident."

The way she said those final words, almost to herself, made Sean look back to her. This was one of those cryptic moments that hinted at something deeper but he knew he couldn't push her.

Which was just as well, he'd pressed her enough for one night. His next best course was to walk away. But before he could take a single step, Ivy whirled on him, eyes blazing.

"Why do you only want me when it looks like someone else is showing interest?" she demanded.

Christ. He should have bolted when she'd had her back to him.

"You're blind if you think that."

Her eyes narrowed at his vague remark.

What he wanted to tell her was that he wanted her all the fucking time. Every minute of every hour of every day. And it only pissed him off when someone showed interest because she was so wrapped around his heart that the idea of someone else having her felt like they were taking away the thing that was keeping him alive.

That's what he *wanted* to say. But he didn't say that, because he knew her well enough to know she wasn't ready for it. Whatever mental block she had that made her believe she wasn't deserving of someone to love her wholly and completely wasn't unblocked. And until it was, there was no point in pouring his heart out. She wouldn't hear it.

So he left it at that. Another fucking stalemate. Super.

"I'm going home." She finally said. "I'm tired."

He nodded. "Fine, I'll walk you."

"You won't."

"Ivy."

"You won't, Sean." She turned and as she walked away, Sean watched another acre grow between them.

CHAPTER ELEVEN

"**P**ick up the pace, ladies!" Erica hollered in her typical *Sports Illustrated* model come drill sergeant tone. "I don't want to see your asses in the air. Keep your form. Jesus, what are you? Beginners? This is an *advanced* class. Read the small print next time."

At six in the morning on a Saturday, Ivy did feel like a beginner as she went down for another boxer burpee. She hated Erica's 'warmups.' They were like a full work out all on their own, but Ivy was avoiding Sean's classes and Erica was the next best option. So here she was, doing her thousandth burpee of the morning, because she needed a way to release all the pent-up emotion that was boiling inside her. She'd forgone her morning run because the rain was torrential and even she had limits from her self-punishment. Little did she know then that Erica's class would be a thousand times worse than running in a downpour.

"Ivy Harrington. I want to see you kiss the fucking floor. Lower!" Erica barked.

They had moved on to push-ups.

"Holy shit," Christine wheezed from beside Ivy. "Who pissed in her cereal this morning?"

If Ivy could have caught her breath, she might have responded, but as it was, 'kissing the floor' was taking every last ounce of her energy.

Christine was right. Erica was a nightmare trainer on good days. She'd earned a reputation for it. Anyone who took her class was going to feel the memory of her tyranny for at least a week in their sore muscles.

Today, though, she seemed off. She wasn't just being a tyrant, she was being a little mean.

"Anna," Wendy gasped the name as she lowered herself into yet another push-up. She barely made it back up, and that was saying something for the Brazilian jiu-jitsu master who could drop push-ups like Ivy dunked donuts. "Fight."

Erica had a fight with Anna? Impossible. They were the perfect couple, the envy of all their friends. They had been trending #couplegoals pretty much the entire four years they'd been together. They were the couple who made Ivy believe that maybe true love did exist, and maybe it could defy all the odds. They'd had spats to be sure, but nothing that resulted in Ivy getting her ass whipped in class at six on a Saturday morning. The whole idea that such a perfect couple could be in crisis burned more than Ivy's thighs midway through class.

Forty-five painful minutes after Wendy's revelation, the supposedly in-shape Ivy, and her two fitness influencer co-workers, lay on the floor of studio one, drenched in sweat and gasping for air. The other students, those that hadn't crawled out early, unable to make it through the drills, had somehow managed to drag their sorry asses out of the room now.

Erica hovered above them, arms folded, lips twisted into a sneer. "Wimps," she muttered before stalking out of the room.

"It must be bad," Ivy said to the ceiling. She tried to blow her bangs away from her eyes, and failed. They were glued to her forehead with sweat.

"Yeah." Christine's disembodied voice floated up from yonder. "She's never insulted us before. Not after class was officially over."

"Bagels," Wendy managed and got a resounding grunt of approval.

Within half an hour Ivy, Wendy, and Christine had showered, changed, and dragged Erica against her will to the bagel shop down the street, where they now sat, staring expectantly at Erica, waiting for her to spill.

She sat slumped in her chair, arms folded over her chest, her dark curly hair a halo around her frown-creased face.

Finally, Ivy bit the bullet and spoke. "Did she cheat on you?"

Beside her, Wendy gasped. Not surprising. Even the suggestion that Anna would cheat on Erica was about as unfathomable as someone divorcing a Hemsworth brother. And yet, it had happened.

Erica stared out the window.

"Is she unhappy about something?" Christine ventured more gently than Ivy had. "Maybe you can work it out. I mean, everyone goes through their ups and downs. Surely you can work out what—"

Erica made a sound that was half sigh, half groan. "She wants to get married."

A brief pause ensued before Ivy dropped her bagel on her plate and thumped her hand on the table, rattling everyone's plates. "Well, that's just fucking unacceptable."

Christine elbowed Ivy in her side. Her sarcastic humor had come through at an inappropriate time yet again, but honestly, she couldn't help it. Anna was a beautiful, intelligent, sophisticated woman who not only adored Erica, but treated her like a queen. It was a shocker that they weren't married already.

Blessed with more decorum than Ivy, Wendy lay her hand over Erica's. "Oh hon, how is that a bad thing?" she cooed in a soothing voice Ivy couldn't have imitated if she tried.

Erica's face crumpled. "I don't know," she cried. "Anna was so damn cute last night, setting the table real nice, made my favorite meal, wore a pretty dress. It was all so perfect, and then she popped the question and I froze. Totally freaked." She dropped her head in her hands and her shoulders started to shudder.

Ivy, Christine, and Wendy looked at each other. Ivy shrugged helplessly. This was so not her forte. In one way, she could totally understand. If anyone proposed to her, she'd freak too. But she was single and very likely staying that way. Erica and Anna were in a long-term committed relationship, the trajectory of which was headed straight to matrimonial bliss. But someone had to say something before hyperventilation ensued.

"Marriage is fucking scary. Of course you freaked." The words were out of her mouth before they'd even fully formed in her head. What the hell, when in doubt, fill the silence with awkward and inappropriate comments.

Christine made a subtle cutting motion across her neck. Wendy scowled, shaking her head.

Erica looked up, eyelashes wet with tears. "Yes. It is. It's *so* scary. I mean, what if we fail? Things are so good right now. Why screw it up? What if marriage ruins us?" Erica hadn't taken her eyes off Ivy as she spoke, as if Ivy held all the answers.

"Hey, do *not* look at me. I am no relationship therapist. I can't even fulfill my mission to find a fuck buddy, so I'm not the person who should be dolling out martial advice."

Wendy fixed her full attention on Ivy. "You're on a mission to find a fuck buddy?"

Why had she mentioned her mission? "Can we stay focused here? All I'm saying is I don't know much about love or commitment. But from what I've seen between Hope and Gabe, I think marriage is one of those motherfucking scary things that you do only because the alternative is even scarier."

"But why can't we keep doing what we're doing? Live together, love each other, and not be married?"

"Because that's not making Anna happy anymore." Ivy wiped the corner of her mouth with a napkin. "She wants more. She wants the formality of marriage to seal her commitment with you. Which, when you think of it, is actually pretty damn special. And romantic."

The silence that followed was deafening, and Ivy took in three sets of eyes staring at her as if she was a specialty showcase at the museum. "What?" she asked the blinking eyes.

"That was a pretty impressive speech," Christine mused. "I didn't realize you were a closet romantic."

"I'm not!" Good Lord, she was the opposite. She was about as twisted and jaded as they came. Besides, she'd hardly call her quest for finding a fuck buddy romantic. "But I do think that what Erica and Anna have is once in a lifetime. Even I can see that. And if you ever have something like that handed to you, you should grab on. That's all I'm saying."

"Like you would do if someone dropped love in your lap," Erica said with a knowing smirk, wiping a tear off her cheek.

"No one is dropping love in my lap, and this isn't about me." Ivy pointed at Erica. "It's about you, and how you've got something pretty damn special that most of us only dream of."

Truth was, Ivy didn't trust herself enough to dream about love and a wholesome relationship. Her travel-blogging parents had all but abandoned her when she became school aged, finding Bali, St. Petersburg, and the African savanna far more interesting than raising the child they'd made together. By the age of five, Ivy was sent to live with her old-fashioned English nana in a suburb outside of Seattle so she'd have more 'stability,' which had felt an awful lot like 'neglect' to young Ivy.

As if her parents jet-setting around the world chasing the next adventure instead of being with their daughter hadn't done enough emotional damage, the assault had happened and dissolved what was left of her self-worth.

Not that she'd had much to start. As a kid, she'd been scrawny and awkward looking, so she created a personality to match—insular and sullen at best, rude and sarcastic at worst. They hadn't called her Wednesday Addams in high school for nothing. She'd earned her reputation. But mostly, she'd created that personality to protect herself from being hurt. If she came across as not caring, maybe no one would bother to hurt her.

The incident at college had pretty much flushed that experiment down the toilet, so afterward, as part of her great reinvention, she'd made adjustments. She'd moved to Portland, stopped dressing like a prep-school goth, started saying hello back to people she passed on the street, smiled once in a while. That kind of thing. Hanging out with Hope helped her have someone to emulate. Meeting Sean had given her a reason not to fake it all the time.

But none of that meant she was anywhere near ready to trust herself or someone else with a relationship. Sex. She needed to learn how to get comfortable with sex first, before she'd even entertain the idea of a relationship. If she could trust herself in that department, maybe she could trust herself in others.

Sean. She still wanted it to be Sean. Beneath her ribs, her heart sighed. How had things gotten so complicated between them? Regret washed over her. It was her fault for making things awkward and for hurting him in the process. She should have never asked him to be her fuck buddy, and the fact that she had was painful and humiliating.

"I think she's in la-la land."

"She's daydreaming about her future fuck buddy."

"She's scaring me."

Ivy blinked back into reality. "Sorry, what?"

Three shaking heads greeted her.

Wendy spoke first. "Girls, I think it is time for a night out. Ladies only, on the prowl, forgetting about our problems." She dug her phone out of her purse. "I'll text Hope. We haven't done anything like this in ages. Nothing to get you out of the funk like the bonds of female friendship, dancing, and copious amounts of fruity cocktails."

A night with the gals should have sounded like fun, like exactly what she'd needed. Something to take her mind off the intense brown eyes that constantly invaded her brain, inciting a desperate longing to nag at her heart.

Yes, she definitely needed a distraction, and this one sounded perfect.

"This is a bad idea."

Ivy hit the speaker button on her phone before she tossed it on the bedspread beside her so she could properly lean over her bent leg to paint her toenails. Hope's voice lectured her as she stroked Fearless Red onto her big toe.

"If I remember correctly, you were the one encouraging me to reclaim my sexuality," Ivy replied in an even voice.

"Yes, but I meant with Sean! Not some random dude from a techno club in a seedy part of town," Hope countered, her voice horrified.

"Sean doesn't want to be a fuck buddy."

"Because he wants *more*," Hope cried. "He wants you, Ivy. What's wrong with that?"

"Plenty. *More* is a big leap from *can-have-sex-without-freaking-out*. I'd end up screwing it up somehow and he walks away."

"You're being ridiculous." Hope sighed loudly through the phone. "At least tell me Sean knows your plan for tonight."

Now she laughed outright. "Are you kidding me? He'd lose his mind."

"Exactly! So why are you doing it?"

"Because he has no right to lose his mind! Because I made an offer and he didn't take it. I have one life to live, and I'm tired of living in this black hole where I feel numb all the time. I want to live again. I don't want to feel the remnants of that night like paint on my skin that I can't wash off. And I don't give a damn if Sean doesn't like it. He didn't have to live through what I did. I don't owe anyone more than I am willing to give." Her words surged out of her on a huff.

For a moment, there was silence over the phone, and she thought she might have accidentally hung up on her friend.

"You're right," Hope said into the silence. "He has no say. But I'm coming with you guys tonight. And we're not going to Silk, we're going to Bowie's."

She suppressed a groan. Hope was turning into a wet blanket. Bowie's was tame compared to the popular nightclub, Silk. Not to mention that she knew most of the regulars at Bowie's and her chances of finding the potential candidate she was looking for were less likely, especially with all her bodyguards present. Bodyguards being Carter and Gabe. She also knew if she didn't compromise on this, she couldn't guarantee Hope wouldn't sabotage ladies' night altogether by doing something stupid like calling Sean.

"Fine," she agreed. "I'll text the others with the location change."

Having appeased her friend, she hung up on Hope and texted the others, who were more than agreeable to the change. Going to Bowie's often meant a generous family and friends discount on the tab.

The rest of the afternoon went by in a flurry of picking and discarding outfits until she finally settled on pairing a low-necked, long-sleeved bodysuit with skinny jeans and killer black heels that raised her short frame a few more inches. She needed to feel herself tonight, or at least the version of herself she wanted to be. Confident and empowered. She studied her reflection in the mirror as she applied a layer of lipstick. Tonight, she'd need as much confidence as she could muster.

Coi Leray's *Girls Is Players Too* came up next on her playlist, and she'd smacked her lips together with a courage boosting *pop* when there was a sharp knock on her front door.

She pulled a bottle of red wine out of her cupboard and set it on the counter, not at all minding that the ladies had stopped at her apartment for a warm up drink.

But when she opened the door, it wasn't the ladies on the other side.

CHAPTER TWELVE

Sean stood in her doorway, with his hands braced on the doorframe above his bowed head.

Ivy sighed loudly. If he was here to ruin her night, he was going to need that look of defeat because she was going to kick his ass. "I don't have time for this. I'm going out."

When he finally looked at her, his dark eyes immediately roamed over her body like, for once, he wasn't searching for injuries. Her skin warmed under his appraisal, which only irritated her more, so she crossed her arms defiantly. Or maybe it was defensively. She had so little armor against this man.

"You're not going," he said matter-of-factly.

"What do you mean I'm not going? And more importantly, how do you even know I'm going anywhere?" Ivy narrowed her eyes at his impassive stare, realization dawning. "I'm gonna kill her."

"It was Gabe not Hope. He caught wind of what your girlfriends and you were up to and thought I'd like to know."

She glared at him expectantly, but he stared back with a

blank look. After a long and awkward silence, Ivy let out a long exhale.

"Fine, I'll bite. Why would you want to know about what the girls and I are up to tonight, Sean?" She tried to sound bored but, in her chest, her heart was pounding. *Why was he even here?*

"Because I care, Ivy."

The casual drop of the "c" word shot a surge of anger up her spine, making her whole body stiffen. How dare he drop bombs like that after his behavior? "What the hell does that even mean?" she demanded, throwing her arms out. "You have some nerve showing up here like an overbearing ass and—"

"It means—" He interrupted, his jaw bunched. He looked her over again, his gaze lingering on the dip of her neckline, where the tops of her breasts were peeking out enticingly thanks to her new push-up bra. His jaw flexed once before he snapped his gaze back up to her face, his eyes flashing. "Are you planning on going out to find your fuck friend tonight?"

She took a step back with a shocked gasp. "Pardon me?" She was so appalled she was nearly speechless. Nearly. "Please tell me that you did not come here, into my personal space, to tell me who I'm allowed, or not allowed to sleep with."

Sean pushed off the doorframe and straightened to his full height, taking up all the space in the world. Then, with one long step forward, he was in her apartment and shutting the door firmly behind him.

"What if I did?" he asked simply. He didn't move again, but he was close enough that the scent of him filled her nostrils and curled into her stomach, warming her from the inside out.

"Then I'd probably have to learn how to hide a body real fast."

Dammit, why did it have to be him? Why did she have to feel this incessant attraction to this obstinate man? The one man who'd never been obstinate with her in their entire relationship, but had now suddenly decided to be a possessive alpha ass.

What had happened to him? To her? To them?

Suddenly, the weight of a thousand defeats fell onto her shoulders.

"I can't do this with you anymore," she said quietly, sadness filling her from the soul up.

"Ivy—"

"Look, I don't know what century you think you're living in. Or who the hell you think you are since I told you my plan, but you don't get to call these kinds of shots—ever." Anger. Anger worked. It never failed to mask the hurt she was feeling, so she let it flood her system as she stepped right up to him and his nerve. "You had your chance, mister, and all I got from you was a big fat *Hell No*. So, guess what, you don't get to stand there all tall and sullen and moody and tell me how to live my life, because—"

"I'll do it."

Those three words froze the rant she'd been spewing right on her lips. Her heart jumped into her throat, then erupted like a fistful of butterflies. He couldn't mean what she'd thought he meant.

"What?" she whispered shakily, wanting him to clarify. Not wanting him to clarify.

"I agree." His voice was hard, his mouth a firm line. "You're obviously determined to find some action, and there's no way in hell I am going to let you get it from a stranger at a bar or from Greg-Fucking-Lewis. So, I'll do it.

I'll be your fuck buddy, your boy toy, your man servant, your sex slave, whatever the hell you want, Ivy. Please just stop your manhunt."

Ivy's jaw fell open, and she was pretty sure she was losing feeling in her outer extremities because she couldn't feel her fingertips when she poked him in the chest.

"Ouch. What the hell?" Sean rubbed the spot on his pec that she'd poked.

Yep, he was solid. Fully present. Moving and breathing in front of her. Definitely not a hallucination.

Snapping her mouth shut, she straightened her back and squared her shoulders. If he was playing, she'd play too. She wouldn't be made a fool of twice by this man. She had more dignity than that. She hoped.

"Well, I am sorry to inform you Mr. I'm-God's-Gift-To-All-Women, but the offer no longer stands. In case you haven't noticed, I am not the kind of girl who stands around and pines after someone once she's been rejected. I asked. You said no, and I moved forward without you. You can't waltz around thwarting my plans left, right, and center because you don't approve of my choices." She took a fortifying breath and continued, "Now if you'll excuse me, I have a girls' night I'd like to get to."

She tried to shove past him, but he caught her hand, stopping her.

"What if I changed my mind?" he asked, his breath caressing her hair, his baritone rumbling right by her ear. "What if I realized I made a big mistake? The biggest. What if I want your choice to be me, like it was when you started down this warpath?"

"I don't understand," she said, the tremor in her voice betraying how dangerously close she was to losing it. "Why are you doing this now?"

"Because I can't do it anymore, Ivy." Deliberately he shifted to face her again. "I can't be the friend who has to watch you be with someone else. I should have told you yes from the very beginning. I guess I hoped—" He cut off, pulling back a bit.

"Hoped what?" Good God, was that her breathless voice? She didn't even recognize it. Didn't recognize him.

His eyes were so dark they were nearly black. They shone like obsidian, revealing an anguished look before he blinked, and the emotion was shuttered away.

"I hoped you'd give up the idea. But you've clearly made up your mind." His voice was cool and remote, opposite to the rough passionate one he'd spoken with seconds ago. He seemed all over the place, which made her feel better about her own emotional turmoil. "You were right. If it's going to be anyone, it should be me. We're—" He cleared his throat. "Friends. And you trust me. I won't break that trust. If it's casual sex you want, I can give you what you need."

Gone was the heated, passionate man who'd appeared at her door making outlandish demands, and egotistically charged declarations. This man was calm, cool...inaccessible. But both men were Sean. Versions of the friend she trusted, and the only one she could ever imagine sharing this part of herself with.

No one else made sense. That much was clear now. He would, like he said, give her what she wanted, and not ask for more.

Before he could change his mind, Ivy nodded. "Okay," she agreed, looking him up and down. Her gaze stopping at the bulge behind his jeans. She never imagined her mouth-watering at the sight. But it did. Her fingers tingled with the need to touch. "So, um, how about now?"

Holy *mother fuck*. What had he done?

Ivy was staring at his crotch like an alligator about to attack, and the reality of his situation hit him. They were going to have sex. All his wildest, dirtiest fantasies were going to come true. He was going to have this beautiful, fierce, resilient woman in his bed once and for all. Everything he ever wanted. And still, he couldn't shake the feeling of dissatisfaction.

It wasn't right. It didn't *feel* right. It was...unsettling, how forced and manufactured this was all unfolding. Not at all like the natural progression from friends to lovers, to everything and more that he'd imagined.

Ivy removed her heated gaze from his groin and turned to walk the short distance to her kitchen. He followed her, pausing when she stopped and reached for a bottle of wine that sat on the counter. Her hand trembled as she removed the wrapper from the top. The movement was slight, but Sean caught it. It was her tell. She might be turned on, but she was also nervous, reminding Sean again that this whole fuck-buddy, friends-with-benefits scheme was a load of shit.

He had no idea where it had come from or what she was about, but she clearly wasn't 100 percent on board with her own idea or she wouldn't be shaking like a leaf as she reached for a bottle of booze.

"How about we have a glass of wine, and then we can, um, move things into the bedroom?" she said to the bottle, not looking up at him at all.

Ya, no. That wasn't going to work for him.

Sean made his way over to her. He'd agreed to this game, so he was going to stick with it, because he also knew Ivy, and once she had her mind set on something, there was no talking her out of it. But that didn't mean he wouldn't do his best to get her out of her head and into the moment with him.

When he came up behind her, she stiffened in a way that a woman who was eager to have sex didn't do. At least not any woman he'd ever taken to bed.

Slowly reaching around her, he took the bottle out of her hands, lowering his head close to her ear, inhaling the sweet floral scent of her shampoo that fuzzed his brain better than any alcohol ever could.

"No wine," he murmured against her hair. "I fuck better when I'm sober." He set the bottle back on the counter. "And so will you."

Sean saw the fragile column of her throat work up and down as she swallowed, her pulse hammering so desperately he watched it visibly thrusting against her skin. As she let out a slow shuddering breath, he watched closely, keeping his movements slow and allowing her plenty of space. If they were going to go any further tonight, he needed to be sure that she trembled only for him, and not whatever ghost was haunting her mind.

When she leaned back so her shoulder blades brushed his chest, he smiled and allowed himself the indulgent pleasure of brushing his lips against her silky hair. She'd left it down tonight, so it fell softly to her shoulders, framing her lovely face.

"Ivy."

"Yes." She breathed the word out. Not as a reply, but more of an acquiescence, as if she were agreeing to something he had not yet asked.

But he was going to ask now. "Can I kiss you?"

"Yes." This time her voice was more of a whine, like maybe she was as needy for him as he was for her. When she moved to turn around and face him, he stopped her, sliding a hand across her stomach, holding her against him. His other hand moved the curtain of hair away from her neck slowly. Slow enough for her to stop him, slow enough for him to stop.

He could have spun her around and kissed her, which would have likely been what she expected. But he wanted to show her the beauty of all the unexpected. The thousands of ways he could put his lips on her and still make her feel like he'd kissed her senseless. He had a feeling she had no idea how much magic could be created between two people when there was trust, affection, and relationship in the mix. And he wanted to show her. Oh, how he wanted to show her.

When she made no move to stop him, Sean watched the pulse hammer against her throat for five more beats, then lowered his mouth and brushed his lips to that pulse so he could feel it pound for him. Her breath left her like a balloon being deflated, and she sagged on his chest.

One upside to this whole friends-with-benefits charade would be getting to know all the things that turned Ivy on. As he trailed his tongue up the length of her neck, he realized he couldn't wait to learn what she needed to come alive under his touch. There was no way in hell it was going to be easy, but it couldn't be any harder than maintaining the boundary she'd drawn between them.

Friendship. Sex. Affection. No sloppy emotions, no heart-shaped boxes of chocolate on Valentine's Day, no love letters covertly slipped into jacket pockets, no shared playlists. No romance. No love.

And fuck was that going to be hard. Not only because he wanted those cliché things, but because he'd already started having feelings for Ivy so long ago, she'd turn tail and run if she knew. Doing this with her, the way she was insisting on doing it, was going to require him to dig up acting skills he wasn't sure he had.

She was out for something casual, no strings, but he was attached to her by hundreds of invisible strings. Like a puppet, she had the power to play him anyway she wanted, and she didn't even know.

Out of sheer necessity, he pulled himself away from her, and nearly regretted it when she moaned in protest.

"Why'd you stop?" she asked, lifting her gaze to meet his. The pale depths of her eyes had clouded over into a silvery gray. That color was only for him. He knew it because he'd only ever seen it after he'd kissed her.

"Well, you've got your friends waiting down in the bar for you. It would be rude if you stood them up."

"You said I couldn't go," she replied, her voice still thick with unsated desire.

He'd fix that and give her what she wanted. Later. "And you said you'd learn how to bury my dead body," he reminded her. "Besides, that was before we agreed to be exclusive."

"Who mentioned anything about exclusive?" she demanded, her jaw setting defiantly as she rounded on him fully, reminding him that this wasn't an arrangement where he should call any of the shots.

Except for one he was going to insist on.

Taking a step closer to her, he lifted a hand to her and brushed his thumb along her lips and jaw. Ivy shuddered, and this time in a good way. She definitely liked to be touched there. Face, neck, shoulders. He filed the information away for later.

"Ivy Harrington, I'll be your sex slave if that's what you want, but I'm going to have one non-negotiable." He tightened his grip on her neck ever so slightly and pulled her up to him, bending his head to meet her halfway, their lips a feather-width apart as he whispered, "If you're fucking me, you're not fucking anybody else."

He released her, and she swayed backward, slightly dazed, before she found herself again.

"And what about you?" she asked. "If I have to be monogamous with you for the duration of this arrangement, then you sure as hell can bet I'll expect the same from you." Her hands were fisted at her hips. Her signature stance.

Did she notice how often she assumed that defensive, defiant position?

"No problem," he said, shrugging casually to prove his point. He hadn't even gotten Ivy into bed yet, but he knew once he had her there, he'd never want anyone else. Ever again.

Shit, he already didn't. Couldn't even remember the last time he'd wanted anyone but her.

He was doomed.

"Come on, let's go." He grabbed her purse from the kitchen counter next to the wine and tossed it to her.

She caught it in one hand.

"What do you mean 'let's go'? This is a girls' night. As in, no penis', no six-packs. Well, except for Christine's. And no testosterone." She trailed after him as he made his way to the door. "We can't talk shit about you if you're there with us."

Sean stopped and turned so abruptly that Ivy crashed into his chest. He caught her up by the shoulders. "We're fuck buddies now, Ivy. Which means we're about to spend a lot more time together. Starting tonight."

"We haven't even, um, done anything yet," she

mumbled, dropping her gaze to her shoes. "So technically we're nothing."

Sean stared at the top of her head and frowned. He really hated when she did that, lowered her head to him, her bangs hiding her eyes. It made her vulnerable and not in a good way. And it killed him, every damn time.

He hooked his finger under her chin and tipped her face up to his, smoothed hair away from her face. "But we're going to be something, Ivy. Soon. Tonight." He watched her cheeks blush pink and decided he liked that look much better. He allowed his gaze to dip to the plunging scoop of her tight as fuck shirt, feeling his body react to the sight of her incredible breasts rising from it as she inhaled.

"Any chance you want to change your shirt?" he asked hopefully, knowing full well he was asking for diatribe.

Ivy glanced at her chest, then back up at him. "But this top enhances my assets, and I have very little to enhance."

Sean looked back down at her *assets*. Was she kidding him? He knew she struggled with self-esteem, and had since she showed up at his gym years ago. He'd thought they'd worked through the worst of it by now.

She'd always been beautiful. Even when he'd first seen her, hollow-eyed, haunted, and gaunt, there was a beauty about her that had drawn him instantly. Now, after years of training, she had a toned, killer body to go with it. How could she not see her many assets?

"Whoever said you had very little was lying. You have plenty to enhance, and every dick in the room is gonna notice. So, it would be great if you could go toss on a turtle-neck or something."

"A turtleneck?" Ivy's lip curled in disgust.

"Or something," he reiterated. Then, because of the look she gave him, he added, with a sigh, "Look, it'd make me a thousand times more comfortable if I didn't have to worry about other guys checking out your—" *Fucking hell.* "Assets."

Ivy snorted. Then outright laughed. "Oh, this is going to be fun, Thompson. Very, very fun." She breezed by him and out the door, leaving any talk of the turtleneck eating her dust.

CHAPTER THIRTEEN

"What's he doing here?" Wendy murmured to Christine as Ivy took her seat at the table.

"I can hear you, you know," Ivy muttered as she looked over her shoulder at Sean, who had paused at the bar to get a round of drinks and say hi to Gabe.

"Great, I was hoping I had used the exact right amount of volume so that you could ignore me if you chose to, but also explain why a hot male is here crashing our girls' night, if you wanted to," Wendy said, all in one breath, then took a sip of wine, looking casually over the rim. "So?"

"He insisted on being here after we came to an agreement." She wasn't quite sure what other way to put it.

"What kind of agreement?" Christine asked as she reached for the bowl of pretzels in the center of the table.

With both women staring at her with avid interest, and no love lives of their own to focus on, Ivy had to drum up something to tell them that was vague enough to satisfy their gossip lust but not detailed enough to leave them asking for more.

Luckily, Hope chose that moment to arrive, shrugging

out of her coat and draping it over the back of the tall bar chair before lifting her elegant figure onto the seat. Looking around the table, she settled her dark-brown gaze on Ivy with her knowing best-friend look.

"What are you girls chatting about?" she asked.

"Ivy was about to tell us about an agreement she made with Sean that has him following her around like a puppy on our girls' night," Wendy supplied.

"Is that so? Well, do tell." Hope linked her long, perfectly polished fingers together and set her chin on them, batting her lashes several times in Ivy's direction.

Crap. There was no hiding when Hope was around.

Ivy shrugged, as if being hours away from having sex with Sean was absolutely no big deal.

"We've decided to see each other. Casually," she added at the resounding gasp and muffled squeal that came from the women around the table. "Very casually. Like super, no strings, having a good time, casually."

"So what, like fuck buddies?" Christine asked, stuffing another pretzel in her mouth. "Why don't you actually date? Everyone knows you guys have it hot for each other."

"Um..." Ivy hummed evasively. The only person at the table who knew about her past, and the supreme damage it had done to her sexual confidence and life in general, was Hope.

But the others didn't know anything, and Ivy really wasn't here to talk about it all, so her mind reeled with other possible explanations as to why she'd agree to sleep with Sean, but not date this highly dateable specimen of a man.

"Sometimes jumping into a relationship right away is too much pressure," Hope piped up, coming to the rescue. "I think it's a great idea to keep it casual, start slow and see where it goes."

Ivy sighed inwardly and shot her friend a grateful look. Hope winked back in return.

"Has the fucking part started yet?" Wendy asked tactlessly, finishing off her wine, then blinked at the looks they all shot at her. "What? I mean, look at him. He's like a Michelangelo sculpture in the flesh. Of course I want details on whether or not he's as good in bed as everyone here thinks he is."

"We haven't," Ivy replied. "Yet. But—" Ivy was cut off by Erica arriving at the table...with Anna.

"Hey guys," Erica said, looking pretty damn bashful with a noticeable flush on her cheeks.

"Hey Erica," Ivy greeted her friend, then turned pointedly to look at a beaming Anna. "Hey Anna. We weren't expecting to see you tonight."

Anna was grinning from ear to ear, her elation obvious. "I know it was supposed to be a partner-free evening, but I felt like a celebration tonight, so I tagged along. Hope you don't mind."

The now visibly tipsy Wendy scooted to the side to make room and pulled a bar stool over from a neighboring table, patting it vigorously. "Of course we don't mind! It's a night for celebrations. What are you two toasting to?"

As if no one had figured it out already.

Anna looked at Erica and smiled. There was so much love in that smile that Ivy couldn't help but feel a surge of giddy anticipation bubble in her chest.

Erica's mouth split into a massive blinding grin, then she lifted her hand to reveal a giant sparkler on the ring finger of her left hand. "I came to my senses and said yes to the best thing that's ever come my way."

"Oh my God!" Hope squealed, jumping from her seat

and tossing her arms around Erica, then Anna. "That is amazing. I am so happy for you two!"

The next few minutes were spent hugging, laughing, and congratulating. Hope ran to the bar to order a bottle of bubbly to be brought to the table, and the buzz of pure joy at the celebration of love seemed to spread through the bar from then on.

Caught up in the energy, Ivy hardly noticed when her eyes went damp. This was love, the wild abandon of taking a leap and finding someone who caught you on the other side. It was incredible, wasn't it? So where was this pang of heaviness coming from? She tried to swallow it down before her night morphed into a pity party. But there was something about seeing this kind of love, the kind that took openness and risk, that made her wonder if she'd ever have what it took.

Just as she thought the thought, there was a familiar tug in her chest. By the time Sean came up behind her, setting his hands on either side of the back of her chair and dropping a kiss to the top of her head, he'd already made his presence known. And somehow, the pressure in her torso loosened.

"Dance with me," he rasped against her ear, making her hair tickle her neck.

That tickle shot right to her core. Holy cow, she was definitely not going to have any issues getting her juices flowing for this guy if he kept up these sexy ear whispers.

"Um, dance? Now?" she asked, even as she slid off her stool and turned to him. "I'm not much of a dancer."

Sean tipped back his head and let out a rumbling laugh. "Bullshit, Ivy. I've seen you tear up a dance floor like nobody's watching plenty of times."

"Well, that's because I generally assume nobody is watching."

Sean intertwined his long fingers through hers and with one single tug, pulled her against his chest. "Then you haven't been paying attention, baby, because I've seen plenty of people noticing you. Trust me."

Without waiting for a reply, he led her toward the crowded dance floor in the middle of the bar. The girls were already going for broke, dancing around the newly engaged couple, arms raised, hips swaying. Ivy moved toward them, but Sean directed her off to the side, where there was a pocket of space away from the main crowd.

"But what about the others?" Ivy asked, her body already not caring about anything but the fact that he was touching her, his fingertips playing gently at her hips.

"Want you all to myself for now," Sean murmured. He started to move with her, in sync with the beat of the music. That unbreakable thread that linked them guided their movements so that it was almost as if they were engaging in a highly choreographed routine and not dancing together for the first time.

Who knew dancing with Sean would be an overload of the senses? The unique smell of him mixed with the subtle scent of cologne, and the gratifying aura of all the happy, alcohol infused bodies around them in the bar. The sounds of the music pumping through the bar, the vibrations of it adding a friction to the air. The taste of champagne still on her tongue from the toast they'd made earlier, making her wonder if he tasted the same. The tickle in the places where his body touched hers. He hadn't pressed himself on her. Their bodies weren't knotted together in a gyrating embrace like many of the other couples on the dance floor. He held her with his eyes, and she felt the touch of them everywhere.

Then there was the visual feast of him, his height, his build, the way his shirt hugged his biceps, and back to his mesmerizing eyes. Ivy let all of it consume her, fill her soul, fusing the thread that connected them more fully to her heart.

This was dangerous, to let him affect her this way. He was too close already. Not only in a physical sense, but an emotional one. She recognized that his keen eyes were seeing more than what was on the outside. He was seeing inside her, and if she wasn't careful, he'd see all the secret places that she was protecting. All the things she never wanted anyone else to see.

But in this moment, she couldn't bring herself to care.

She lifted her arms, swayed her hips as she turned in a slow circle for him. Boldly, she stepped toward him, so close but still not fully touching, and mirrored his movement. She watched as his pupils dilated, until his eyes were more black than brown, and she let a healing sense of power fill her. For the first time in her life, she had a sense of being both fully in control and fully surrendered.

As one song blended into another, time passed, people talked to them, moved beside them, around them, and it was all one big part of this intricate dance she hadn't realized she knew all the steps to. With each movement, her body became more and more alive with wanting, and with it the absolute knowledge that this was the man she had been moving toward since she arrived in Portland. This was the man who would help bring her peace.

Her heartbeat echoed everywhere. Her chest, her ears, her throat, but the pulse between her legs beat the loudest.

It was a lusty ache that begged to be seen to. It was so unfamiliar, so demanding, Ivy pulled back, stunned.

"Now." The urgent plea tore from her lips before she could explain herself.

"Now," he repeated with a brisk nod, knowing, of course, exactly what she meant. Desire burned in his opaque eyes.

"Right now." Ivy mirrored his nod. "Or I'll explode."

A tight, knowing laughter rumbled out of him as he grabbed her hand, pulled her through the throng of people, past the table where their friends sat calling after them.

"Where are you going?" Christine asked.

"We just ordered another bottle of bubbly," Wendy added.

"Um, have a glass for me. We've, um—we've got to go."

Before they even made it halfway across the bar, Hope appeared in front of them, halting their progress, her brown eyes sharp as laser vision. Hope glanced up at Sean with a sugary sweet grin. "Sean, Ivy forgot her purse at the table. You don't mind getting it for her, do you?"

Sean's gaze flicked between the women, then focused on Hope. "Of course not." He headed off to where they'd been sitting.

Hope locked eyes with Ivy. "This is happening?"

Ivy took her friend's hand and gave it a squeeze. "This is happening."

Hope just stared at her for a moment, then nodded. "Call me in the morning, first thing. Or before. I'll have my phone on me all night. I can sleep over in my old room if you want? Whatever you need. Just say."

Ivy dragged Hope into a hug. She didn't deserve a friend like this. Didn't know what she'd done to get lucky enough that Hope had moved to the same city, so she had access to her love and support every day. Most of the time, Ivy needed it. But tonight, in this moment, filled with a sense of resolution, she didn't need Hope. The only person she needed was already heading back her way.

"I'm fine. This is right. I can feel it," Ivy whispered, feeling her friend's nod against her shoulder.

By the time Sean pulled up next to Ivy, holding her purse, they'd pulled apart.

Hope looked up at Sean, bright-eyed and serious. "Sean Thompson," she said, "hurt her and die."

The vehemence in her voice was so out of character that Sean's eyes widened in shock. Ivy swallowed a laugh. It was funny/not funny. Anyone who didn't know what had happened to Ivy might have thought Hope's caustic sentiments were an attempt at humor. But Ivy knew better and had no doubt Hope would cast aside her sweet nature in a heartbeat to bring down anyone who dared hurt Ivy again. She'd done exactly that when Adam confronted them at Bowie's not long ago.

And even in this immensely opposite situation, Ivy appreciated her best friend's support and sentiment.

Sean reached for Ivy's hand and tugged her against his side. "Noted."

"Oh-kay." Ivy steered Sean toward the exit. "Time to go."

From behind them, Hope hollered, "Have her home by 9 a.m.!"

Jesus. "Yes, Mom," Ivy groaned under her breath, while tugging Sean more firmly toward the door, immediately feeling bad because she knew Hope had every right to be concerned. Pausing, she turned and blew her friend a kiss, then mouthed, *I'm good.*

When she finally glanced up at Sean, with a big toothy grin fixed on her face, her heart sank to her stomach at his expression. His brow puckered and jaw clenched, his hand flexed against hers.

Uh oh. She couldn't let him second-guess his promise to her and change his mind. Not only had she realized that she'd been kidding herself when she thought she could share this moment with anyone but him, she was now achingly aware of how much she wanted *him.*

Her whole body was alive with wanting. Her palms itched to touch his skin, her heart fluttered erratically in her chest, her breasts were sensitive against the satin of her bra, and between her thighs she was drenched for him. Her mind, for the first time in a long, long time, matched all the physical things happening to her body. They wanted the same thing. And that thing was Sean.

Now. Immediately.

This was happening. Nobody was backing their way out of anything tonight.

It was time to put the past as far behind her as she could shove it.

CHAPTER FOURTEEN

She looked like she wanted sex. She talked like she wanted sex. And she was walking like she wanted sex. But for the first time in his whole damn life, Sean had no idea if the woman he was about to fuck actually wanted sex.

Ivy dragged him through the bar with a fierce grip on his hand, as if she were afraid that if she let go, he'd run off.

Well, she was crazy if she thought that, because he had no intentions of running. If she wanted him, she had him, but he sure as shit needed to know for a fact she wanted this before they went any further.

He let her pull him into the quiet hall that led to the stairs up to their apartments before he tugged at her hand and pulled her to a stop.

She staggered back, looking up into his eyes. Panic shifted through them but was gone as quickly as it came, a mask of cool determination coming down in its place.

"What?" she demanded breathlessly. Her lips parted, moist from her tongue. Her cheeks flushed, bringing a pretty pink blush to her pale face. Christ, she was so crazy beautiful.

"Ivy, what was that?"

"What was what?" she replied innocently. Yeah, she knew exactly what he was talking about.

With a dramatic sigh, and her signature eye roll, she said, "Hope is the ultimate mother-hen. She worries about me. Needlessly."

"Needless? Really?"

Here was the elephant in the room between them. The incident in the bar several months ago that they never spoke of. He beat the shit out of a man for her, and didn't even fully know why. All he'd had was a gut feeling and the instinctive knowledge that the bastard had deserved more than a beating.

But that had only been one piece of the puzzle. Her 'play dead' routine when he'd gotten on top of her on the couch had been another. Then Hope's mama-bear routine a moment ago. Not to mention the state Ivy had arrived in when she appeared at his gym all those years ago. The picture was shaping up to look terribly grim.

"Ivy, look, I'm not going to lie. I want you so fucking bad I'm going crazy with it. But if there is something I need to know before we do this, now is the time to tell me."

Ivy shrunk from him and tried to tug her hand free, but he held fast. Her pale eyes did the darty back-and-forth thing they did whenever he picked at her like this. As if he was getting close to seeing something she didn't want him to see, and she was searching for a place to hide. Skittish. Like a trapped kitten. And he hated himself every time because people shouldn't be forced to tell their stories if they didn't want to.

But they'd never been a flight of stairs away from fucking before, so Sean braced himself against his guilt and pushed on. He lifted his free hand to her face, let his palm curl over her cheek, holding her like that until she leaned into his touch and released a tiny sigh.

"The other week, when we almost—" He bent his neck to keep her eye contact. "When I got on top of you, you froze and I lost you. You went somewhere else. I don't want that to happen tonight. But I need you to meet me halfway." The callus of his thumb stroked the soft skin right under her eye. "Tell me," he gently urged, his voice quiet, but determined.

"I was in a bad situation before," she started haltingly. "I made poor decisions about who I left a party with and the consequences were—unpleasant. Hope was there when it happened. She doesn't want it to happen again, obviously. Neither do I. But this is different." She looked up at him, her blue eyes melting into a pleading look. "So different. And I don't want it to stop. I don't want you to go."

Schooling himself not to react to what she'd told him had been the biggest exercise in restraint he'd ever experienced. She hadn't given many details, but he could read between the lines enough to know what had happened was a hell of a lot more than 'unpleasant.'

"That jackass, Adam, who showed up in Bowie's—was he involved in this *bad situation*?" Sean asked, knowing the answer but needing to hear her say it.

Ivy dropped her gaze to the floor.

"Ivy."

"Yes." Her reply was barely a whisper, but it echoed like a scream in his head.

He should have killed the bastard when he had the fucking chance. "What the fuck—?"

She cut him off with a look, crystalline eyes flaring to life, burning with a new intensity. "I've said all I'm going to say on the matter. It was a long time ago. I don't want to give it another single moment of my life. That's why I'm here, Sean, with you. I don't want to look back. I want to look forward. I want to move forward. With you." Slowly, tentatively, she slid her palms up his chest, gliding them over the planes of his abs and his pecs.

Her touch, even through his clothes—Damn, it brought his desire right back to life. Guilt swamped him for wanting to take her the way he was imagining—hard and all-consuming, until there was no difference between him and her, until they were only one.

"Please don't let this change things. Please don't walk away." Her voice was so defenseless, so pleading, he would have done anything for her in that moment. Fucked her against the wall if she'd asked. But she wasn't asking for a fuck against a cold wall in a concrete hallway. She was asking to move forward. Away from an old memory and toward a new one. A better memory.

And, God help him, he was going to give it to her.

"I don't think I could ever walk away from you." *Not in this lifetime, and not in the next.* He kept that part to himself for now, but he lowered his head and covered her mouth, sealing both his spoken and unspoken thoughts like a vow.

She bloomed under him instantaneously. Rising on her tiptoes, she looped her arms around his neck, and he drew her in, lifting her up so she could wrap her legs around his waist. With their height difference, this seemed to be their go-to pose when they kissed, and he was more than fine with it, because it meant he could be closer to her.

He took the stairs with Ivy wrapped around him. Thank God he knew this staircase like the back of his hand since he was essentially climbing it blind with his lips suctioned to hers, eyes closed, his mind already in the bedroom. When he broke through the upper door and into their hallway, he paused before making the split-second decision to turn right toward Ivy's apartment. If they were going to do this the right way, she'd be more comfortable in her space.

Releasing her, he relished the soft weight of her body as it slid off his. Meanwhile, his body was so hard and tight with pent-up need, he wasn't sure he'd make it across the threshold.

Ivy made quick work of opening her door, and he followed her inside. The mood shifted as soon as the latch clicked shut behind her. Her anxiety became a palpable entity in the room, like the churning in the air before a storm.

She stood there, her back to him, hand on the doorknob, like she was contemplating whether she should bolt and run.

Sean couldn't imagine what she'd been through, and that worried him. He needed to know how she'd been hurt and where, so he wouldn't hit any of those triggers again.

From their last encounter on her couch, he'd learned she didn't like being underneath, that she needed space, a way up and out. So he'd start there.

Slowly he moved up behind her, letting his footfall make noise so she knew he was coming. He placed his hand over hers on the knob.

"Don't say it." The irritation in her voice surprised him. "I know what you're thinking, Sean, and don't even think about saying it out loud."

Sean lifted her hand and brought it up to her chest. He drew her back against his own chest and they stood there, Ivy cradled against him, their fingers interlocked against her heart.

"And what exactly am I thinking, Ivy?" he murmured

above her head, a smile quirking his lips at her surly, stand-offish tone.

"You're thinking that we don't have to do this. And if you say it, I'm gonna kick you in the nuts."

"We don't—"

Ivy whirled, as he'd anticipated, because if she was anything, she was true to her word. He moved to the side in the nick of time, as her knee came up.

"Whoa, we're going to need those for what I have planned tonight, so careful where you put that knee, sweetheart." He chuckled at the expression on her face, half pissed, half aroused.

"W-what do you have planned? You don't want to stop?" she asked timidly, her vacillating mood softening every part of him.

Well, nearly every part.

Sean tipped her chin up, catching the crystal blue of her gaze. "Do *you* want to stop?"

"No." She resolutely shook her head. "No, I don't. I want to have sex. Lots of sex. Lots of casual, no-strings sex. With you."

For him, it was way too late for the no strings part. He had strings all over the damn place that he craved to tie to her strings with neat little double-knotted bows that never snapped. But apparently, she was still on the friends-with-benefits train, and he was starting to understand why. So, he wouldn't call his own bluff yet.

"Okay then. Sex it is. But I have one more condition."

Ivy inhaled deeply, then squared her shoulders like a soldier preparing for battle. This wasn't turning out to be the romantic evening he had in mind.

"Okay. What is it? But I tell you this right now—no

bondage. I need—" Her eyes flitted back and forth. "I don't want to be tied down."

Strange that she went there with him. Did he look like a bondage sort of guy? He didn't want to tie her down so much as he wanted to...connect himself to her.

"Understood," he said, matching her business-like tone. "But that wasn't my condition."

"What is it then? I'm on the pill, but I have condoms in the bedroom. And I've been checked."

Holy fuck, what was this, a business merger? Did this woman know anything about romance? Seduction? The answer slugged him in the gut. It'd been robbed from her, along with her confidence and desire, after whatever had happened to her.

"I've been checked too, and never have sex without protection, and haven't had it at all in—well, too damn long," he admitted. Not since he'd moved in across from her, that was for sure.

Anytime he'd been with a woman since he'd met Ivy, he'd never experienced any genuine fulfillment. His body might have been sated but his soul was still hungry. As though what he'd been doing was right, but with the wrong person. Eventually, he stopped altogether, because it wasn't his body that needed satisfying.

"So, what then?" She fisted her hands at her hips, looking irritated.

"If you'd let me get a word in, I'll tell you that my condition is that this first time, between you and me, right here, right now, you lead."

Ivy blinked up at him, as if slowly letting the information compute in her brain. "I lead?"

"Yes. You say what and when. You make all the moves. Whatever you want, how far you want, how fast you want.

You're in the driver's seat. You control *everything* that happens tonight."

Because regardless of the details he was missing, one thing was clear: control had been taken from her before, and tonight she was getting it back.

"I don't know how to be in the driver's seat," she said, sounding a little stunned.

"You do know, Ivy," he reassured her. "You know what to do by how you feel. Let that guide you."

She continued to stare at him blankly, so he moved to the kitchen, because maybe she did need prompting.

"Where do you keep the candles?" he asked, opening random cabinets.

"Candles?"

"Yeah, you know, the waxy things that have little strings that light up if you hold a match to them."

That got her attention. She stomped over to him, shoved him out of the way, reached up to a cupboard she could barely touch, and took down a couple of stubby off-white candles.

"I know what a candle is, genius. Why do you want them?"

He picked the candles out of her hands and pressed a kiss to her lips. "To set the mood." Then, because he loved that smart mouth, he kissed it again. "So, where do you want me?"

She gazed up at him, a little dazed. The look he loved best because he knew he'd put it there with his kisses, and he almost dropped the candles and pulled her in for another one, one that didn't end until they were both panting and spent, except that didn't exactly align with his earlier declaration that she lead, so he stayed focused on his task.

"Ivy, sweetheart, where do you want to do this? The couch? Your bed?" He crouched a little to look into those gorgeous blues, and gauge where she might be at.

Was she second-guessing? Did she need an out? Was she still full steam ahead?

She grabbed him by his shirt collar and marched him toward her bedroom.

Full steam ahead it was.

In the bedroom, Sean moved to close the door, but she stopped him. "I need it open."

Sean nodded—her game, her rules—then set the candles on the top of her dresser. Using the lighter he'd snagged from the cabinet, he lit the flames. When he was done, he savored the moment of taking her in by candlelight.

"You're so beautiful." He wasn't sure he'd ever told her before, but he was telling her now, because the way the light flickered off her skin and made her eyes shine like they were made of crystal, it was the God's honest truth.

Her beauty was otherworldly.

She likely wasn't used to being complimented because even in the candlelight he saw the blush creep up her neck, but she'd have to get used to it, because he had a whole lot more where that came from. As part of this, he wanted her to learn how to accept his affection, not cringe from it. She deserved to be romanced in this relationship.

Friendship.

Arrangement.

Whatever the fuck it was.

Sean buried the annoying ambiguity of their situation under the depths of his soul. He'd deal with the inevitability of his heartbreak later. Tonight, nothing was going to ruin this moment.

He wanted, no *needed*, this to be special for both of them.

When Ivy did nothing more than stand there, lips parted, breathing unevenly, he stepped toward her. He wanted to touch her so badly his fingers twitched with it, but he held the line.

"So, what do you feel like doing?" He wasn't completely surprised by the hoarse sound of his voice, but he resisted the urge to clear it. "What do you want, Ivy?"

She glanced up at him, eyes wide and luminous, like she was looking at something brand new and amazing, and was a little awestruck. It filled him with a primal male satisfaction and pride. That look was all for him.

In the room, there was no sound, only the candlelight flickering, and their mutual desire heating the space around them. And Sean was more turned on than he'd ever been. He was pretty sure if they stood there long enough, staring at each other like this, he'd come right where he stood, fully clothed, from her eye-fucking alone.

"Tell me. Whatever you want."

Eventually, Ivy inhaled deeply and opened the snap of her jeans, then fumbled with the zipper.

"I want to take my clothes off." Her hands were trembling but determined as she pushed her jeans down her legs, revealing more creamy skin. "And I want you to do the same."

Her shirt came off next, and then she was standing in front of him in a black bra and panty set before he even had a chance to inhale his next breath.

Okay, so he totally had not expected this boldness from her. With Ivy, things had always been intuitive. Most times, he had an innate sense of what she needed, what she was going to say, how she was feeling. But lately, she surprised him by doing the exact opposite of what he anticipated. Like right now.

"Your turn. I want to see your body, a-and I want to touch it." Words were coming out of her mouth he'd only ever dreamed of, and, like a sub to his dominant, he did as he was told and pulled his shirt over his head in one swoop, then dropped his pants with the flick of a wrist.

They stood before each other in their underwear, and when her gaze dropped to his crotch, he had to close his eyes to regain some control.

"I want to see you," she murmured shakily, her voice impossibly quiet. A whisper over candlelight. A plea.

Sean opened his eyes. She was standing there nearly naked, short hair brushing her shoulders, bangs mussed, blue eyes twinkling in candlelight. Innocent and vulnerable, yet hungry.

And he was hungry for the same thing, so he held her gaze steady and slowly dropped his boxer briefs and stepped out of them.

The way Ivy's eyes widened, her mouth forming a perfect little 'o,' would have made any ego grow, his notwithstanding. Sean took pride in his body, had built a career out of it. His body was his best advertisement for the gym, so he made it a practice to stay in peak physical condition. Did the fact that Ivy was clearly appreciating his efforts go straight to his head? Hell yes, it did.

"What now?" he asked gruffly.

She was still wearing her bra and panties, but he wasn't going to point it out. This was her rodeo. She could keep them on all night if she wanted. Although he prayed that wouldn't be the case.

Her gaze was still fixed on his midsection, which was

starring his very eager erection. The 'o' of her mouth grew bigger when he took a step toward her.

"Ivy?" he questioned through a smile. He loved her like this, all stunned and heated and turned on by him. It was the 'by him' part he liked best.

She blinked and looked up at him, clearing her throat. "Um, can you sit on the bed? Please." She was so damn cute and innocent that he did as he was told, sitting himself on the edge of the mattress in front of her.

"I, um, I don't really know. I..." Her gaze roamed over him, her hands fidgeting. She did a little shuffle from side to side, and nerves started to creep into her aura again, fading the glow of desire he'd been admiring.

"Ivy." To still her hands, he laced his fingers with hers. "Look at me."

And she looked at him, her trust humbling him to the core.

"Keep looking at me. Just look into my eyes. As long as you keep looking at me, we'll be fine. We'll stay connected. I'll be able to see everything in your eyes, and you'll be able to see everything in mine, and we'll be in this moment together. Okay?"

As he spoke Ivy's tension eased, until her hand was soft in his, the nerves stilled. For now.

She nodded, then to his surprise, reached behind her to unhook her bra, letting the straps fall from her shoulders. For a few heartbeats, she held the silky fabric to her breasts, not letting it fall fully away from her body. Her eyes locked onto his until, with a sigh, she let it drop, revealing two of the most perfect breasts he'd ever seen.

He had to make every damn effort to not let his tongue loll out like an over eager dog.

She slid her fingers into her panties next, pulled them

down slowly until she was standing fully naked, in all her goddess-like glory. And every horny teenage daydream he'd ever had came true in that very second.

He was full on ogling her stunning tits when she took his hand and guided it to one of the objects of all his attention. His fingers sunk into the soft, giving flesh.

Okay, he was wrong. Now, every dream he'd ever had had come true.

CHAPTER FIFTEEN

Ivy couldn't remember a time ever in her life where she had been this aroused. There wasn't a single part of her that didn't ache for sexual release. And the way Sean was looking at her, like she was a tall glass of water after a long run through the desert, was giving her a confidence she'd never experienced before. Ever.

She hadn't realized how much she needed the control he was giving her. Honestly, she hadn't known what to expect, but she hadn't expected him to understand, so intuitively, what she needed. Knowing that he wouldn't be making any of the moves tonight took away her anxiety and uncertainty about what might come. Any worry she might have had about how she'd react if he did something she didn't like vanished because he wouldn't be doing anything she didn't tell him to do. She was in control. And she liked it. Even nervous as hell, she liked it.

So when he'd simply sat there, staring at her boobs, she'd brought his hand to her sensitive skin.

A slow smile spread across his wide lips, as he ran his fingers along the taut peak, then spread his big palms over either side of her rib cage, running his hands down the dip of her waist and back up again.

Ivy inhaled sharply at his touch.

"Can I kiss them, honey?"

She nodded enthusiastically.

Taking his time, Sean bent forward, tugged her toward him, covering her right nipple with his mouth.

Moisture shot to her core like an arrow, flooding the area between her legs. She pressed her thighs together to relieve the pressure.

Sean's mouth moved over her nipple and breast with an expertise she didn't want to dwell on too much. He had skill. It was part of the reason she picked him. How he acquired it wasn't something she wanted to overthink. She focused on the fact that he was with her now, in this room, with his mouth on *her* breast, his groan of pleasure vibrating through *her* body.

Wanting to touch him, she lifted her hands and ran them through his hair. Eventually, he traveled to the left breast, imparting the same treatment, and her head fell forward, moaning as she watched his tongue lap and tease her nipple into a stiff peak.

"Oh God," she sighed and took a step closer to him.

His erection bobbed against her thigh, hard but smooth, and he hissed in a breath at the contact.

"Does it feel good?" she asked.

Sean pulled away from her breasts and gazed up at her with a curious mix of intense desire and agony. "Ivy, sweetheart, I feel more than good. I feel, fuck, can I touch you? I really need to touch you here." He brushed his fingers over her aching center, the light touch ripping a little cry out of her.

Lucky for him, she was dying for him to touch her there. "Yes."

Sean slipped his fingers between her flesh and let out a rough groan of satisfaction. Ivy widened her stance a bit and watched him. Seeing his fingers slide over her, glistening with the evidence of her desire, caused a desperation to course through her.

He looked up at her, his eyes bright and questioning. She nodded, understanding him perfectly.

Never breaking eye contact, Sean dipped two fingers inside her, and she braced her hands on his shoulders, her knees nearly buckling under the exquisite sensations. He worked her into a frenzy, his fingers curling and pumping as his thumb rubbed circles over the bud at her core. After a while, he dipped his head and his tongue stroked and teased her nipples in time with the movement of his fingers.

"Sean—" she gasped, sucking in air as he continued his ministrations over and over until she couldn't take any more. Until the blinding pressure erupted and wave after wave of ecstasy washed over her.

Sean's free hand held her hip firmly, holding her steady when she would have collapsed. Finally, the sensations ebbed, and her vision returned as she locked eyes with him, re-centering herself.

"That was the sexiest thing I have ever seen in my entire fucking life," he said, his voice low and thick and a little breathless.

Ivy could only think to say one thing.

"Again." She launched herself away from him and raced to the side of her bed to pull out a condom from the bedside table, rushing back to him so quickly her legs caught the corner of the bed and launched her forward.

Laughing, Sean caught her before she dove headfirst

into the wall. "What's the hurry, gorgeous? You've had your turn."

He steadied her, and she took the opportunity to curl into his embrace. His body was slick and hard, primed and needy, but controlled, his arms around her tender.

She could have stayed like that all night, tucked into the protective shield of his body—but she didn't want to. Eager, Ivy pushed him onto the bed, all the way this time, so he was lying on his back.

"I want another turn," she demanded as she climbed over him, straddling her legs on either side of his powerful thighs. "And I want it now."

His eyes went from bright and laughing to molten and serious in a second. The deep growl that came from his throat, as he took the condom from her and rolled it down his shaft, went straight through her, reminding her body how ready she was for round two.

This was it. The first time a man would be inside her body since that night. She hovered over him, poised, staring down between them where his cock surged upward, aiming for her, straining for her.

Ivy swallowed as a memory she didn't want threatened to invade her headspace. It hovered around the edges, like an unwelcome thief peeking through windows, looking for a way in. She closed her eyes tightly and tried to breathe through it. She wouldn't let anything ruin this for her. She wouldn't let that night touch this one.

Everything so far had been perfect, and this would be perfect too. She just had to—

A low voice called her name. Warm hands wrapped around hers. A familiar tug pulled at her heart. "Look at me."

She opened her eyes and met warmth. Patience. Trust.

"I'm your friend, right?" Why was it that the way he said the word, like it meant so much more than any friendship she'd ever had, made tears flood her eyes?

She nodded. "My best friend." Her lips trembled over the words, making her voice wobble.

And he was. Hope was her sister-from-another-mister, but Sean was her very best friend.

Sean grunted in approval. "And you trust me to catch you when you fall, right?"

Again, she nodded, because she did. Absolutely did. *You're my trust fall.*

"I'm the kind of friend who will never let you fall, not ever. I'll never hurt you. I'll always keep you safe. Every time, in every situation. Tell me you believe that?"

This time when she nodded, a tear slid down her cheek. "I believe it."

"It's you and me. No one else is here. Only us. Touching each other, holding each other, together. Be here with me. In your room, in your apartment, with candles, on your bed. Look at me and be here with me." Sean threaded his fingers through hers, joining them.

Ivy looked down at their hands, then back into his eyes. "Sean."

He nodded. "Yes, Ivy. You. Me. Us." He came up and gave her a gentle kiss on the lips, leaving his eyes open, never breaking contact with hers. Then he kissed her again, longer and deeper. As the kiss heated everything inside her, something in her heart and mind melted away.

"Say my name again," Sean murmured against her lips.

"Sean," she whispered, and she leaned her forehead to his.

"Nothing happens that you don't want. I promise. We can just lie here. All night. Let me hold you."

His tone, so gentle, so honest, made her tears flow freely. Deep in her heart, she knew he meant every word. He'd be happy to lie with her, if that was what she wanted. But it wasn't. It really wasn't. Reset with new resolve, she leaned into him again.

She kissed him fiercely on the lips, hot open-mouthed kisses of gratitude, respect and awe for this man. It didn't take long for the kisses to turn hungry. She devoured him, taking everything she could.

Ivy let the kisses drive her into a frenzy until she was so desperate she urged him back down onto the mattress. Palms flat against his chest, she held eye contact with him, looking deeply into the brown depths until she saw nothing, sensed nothing, but him.

And holding that gaze, she sank onto him. The feel of him stretching her, filling her, was so exquisite his name fell off her lips with brand-new purpose, and he responded by gripping her hips, holding her still while he caught his breath.

Maybe he was caught up in the same storm as she was, lost somewhere between the disbelief that this was happening and the satisfaction that came with finally experiencing something that had been a longtime coming. She wanted to savor every second.

"Look at you," he whispered, using his fingers to thread the hair away from her face. "I wish you could see how beautiful you look while you're taking me. You're perfect."

It was his praise that gave her confidence. His words, spoken so candidly they had to be true, urged her to take what she wanted. And she did want it, so, so badly.

Slowly, Ivy lifted and dropped her hips over him, tentative at first, adjusting to his size and presence inside her. At some point between exploration and need, her body took over, moving faster and harder as momentum grew around them. Sean was patient, only the pressure of his fingertips pressing into the flesh of her hips giving away a hint of his desperation. That and the glisten of sweat spreading out over his skin, showed Ivy how his control was costing him.

What would it be like if he completely let go? How wild could he be? How dominant? Part of her relished the idea of one day finding out. But this encounter now, with her on top, staying his power, controlling his climax, it gave her a thrill she'd never experienced.

Their eyes held, and she watched as his mouth opened, unintelligible words and her name falling out of it over and over as they moved in unison. His grip never left her hips as he held her closer, encouraging her to go faster as she chased the feeling that grew every time she bore down and he reared up, hitting the deepest part of her.

Their connection never faltered as they rode the moment together, until finally, everything around Ivy blurred into one. The pleasure of their joining hitting a pressure point so intense she broke eye contact only to throw her head back and cry out his name, loudly shouting it so the whole world could know who it was that had brought her back to herself. Who it was that had made her feel again.

Distantly, through the haze of her own pleasure, she heard her name tearing off his lips right before he tensed beneath her.

She had no idea how long it went on. It was an orgasm that probably deserved a place in the *Guinness World Records* for length and intensity, but eventually, it did subside. And when it did, Ivy dropped over Sean's chest heavily, spent and exhausted. Instantly, his arms came around her, caressing her back, uttering praise she didn't realize she needed to hear.

"You're amazing," he murmured into her hair, his voice raspy. "Everything about you is amazing."

Ivy nuzzled against him, letting his words wash over her, giving herself permission to, if only for this moment, believe them. After a minute, once their breathing regulated, their heartbeats settled back to normal, she turned in his arms.

"You can hold me now. If you want."

Any insecurity she had left melted away when he smiled and turned her to her side so he could curl up behind her. He pulled her close, and wrapped an arm around her body, dropping his palm low on her belly.

"Just try to get rid of me." Sean's arms squeezed around her, and Ivy snuggled, fully content, as they lay there, in this moment they had created together, candlelight flickering around them.

Her eyes had been closed for no more than five minutes, and already there was a nudge against her backside. If this was sexual liberation, she'd have to rethink her strategy. Sleep was sacred, and since she wasn't used to getting much of it at the best of times, she wasn't sure she wanted to sacrifice any more. Not even for the treat that sex with Sean had turned out to be.

Another nudge. Well, she could always sleep when she was dead, she figured as she rolled over in the heated cocoon of her comforter to face Sean. Except he wasn't there. At least not on the mattress beside here, where she could have sworn she'd seen him five minutes ago.

Instead, he stood by the side of her bed, wearing nothing

but a pair of running shorts and his six-pack, grinning at her like a Cheshire Cat with a death wish. He leaned down and poked her again.

"Wake up, sleepy head. Run time."

"Are you insane?" she croaked in her sleep-thickened voice. "It's the middle of the night."

Sean chuckled as he pulled on a long-sleeved athletic shirt. "It's six in the morning, Ivy. And I know you like to run before sunrise. Run time." He grabbed the comforter and, with one fierce tug, pulled it right off her.

Ivy screeched and scrambled to find something to cover her naked body. There was nothing. The sheet had gone with the comforter. So she gave up and grabbed her phone. Sure enough, it read 6:03. She blinked in confusion. Had she slept for six hours straight, without waking, dreaming, or even moving? When was the last time that happened?

And now she was even more pissed he woke her. How much longer could she have slept?

Sean had rounded the bed and was crouched in front of her. He kissed the tip of her nose. "You'll be more pissed if I let you miss your run."

Dammit, he was right. He was going to make it difficult to keep things casual between them if he kept reading her inside out like this.

Ivy dragged her butt out of bed and pulled her running clothes on. An hour and a half later, having run along the Willamette River with Sean, watching the sunrise over the city she loved so much, the cold fall air pumping through her lungs, a familiar peace settled in her heart. They didn't talk as they pounded the pavement in unison. Sean's long gait easily ate up the miles, but Ivy had built endurance over the last few years, and keeping up with him today was easier than the last time they'd run together. He also hadn't set a punishing pace like last time, which helped.

By the time they'd arrived back at their apartments, Ivy was more revitalized than she had been in longer than she could remember. Between the sex, the sleep, and the run, she was ready and eager for another round with naked Sean.

Maybe he'd be open to showering together? Maybe she could lick the water droplets off his moist body afterward?

Her deliciously naughty thoughts were interrupted by the sound of Sean's phone going off. His gaze darted down to the screen, and he instantly stilled. He held the phone in his hand, staring at it until it went silent, then continued to stare at it for another beat, before shoving it roughly back into his pocket.

To the untrained eye, it would probably have gone undetected, but Ivy had been checking Sean out for long enough now that she could tell by the way his jaw tensed slightly and his eyes darkened almost imperceptibly that he'd been rattled by the phone call. Something wasn't right.

"You want to talk about that?" Ivy heard herself asking, regretting it immediately when a shutter came down over his eyes.

"Talk about what?" he asked casually, pushing her away with his denial.

If this was how he wanted to play it, she'd back off. Should have backed off. And yet, damn it, whoever had been calling him had ruined his mood in five rings flat, taking her plans for an erotic shower with it, and she wanted to know who it was.

"The phone call you stared down but didn't answer. You looked at that caller ID like the Ghost from Christmas Past was calling. Thought you might want to talk about whoever it was."

Maybe it shouldn't have, but his casual shrug hurt.

"It was nothing. Long distance number. Probably some salesperson telling me I've won a free vacation."

Okay, he was going to play it like that, was he? Ivy tried to ignore the pang of disappointment that rang through her at his evasiveness and failed.

Sean moved toward the door to his apartment. "Look, I'm gonna hit the shower, then I've got to head into the gym to finish a few things in the office, but maybe we can catch up later?"

His tone was neutral, but Ivy could tell when she was being blown off.

It shouldn't have bothered her. It definitely shouldn't have hurt. He had a right to his private business, which had been her idea really when she insisted that she wanted to keep this thing between them casual in the first place.

Honestly, it was hypocritical wanting to know all his business, considering the huge part of her life she hadn't shared with him. But until this moment it hadn't occurred to her that there was a part of his life he'd chosen not to share with her.

She lifted a shoulder. "Sure. Later."

The silence echoed through the hallway between their apartments. And for the first time things between them were truly awkward.

As Sean watched her, she held her breath, hoping he might do or say something to bring back the light mood that had existed between them all morning. But instead, he went inside his apartment, leaving her alone in the hallway, wondering what had happened to make things change so quickly.

CHAPTER SIXTEEN

On Tuesday morning, Ivy walked through the front door of the gym only to be faced with Wendy, Christine, and Erica leaning up against the reception desk, chins in palms, waiting for the firefighters to arrive for their training session. As had become a habit over the last few weeks.

"You guys are ridiculous," Ivy said grumpily, swinging her bag off her shoulder and dumping it on the floor behind the desk.

"Somebody needs a pumpkin spiced latte," was Wendy's reply.

Ivy ignored her. She did need a pick-me-up, but hell would freeze over before she admitted that to these three. "What are you going to do in a couple weeks when the charity fight is over and the guys don't show up for training anymore?"

"Ugh, I don't know." Christine sighed dejectedly. "Start a fire?" She glanced at Ivy as she twirled one of her boxer braids between her fingers.

"I'm hoping they'll keep coming back. I mean, why work

that hard to get bodies like they have and then drop it altogether? Maybe they'll take some of my classes. I should tell Sean to give me a plug before he sets them loose." Wendy flipped her straight, ebony ponytail over her shoulder as she turned to face Ivy. "Speaking of Sean. What's the scoop on Saturday night?"

"I have no idea what you're talking about," Ivy evaded. She hadn't seen Sean since their awkward moment in the hall, which was unusual because they usually saw each other daily. She was trying not to read too much into it.

"So, you didn't leave our girls'-night-out-turned-engagement-party early to go fuck his brains out in your apartment?" Wendy asked with a flutter of eyelashes.

"You know, for someone so sweet looking, you sure have a filthy mouth on you," Ivy said, hoping more than anything to avoid the conversation Wendy was angling at.

"Oh please, if all the sexy as hell guys around here can swear up a storm, why can't I? I'm so over all the fucking double standards."

True. Still, Ivy didn't feel like discussing that her newly discovered sex life might have dried up as quickly as it had come. But since she couldn't seem to divert the conversation, she'd have to change the subject. She pointed at Erica.

"Hey, didn't you get engaged over the weekend? Does Anna know you are sitting here waiting for hot guys to walk by so you can ogle their asses?"

Erica looked from Wendy to Christine. "She's deflecting."

"She is," Christine said, looking at Ivy as she spoke. "Could mean one of two things. One, it was bad. Or two, it was amazing, but it hasn't happened again and now she's worried that she did something wrong."

"Hmmm. I'm gonna go with door number two," Erica guessed.

"Oh, for Pete's sake!" Ivy threw up her hands. "You guys are hopeless. Maybe I don't boink and tell. Has that ever occurred to you?"

Wendy gave her an astonished look. "*Boink* the hottest guy in the gym and not tell your girlfriends about it? It's simply not done."

"Co-workers," Ivy corrected on instinct, and all three women snickered.

"Cute," Christine said. "She still tells herself we're not friends."

Ivy frowned, not appreciating the tone, but the truth hit hard, regardless. When had these women wormed their way into her heart when she'd made every effort to keep her walls up and not let anyone in?

Luckily, the firefighting quintet came through the doors at that moment, saving the day.

"Hey ladies," the tallest one drawled.

When Wendy visibly melted against the welcome desk, Ivy rolled her eyes.

"Are you ladies planning on coming to fight night to cheer us on? It's in less than two weeks, you know," the dark, chiseled cheekbones one asked.

Christine rested her breasts against the countertop, leaning in suggestively, her boxer braids tickling her cleavage. "Is that an invitation, handsome?"

Mr. Chiseled had no problem propping his elbow on the counter next to Christine, homing in on her personal space. Not that she seemed to mind.

"Only if you want it to be." He winked at her and she sighed.

Oh, for the love of Pete! Ivy thought as Christine and her firefighter eye fucked each other across the counter space. Next thing, they'd be fondling each other. She needed to get out of here before that happened. Picking up her bag, she made her way toward her clinic to prepare for her first client.

She determinedly did not look toward the back of the gym where Sean would likely already be in the ring prepping for a training sesh with the Casanovas.

Since Sunday morning and the cryptic phone call, she hadn't talked to him. True, they'd both been busy, and he didn't owe her phone calls or explanations, but still, she had thought that he'd at least reach out to her, especially given their...arrangement.

Yesterday, they'd made eye contact a few times, and Ivy got her ass whipped in his kickboxing class, but they hadn't exchanged many words in two days.

She was trying hard not to stress about it. After all, he knew where to find her if he wanted. Clearly, he didn't want to. Maybe he was already over it. Meanwhile, she couldn't seem to think of anything else. Every time she had a free minute for her mind to wander, it wandered right back to her bedroom, and all the things they'd done in it. Try as she might, Ivy had not been able to recreate an orgasm that intense.

The thought of that being the beginning and the end of their arrangement was unacceptable. And yet, what the hell was she supposed to do? Strut up to him and demand sex? Ask him when he'd be free for the next booty call?

Is that what people in these situations did? Because if so, she really wasn't cut out to be a fuck buddy. In hindsight, she probably should have done some research first. *Hey Google, how do you become an expert fuck buddy?*

The reality was, she didn't know the first thing about

enticing a man, let alone a man like Sean—alpha, ultra-masculine, testosterone fueled, confidently sexual—honestly, where did one even begin? She didn't have what it took to keep a man like that on the hook. Not even for a string of emotionless sexcapades.

Disheartened, Ivy thought back to Tina. The voluptuous cookie-baking goddess, with her figure-hugging wrap-around dress and D-cup breasts. Soft, curvy, sexy, and all woman. That was the kind of woman Sean deserved to have as a friend with benefits.

Ivy released a monumental sigh, the kind that clearly said, *Hello, it's me, I'm in the middle of the biggest pity party of my life. Please pass the Oreos.*

She really wished she could have a do-over with how she'd nagged him about the phone call. Damned phone call. Was it terrible that she still wanted to know who had called and soured his mood? If she'd been intrigued before, she was desperate to know now. Everything had shifted after that call, and they hadn't been able to get back on course since.

Oreos never magically appeared in front of her, but she could go for the next best thing. Grabbing her bag she walked back toward the doors.

"Where are you going?" Erica asked.

"To get a round of pumpkin-spiced lattes."

By noon she'd worked on a recovering Achilles injury, dealt with a stubborn client who had not been doing any of the exercises she'd prescribed for his hand injury but who still insisted on resuming his fight training, and lectured an older athlete who was training like she was in her thirties and blew her knee because of it.

Somewhere between the blown knee and a quad injury, Ivy was sitting at her desk wolfing down a yogurt when there was a tap at her door.

"Hey stranger. You got a minute to say hi to an old friend?"

Ivy popped her head up and gasped in surprise when she saw Joel Morgan standing in the doorway of her clinic.

"Joel!" she cried happily as she sprang to her feet and rushed over to him.

When she threw her arms around his neck, he'd laughed, picked her up, and gave her a little spin before setting her back on her feet.

"You look good." He ruffled her hair.

Ivy made a face. Despite him seeing her stripped of all her innocence at the lowest point in her life, he still treated her like his kid sister. Worse than his kid sister sometimes. He never teased his real sister, Hope, as much as he teased Ivy. And Ivy often wondered if all that extra teasing was to lighten the darkness he knew lived inside her.

"What are you doing here?" she asked.

Joel lived in San Francisco, running the family company, but now that Hope had settled in Portland he visited from time to time, and for that Ivy was exceedingly grateful.

He was one of the most socially intelligent people Ivy had ever met. Acutely aware of those he loved, he handled situations, resolved conflicts, saved the day, and was fiercely loyal while doing it. Everyone could count on Joel Morgan. He never let anyone down. Least of all her.

They'd been virtual strangers when she'd called him one fateful day. Three minutes on the phone and he'd dropped everything to come help her and Hope. And she never forgot it.

"I'm in Portland for a few days sniffing around a property we might be interested in procuring." He walked into her clinic with a casual gait that belied his sharp mind and even sharper eye.

Ivy knew he was checking out every inch of her clinic, making sure it was good enough for her. He wouldn't accept anything less for someone he cared about.

"You mean you're spying on your sister, your brother-in-law, and your niece?" Ivy retorted, and he laughed.

"Can't say I don't miss them," he admitted, and she believed him.

The Morgans had worked hard to get where they were as a family.

Now that they'd found their way back to each other, having the geographical distance between them hadn't been easy. But between regular visits and frequent video calls, they made it work.

Ivy hadn't seen her own parents in over a year and was sure that the idea of calls—online or otherwise—didn't even occur to them. They were currently in Ghana, posting their adventures on their YouTube channel. Or maybe it was the Ivory Coast. She'd lost track. It was her nana that she thought of first when she thought of family, and while she tried to check in at least once a week, she knew she could do better in that department.

"But now that you mention it," Joel said, interrupting her mental note to call her nana at the first opportunity. "Hope's been quiet lately. She hasn't texted me in over a week, and Mom said there hasn't been a FaceTime call in a couple of days. You know what's going on with my sister?"

A pang of guilt pierced her heart. She'd seen Hope plenty, but most of the time, they talked about Ivy's friend's with benefits mission. Which was mostly because Hope was trying not to dwell or think or talk about the fact that she still hadn't gotten pregnant. Ivy knew it was weighing heavily on her friend's heart and mind.

Not that Hope would appreciate Ivy telling her brother that. So instead, she shrugged. "She has Ruby, the bar, her art, a husband. Basically, she has a life—unlike us."

Joel nodded, not quite looking like he was buying it, but also not pushing the issue. He picked up a photo from her desk. The one of Ivy and her nana that had been taken right before Ivy left for college. Before everything changed.

"How are you doing?" he asked, his steel-gray eyes watching her carefully, and she knew what he was getting at.

A few days after her assault, Ethan and Adam had been accused of cheating on their business finals. Because Hope had been in some of their classes, they accused her of helping them cheat by getting them copies of the exam. It had been a lie, of course, but they knew they could use Ivy's fear to manipulate Hope into taking the fall for them.

Ivy could have blown the whistle then. Reported the assault and filed charges. But she hadn't. Instead of fighting for Hope, the way Hope had fought for her, she'd taken the coward's way out and called Joel. He'd come, bailing out his sister and saving Ivy from having to disclose the thing she hadn't even been ready to acknowledge.

In the process, Joel had found out what happened. Telling him had been almost unavoidable and given what he'd done for them, the truth was the least he deserved. Which made him one of a handful of people who knew what those college business students had done to her at that frat party one night.

"I'm good," she promised, then sighed when his gaze didn't falter. "Honestly, Joel, you don't need to worry about me anymore. I'm happy here. Best decision I ever made was to come to Portland and open this clinic." She spread her arm wide, gesturing around her. "It's my pride and joy. My happy place. When I am here, all is well."

Which wasn't an exaggeration. What she'd accomplished in the last three years was her saving grace. Her clients gave her a reason to get up every morning and keep going. They needed her to help them heal, and in doing so, she found she healed a little more every day herself.

As if on cue, the door to her clinic opened and her next client limped in. Ivy waved at the tall redhead, who'd injured her quad pretty badly playing in a college basketball game a week earlier.

"Hey Sarah," she said and gestured toward the far end of her clinic. "Get settled on the mats. I'll be right over."

Joel took the hint and moved toward the doors. "Have dinner with me tonight. We'll catch up properly. It's been ages."

It had been ages, and the thought of getting out with someone that didn't know about her and Sean, and therefore couldn't nag her about it, sounded appealing. "Sure. I should be done here around six."

"Great, I'll pick you up at your apartment around seven, then. Give you a chance to get ready." He leaned in and gave her a peck on the cheek. "I've missed you, Squirt." And then he was gone.

Sean was in a bad mood. Had been since he'd left Ivy standing in the hall on Saturday morning after his brother had called him for the third time that week. Or rather, after he'd ignored his brother's call for the third time that week. The morning had not ended how he'd thought it would, and he'd been ruminating about it all week. Now if only he could figure out a way to fix it, then maybe he'd be less grumpy.

But today, he was even grumpier, and he knew exactly what had triggered his foul mood. It was seeing Joel Morgan leaving Ivy's clinic, hands in his pockets, casual as can be, looking mighty pleased with himself. Like he'd accomplished something Sean had not this week—quality time with Ivy.

Should it have bothered Sean that Joel and Ivy had spent time together? No, it should not have. And it never had before. But today, it did.

Sean had met Joel enough times over the last year to know he was as good as a guy could get. Smart, successful, charismatic, family oriented. He was a fucking catch, and it was a damned mystery why the guy was single. Today, for the first time, Sean wondered if it had something to do with Ivy. They obviously had a connection. Sean had always believed it was because they were as good as family, but now Sean wondered if maybe it was more. He'd never had the thought before, but his paranoid mind had it today.

So, he'd watched Joel leave his gym, after having had a private visit with the woman Sean was sleeping with (okay he slept with her once, but he planned on making it a habit as soon as he got over himself) and sulked the rest of the day.

He was still sulking when he finally dragged his sorry

ass home from the gym at 9:30 that night after a long day of training and teaching classes. His plan had been to work himself into such exhaustion that he'd collapse into restful sleep for the first time in days. But his plan was starting to change the closer he got to home. The closer he got to Ivy.

He'd been a dick of epic proportions. He'd slept with her, had the best sex of his entire life with her, gone on an invigorating run with her in the morning, and then dropped her like a hot potato because his brother had called him. Seeing Jordan's name flash on his phone screen had been enough to stop him in his tracks and remind him why he needed to proceed with caution when it came to Ivy.

Everyone had a past. He got that. Ivy obviously had one she was reluctant to share. But he had an inkling of her past, and when she chose to reveal it, it wouldn't change one iota of how he felt about her. Whereas his past—

Well, his past was three unreturned phone calls closer to coming back to bite him in the ass, and he wasn't sure if *he* could handle it, never mind asking the woman of his dreams to.

Jordan's existence pretty much nullified the reputation Sean had built for being a chill, upstanding, easy-going, Mr. Nice Guy.

But regardless of how his brother's return to his life gnawed at him, he had no excuse for treating Ivy as he had the last few days. The reason he hadn't been sleeping well was because he wasn't sleeping beside her, and tonight was the night for that to change.

But first, the truth.

With a renewed determination, Sean jogged up the staircase to the apartments, taking them two at a time. He was debating whether he should go home and clean up or head straight to Ivy's when her apartment door opened.

Perfect, decision made. He'd go straight to her, which is where he'd wanted to be anyway.

Except, not perfect because it wasn't Ivy coming out of her apartment. It was Joel. And the bastard had a self-satisfied smirk on his face that told Sean he'd spent some more quality time with his girl.

CHAPTER SEVENTEEN

Sean calmly instructed every muscle in his face not to move as Joel looked at him, his features relaxing into a friendly smile when recognition hit. After all, he had no reason to believe Sean wanted to shove him against the nearest wall and demand what he'd been doing in Ivy's apartment.

It was no secret Joel Morgan considered Ivy a close friend. It wasn't new or strange for him to spend time with her when he was in town, and Sean hadn't been jealous or concerned about it before. But things were different now, and suddenly, without having any sound reason for it, every male within ten feet posed a new threat.

Which irked him to no end, because he wasn't the envious type. Hell, he'd never been invested in anyone enough to warrant the emotion. But this thing he had with Ivy, this pseudo-relationship that was supposed to be casual and felt anything but, left him in a free fall between the certainty in his heart that she completely owned him, and the insecurity of not knowing where he sat in hers. He wasn't handling it well clearly, because he was reacting in ways that he normally would never react.

Like punching the lights out of a good man who'd never posed a threat to him or Ivy before.

Joel closed the door behind him and strode into the hall toward Sean.

"Sean," he greeted, extending a hand. "Good to see you, man."

Sean shook Joel's hand, making sure not to crush any fingers.

"Joel. I didn't realize you were in town."

Joel held a steady gaze, likely picking up on the tension Sean was clearly not doing a good job of hiding.

"I was at the gym today. Saw you out of the corner of my eye, but you looked busy, so I let you be. Thought I'd catch up with you at some point anyway, since you live here now." He gestured to Sean's door.

Sean nodded. He wanted to know every last detail of what Joel had been doing with Ivy behind that closed door, but instead he asked, "What brings you to town?"

Joel cocked an eyebrow. "I have a sister who lives here, and now a niece and brother-in-law. I'm visiting. With a bit of business mixed in, of course."

"Of course." Joel was always working. It was probably why he was a closet billionaire. And single. Unless he wasn't anymore. Single, that is.

Sean jerked his head toward Ivy's door. "You staying with Ivy?" He forced the words out, trying not to choke on them, because if the answer was yes, he was going to—

"No," Joel said, a new light in his eyes, as understanding dawned. "I'm staying at the Heathman."

Sean widened his eyes at the reminder that this guy was richer than sin. The hotel was iconic and insanely expensive, considering there were numerous free options in town for him to stay. But then again, Joel wouldn't be one for couch surfing.

"It's close to a property I've got my eye on. I'm all about convenience," Joel explained, staring at Sean's apartment door. "As, it seems, are you."

Sean tensed. "What's that supposed to mean?"

"Only that it gives me peace of mind knowing you are so conveniently located across from Ivy. As I am sure it gives you." Joel grinned and clapped Sean on the shoulder.

Sean didn't budge a single inch.

"You don't have to worry, man, she's like a sister to me. That said…" Joel leveled him with a steely look, hard and unyielding. "If she ever gets hurt again, I'll kill the fucking bastard who does it. No matter how much I like him." Holding eye contact for another breath, Joel gave a curt nod, then strolled to the staircase.

Sean stayed where he was, immobilized with a new realization. *He knew.* Joel knew what had happened to Ivy.

Why? How? It grated, though it shouldn't have. For years, he thought he'd known her so well. He'd learned so many of her nuances.

The little details of Ivy filled his mind. How she poured chocolate sauce into her coffee on Sunday mornings as a treat. That her favorite rap artist was Lil Baby, who pounded through her AirPods most times she worked out. He knew her favorite color was purple, and that she loved roses but was embarrassed admitting it because it was so cliché. It was why she'd randomly picked Portland to move to after college. She liked the idea of living in the City of Roses. She'd also wanted to be closer to her grandmother, who lived outside Seattle.

He knew she hated raspberries, but loved blackberries,

and had what he would classify as an addiction to flavored carbonated water. He could pick her out of a crowd by her floral shampoo scent alone. And yet, he had no idea what had happened in her past.

It was a frustration that picked at him, because when he broke it down, it meant she didn't trust him with the dark parts of herself. He could know the fun little things, the quirks, and the joys. But when it came to the hard stuff—the shadows lurking in the past—she blocked him out.

But then, wasn't he guilty of doing the same?

He inhaled deeply and counted to ten. Then entered his apartment, stripped himself down, and stalked to his shower, turning it on full blast and standing under it, the temperature as cold as he could bear. He needed to clear his mind. There was so much pinging around in there it was starting to feel like a Bingo machine. Random thoughts and worries flying around, all of them stressing him out, and none of them landing where he needed them to.

And then there was the lust. Insatiable and ever present. Even under the freezing water, he was burning for her. Imagining her there with him, her tight little body fit snugly against his in the shower stall. The water running off her strong, lean muscles. Those gorgeous eyes rimmed with wet lashes. Her small hands rubbing soap all over him.

Fuck. He had the water cranked to maximum cold, and still he had an erection that wouldn't quit. Just like his desire. He'd always wanted her, but now that he had her, he couldn't stop thinking about the next time he could get inside her again. There had been nothing, nothing, like the feeling of her moving over him, enveloping him in her wet heat, her scent, her look of determination blended with passion, the way her eyes melted into a liquid ice.

His senses were in overdrive, his heart banging in his

ears, echoing like the surround sound in his bathroom. Deep breaths sputtered against the water. He braced his hands against the tile walls and willed his body into submission. His desire was like an addiction. If he didn't gain control, it'd get away from him. And with Ivy, he had to be in control. Always.

When he killed the water, he realized the banging had not been his heart, but was booming through his apartment from his front door.

Wrapping a towel around his hips, he walked toward the sound. The knocking was so incessant it was shaking the door in its frame, and he knew exactly who it was.

Stealing mind and heart, he prepared himself for the sight of her, then gripped the knob and opened the door.

~

D*rool.*

Ivy was pretty sure it was drool pooling at the corners of her mouth as she stood gaping at Sean, who was wearing nothing but a white towel wrapped around his hips, his entire ripped body on full display and glistening with water droplets.

Close your mouth, she told herself, channeling her old English nana's firm disciplinary tone. *For God's sake, Ivy Harrington, close your mouth. Do not let him know how delicious he looks right now. He doesn't deserve it.*

She made the concerted effort to close her mouth in as casual a way as she could muster. Proud of not making a total fool of herself by melting at his feet, she lifted her head and looked him straight in the eye. Not lower. Any lower and she'd give in to the need and lick the water droplets off his hardened nipples.

"We need to talk," she said. She was prepared for him to put up a fight. Maybe make an excuse for why it wasn't a good time or shrug her off and say there was nothing to talk about. But he surprised her by giving her a single nod, side-stepping to hold the door open, gesturing for her to enter.

Ivy moved into the living room. The apartment was a carbon copy of her own in layout, but near opposite in decor. Where she went for vibrant color and comfort, Sean's apartment was all sleek, modern, and minimal. No over-sized, colorful cushions or cozy throw blanket on his steel-gray L-shaped couch. Only the couch, big and wide, with a massive flat screen situated in front of it. A rack of weights sat in the corner by a heavy bag that hung from the ceiling.

Whenever she was in this apartment, she understood why they did most of their Netflixing at her place. He had the better TV, but she had the atmosphere.

The one ode to color was the purple heart-shaped throw pillow she'd gifted him as a moving in present. It sat on his couch, as it always did, looking lonely and out of place.

She turned and faced him where he still stood in the entryway between the main door and the living room.

"You're avoiding me. Why?" She cut to the chase. With him, she had to, or she'd get distracted too easily. Briefly, she'd considered asking him to put some clothes on, but quickly decided it would only be a disservice to her if he did.

Sean sighed deeply. "I've been a dick. I'm sorry."

Ivy folded her arms and nodded, saying nothing. She wasn't one to disagree with the truth, but she did have to admit to herself that his mature response was a lot less satis-fying than the fight she'd been jonesing for.

Moving into the living room, he rubbed a hand over his head, as was his habit when he was frustrated, at a loss for words, or otherwise not in an agreeable mood. "It had nothing to do with you. I... That phone call—" He stared at her, dark-brown eyes filled with an emotion she couldn't pinpoint. Then he looked down at himself. "I should put on some clothes."

"Don't do it on my account," she returned, and it tugged a half-smile out of him. Her heart melted a little at the sight.

He was so damn drool worthy when he smiled half naked.

"Give me a minute." It took less than that before he returned wearing athletic pants and a plain black t-shirt stretched tight over his biceps. "Can I get you a drink? Water, wine, tea?"

This time, Ivy sighed. He was evading. Stalling for a reason she couldn't determine, making things awkward between them when awkward was the one thing they'd never been.

To diffuse the tension, she walked up to him until she was in that personal space zone where things between them started to hum, and heat, and relax. "The phone call," she prompted. "It upset you."

Sean stepped closer to her as well, surprising her by bending low to scoop her up into an embrace, tucking his head into the crook of her neck and breathing deeply. Like inhaling her would give him the courage to tell her what he was clearly gearing himself up to tell her.

"My brother," he murmured against her neck.

Ivy stroked her hands down his back, enjoying the feel of his muscles rippling over her fingertips as she went. She knew he had a brother. There had been brief mentions of him, usually in reference to Sean's childhood. He didn't often talk about his family, and she didn't push, knowing he'd lost both parents prematurely, and both brutally, one in an accident, and the other to a vicious, relentless illness. But when he talked about them, it had always been fondly.

He'd only ever mentioned his brother within the context of a memory, never specifically. Whenever she'd probed for more, he simply said he was still living in Chicago—and left it at that.

He pulled away from her, then led her to the couch, where he sat, pulling her down on his lap, and wrapping his insanely muscular arms around her. Holding on.

"Jordan served time in prison for theft and drug possession." As he spoke, he looked directly into her eyes, never wavering, and because she realized he was watching her for a reaction, she purposefully didn't give him one.

She kept her face neutral, giving nothing away, not wanting to influence what he was going to tell her.

"He recently finished parole. He's officially a free man. He called me because he wants to come here to see me. I haven't seen him since the day he was arrested."

When he didn't offer any more information than that, and the silence had sat for long enough, she asked, "Do you want to see him?" The question sounded simple to her, but she saw pain flicker across his eyes, pinching the edges.

"He's my older brother. The only blood family I have left. His whole life he's made a shitload of stupid mistakes. Most of them landed his ass in hot water, but never bad enough to get him locked up. When Mom was really sick and money for treatment was drying up fast, things became —desperate." Sean's eyes darkened with more devastation, more regret.

She could almost see the past clouding his gaze, his vision blurring with memories. When his eyes gave way to a distant look, she knew he was somewhere else. Likely the same place he'd gone that day in the ring, when he'd lost control of the fight. She tightened her hold, pressing closer, wanting him to know she was there with him, wherever he was.

"Jordan ran with some bad dudes. Our neighborhood was full of them. Street gangs all over the place. For kids like us, growing up in the bad end of town, surrounded by poverty, stacked on top of one another in low-income apartments—there weren't many opportunities to dream big, less to find a way out. Most of my friends joined gangs, dealing in low-level misdemeanors that sometimes led to high-level crimes."

Ivy tried to imagine it. There were plenty of shows, news stories, and documentaries that featured the worst neighborhoods in Chicago. It seemed that life in big cities like that were divided into two halves. Those who have, and those who have not. She knew Sean's upbringing hadn't been stellar, but he'd never described it as awful.

His father was a working man, but his lack of education, among other things, stunted his ability to pull his family completely out of the cycle of poverty. Nevertheless, he'd worked hard enough that his children were provided with more opportunities than others had. She knew that because Sean often talked about the dojo his dad used to take him to after school. It was where he'd first gotten a taste of the martial arts.

But she was only realizing now how little she knew about his life before Portland, or the impact it had.

"I had a knack for school and was blessed because my family saw it early and tried to protect me from losing focus or dropping out like so many did. Keeping me on the right track became the priority, even for Jordan. He didn't let me hang out with him and his friends." Sean snorted a mirthless laugh. "He was an ass about it most of the time, but I learned pretty quickly that he'd been doing me a favor." Sean played with her hair, tugging softly as he wrapped the strands through his fingers.

Ivy leaned into the sensation.

"For the most part, I didn't know what he and his friends were up to, or I turned a blind eye when it was clear some of their activities were less than above board. I never joined them, was never asked to. But then Mom got sick she couldn't work, and the medical bills started piling up. Dad was long gone. My part-time jobs weren't making much of a dent. Jordan sometimes brought money home, and we used it, not asking too many questions about where it came from. But soon we needed more. Things were getting worse; time was running out."

His body grew tense the more he spoke, muscles tightening under her, his skin growing colder. Ivy rubbed her hands over his shoulders, down his arms, and cuddled into his chest more deeply. He drew her in, dropped a kiss onto the top of her head, and lay his cheek against her hair. Time passed—enough of it that Ivy thought maybe he was done with the story.

Then he started talking again, his rumbling voice breaking the silence around them. "His money didn't come in as steady as mine, but when he brought cash home, it was a lot more than I could make in two weeks at the pizza place I was working at. I remember seeing the wads of bills come home and not even questioning what he did to get it. We needed that money." Sean inhaled deeply, his nose to her hair. "God, you smell good. Like honey and roses."

"New shampoo," she whispered, her body responding to the way his breath tickled her cheek and neck.

"Nah. You've always smelled like this. So sweet." He

inhaled again and hugged her closer. "Tell me if I'm crushing you."

In response, she sank into his grip, wanting nothing more than to crawl inside him and embrace his heart.

"One night, a deal went south. Jordan got arrested and ended up in prison." His words were muffled against her hair.

"Oh, Sean." She tried to imagine what it must have been like for him as a young man. He'd lost his father, his mother was dying, and then his brother got taken away. There was nothing to say, so she simply held on to him, so grateful, and humbled that he was confiding this to her.

"The funny thing is," he went on, not laughing at all, "it was all for nothing. Mom died two weeks later."

Ivy's heart bottomed out at the quiet statement. She'd known there wouldn't be a happily-ever-after ending, but this one seemed cruel.

"When Jordan was in, I never went to see him. I just— didn't. Not even after Mom died. I sent a message through the prison to let him know." Sean sighed, and it was a weighted sound. "Now he's out, parole done, and all he wants is to see me."

Shame. She could hear it lace every word he spoke. It was a brutal thing. She'd been paralyzed by it before, in many ways she still was, and knowing that Sean shared an understanding of that was both comforting and heart-breaking in one.

Ivy pulled back, locking eyes. She cradled the side of his face with her hand, stroking the rough stubble on his cheek. She'd never seen him look anything other than calm and at ease. But lately, with her, he'd let more slip through the veneer, revealing more of himself. He was letting her see his vulnerability, his shame, his regret, his guilt. And it wasn't a gift she took lightly.

"He made those choices himself, Sean. No one forced him. He knew the consequences; they were worth it for him."

He said nothing to that.

So she stroked her thumb along the soft skin beneath his eye. "Do you want to see him?"

"Yes." There was no hesitation in the word. "But it feels complicated. Like too much time has passed. And I have this great life here. I've changed myself so much. I don't think he'd even recognize me as the brother he once knew."

"How so?" She couldn't imagine he was that different.

Sean was smart, strong, resilient at his core. She hadn't known him back in his Chicago days, but she couldn't believe his foundation had changed.

"Ivy, here in Portland, people know me as the easy-going, relaxed dude, who doesn't let much phase him. I might be a hard-ass in the gym, but outside, I'm everyone's friend. Mr. Nice Guy. But back when I was younger, that wasn't me."

Silence begged the question. "Who were you?"

"I was dark and quiet. Hopeless. I saw no way out, even though my parents always told me I was smart enough for college, that I would make something of myself. I still felt trapped. There was nothing to look forward to in that life. No joy, if that makes sense. And everyone kept dying. Fuck, it was awful. Knowing that you were going to be all alone. I was a moody bastard because of it."

A few weeks ago, Ivy would have been surprised by that description of him. Moody and sullen weren't aspects of his personality she'd ever seen before. But over the last few weeks, she'd seen it all. She'd seen it after she'd proposi- tioned him and he'd said no. When she went out with another man. When their friendship had been tested like it never had before. Hopelessness. Moodiness. Frustration.

Was that the trigger? When he couldn't see the way forward? When he thought he was losing the people he cared about?

Slowly, the man that was truly Sean Thompson started to take shape in her mind.

"I came here and pretended to be a whole new person. I created a whole new persona and left all of that shit behind. My parents dying, my brother rotting in a jail cell. I left it like it had never existed, and I started fresh. Happy. Optimistic. The trainer who motivated people to do better and be better, and I became the image I was selling. Truly, I became it. It's not fake, Ivy. I am happy here. I found everything I could ever need right here."

The way he held her, cradled on his lap, tucked into his arms like he was holding his whole world, had her wondering if his words had a double meaning, like maybe everything he needed was right there, on his lap.

But she could relate to what he was saying. After she'd arrived in Portland, she'd created a new version of herself, as well. Decimating the weak, powerless girl she'd been when she arrived had been her only objective. There wasn't much left from the old version of her that anyone would recognize.

There would always be something left, though. The past was never completely gone. She knew that better than anyone. And it never would be until there was an opportunity to let go of it. Sometimes the opportunity landed in front of you, and other times you had to create the opportunity yourself. Her whole friend with benefits endeavor had been about exactly that—confronting remnants of the past that haunted her. Maybe Sean needed to do the same.

"You should see him," she announced. "Make peace with

it, with him. Close the circle and move on." There wasn't any reason for him to live in regret and shame if he didn't have to.

"Maybe," he murmured half-heartedly, his eyes closing, and she read between his words. It wouldn't be that easy. Facing ghosts never was. She was still working on it herself, wasn't she?

Ivy brushed her fingertips over his closed eyes, enjoying the silky softness of his eyelashes under her touch. When he opened them again, his pupils were dilated. Dark and deep, telling her he was done talking for the night. And, quite frankly, so was she.

CHAPTER EIGHTEEN

Sean had revealed a big piece of himself, and it had clearly cost him. Sitting this close, Ivy noticed the exhaustion etched in the fine lines at the sides of his eyes. For maybe the first time since she'd known him, he looked tired. It was a vulnerability she had never seen in him before.

Going off instinct, she leaned in, brushing her lips against his, then continued to hold them close so that when she whispered, her words breathed right into him. "I've got you." *This time, I've got you.*

There was no hesitation in his response. It was knee-jerk. His hands combed through her hair, gripping her skull, angling her closer. His lips latched onto hers and drank everything she was offering. Mouths opened, tongues twisted, his arms tightening around her, drawing her inward. There was a strength and dominance to his move-ments that hadn't been there the last time, like for a moment he'd forgotten she was the cracked and fragile glass that needed gentle handling. And she was there for it.

Knowing that he needed this from her as a means of

comfort and not a power play, as a gift and not a conquest, was incredibly empowering. She'd never imagined sex could be like this, not even before the assault. When she was with Sean, he wasn't shy about expressing his desire and his need, and she knew it came from a place beyond the physical.

He cared for her. Deeply. She sensed it right down to her soul. The realization had her jolting back. His eyes had gone opaque, his breath uneven.

"You okay?" he asked, and she could visibly see him scrambling for control between hard inhales.

Was she? She had no idea. The lines between them were blurring at lightning speed, and she had no idea what to do. Her broken bits were still broken. Her soul damaged and tainted. He deserved so much more than that. She wanted more than that for him.

Ivy breathed, or tried to, but her heart was hammering in her chest, and her mind was reeling. Breathe, focus. Stay in the moment. All the things he'd taught her. All the things she held on to like a lifeline. She clung to them now and thought about her next move.

What if she could be the woman he deserved? Could give him the thing she knew he was hungry for? The one terrifying thing she'd never be able to give anyone else. No one but him. And she'd give it freely, because she trusted him.

"I want you to take control tonight." She said the words even as her lips trembled. "Whatever you want." Her stomach knotted, tightening painfully.

He wouldn't hurt her. He'd never hurt her. She knew it, felt it. Still...

"Ivy, you don't have to—" Sean tipped her face up so he

could meet her gaze. His eyes were earnest when he told her, "That's not how it works."

"I want to do this," she insisted. "For you."

Breathe. She told herself. *Just keep breathing, and you'll be fine.*

His eyes warmed. The look of sympathy filling them was so genuine she almost couldn't stand it. She couldn't take his pity, not after everything.

"I mean it, Sean. Tonight, it's whatever you want. Don't argue with me."

She thought he'd put up a fuss. Had fully expected him to. He'd been so damned gentle with her, she had started to feel like glass. Tonight she wanted to show him she could be normal in bed and not choke.

But he surprised her when he nodded, stroking a hand down her arm, then up her side, over the swell of her breast, and playing across the nipple, which came to full attention at the contact.

Before she knew what was happening, he was moving, lifting her up as he got off the couch.

"Wrap your legs around me," he told her, and the tone of his voice made her body obey instantly.

She locked her legs around his solid trunk of a waist, and he turned, moving toward his bedroom. The room was dark, and she couldn't see much, which was why she let out a little yelp when he dropped her on the mattress.

"Don't move," he commanded, his voice moving farther into the room.

At the loss of physical contact, and in the darkness of the room, Ivy started to slip away, to another dark room, to another dark night. A shiver started to tremble through her body, starting in her hands and moving inward, and she scrambled to find her focus.

A panic attack was not supposed to be on the menu tonight. Tonight was for him. Her gift to him. The one thing she could give him. What good was a friend with benefits if there were no benefits? Or if she had a panic attack every time the benefits started rolling. Or if the benefits meant she had to be in control every single time.

Her heart sped to keep pace with the runaway thoughts in her mind. And then suddenly, there was light.

A flicker, and she saw Sean's face in the candlelight. He set three wide, stubby candles on the dresser, then moved to light two tea lights which he placed on the nightstands on either side of the bed.

"You really love your candles, don't you?" she said, immediately soothed by the soft dance of light in the darkness.

"I look better in candlelight," he deadpanned. When he was done, he stood at the foot of the bed, holding her gaze steadily as he removed his shirt. He continued to watch her as he dropped it on the ground. His pants and briefs followed suit quickly.

Ivy swallowed. God, he was impressive. And hell yes, he looked amazing by candlelight. Although, really, six-packs tended to look good under any light.

"Do you want to take off your clothes, Ivy?" He stood in front of her, completely naked and fully aroused. In the shadows, his face was dark, but his eyes sparkled as they stayed trained on her.

"I want you to do it." She surprised herself by saying this, not because it wasn't true, but because she'd never imagined a day where she'd be okay with someone removing her clothes.

Then again, she'd never imagined someone like Sean.

He nodded, and came forward, kneeling on the bed as

he grabbed her foot and pulled off a sock. Then moved to do the same on her other foot. He leaned over farther and unbuttoned the top of her jeans. When she inhaled sharply, he paused, found her eyes, and bent to kiss her, slow and deep, bringing her right into the present again. The moment where all she could do was taste and feel and smell only him.

"Stay with me," he whispered. "Watch what I'm doing."

And she did, mesmerized as his long fingers unzipped her jeans and deftly tugged them off.

"Sit up," he said.

She did as he asked.

"Lift your arms. Don't take your eyes off me."

She lifted both arms above her head. His hands came to the hem of her shirt, and she gasped at the soft touch of his fingers against her midriff. Liquid heat shot right to her core, and moisture pooled between her thighs.

All things considered, he was being very mechanical with his movements. No sweet caresses, or even a passionate tearing of panties. It wasn't necessarily erotic or sexy. He was simply removing her clothes, as she'd asked him to do, and yet she'd never been more turned on in her life.

He paused at her gasp, his fingers stilling on the hem. He watched her carefully, searching her eyes. Ivy tried to close her mouth and failed. Was it normal that she was seconds away from panting? She wanted him to touch her so badly, she was ready to tear her own shirt off herself, but this was for him. She wanted him to have control tonight.

So she remained still, her mouth parted slightly as she inhaled again, holding his gaze as he'd requested.

A few pounding heartbeats later, he continued, pulling her shirt up and over her head. She was now sitting in her bra and panties, willing him to move faster. Finally, he reached around her and unclasped her bra. It got tossed over his shoulder with the rest of her clothing, but her panties stayed on.

"Lie back." Sean gestured to the bed, and she scooted back until she could lie down, her head sinking into the pillows. Sean followed, coming up beside her.

He kissed her mouth, her cheeks, and forehead like it was a reward for good behavior, and Ivy released a sigh of satisfaction.

"You're perfect," he murmured against her skin before he trailed kisses all the way down the side of her neck and across her collarbone.

Okay, that was it, cue panting. Breath raced in and out of Ivy's lungs like she'd come back from a run.

"What do you like, Ivy?" His baritone rumbled through the haze of her lust like a drug, but she was already too lost in the sea of a desire his touch ignited that she couldn't focus on it.

Her skin was alive with sensation, the wet trail of his tongue leaving her cool and tingling. When he pulled his head up, she whimpered. Whimpered! Who was she?

"Answer me, sweetheart. What do you like? What don't you like? What turns you on? What turns you off? I need to know."

Realizing that she'd have to provide an answer if she wanted more of what was happening, she tried to regulate her breathing by taking a shaky breath, then told him the truth. "I don't know."

His eyebrows shot up. "You don't know what you like and don't like."

"It's been a while before you." Her face heated at the admission of her inexperience, killing the desire a bit. "And before that, the last time, well... Nothing was good. So, I don't know."

When his face darkened at her words, she scrambled to recover the mood with more truth.

"With you, everything feels good, Sean. Everything. More of this, for the rest of the night, or however long, and I'll be happy." She meant it. She didn't know if it was that enough time had passed, and she had enough pent-up sexual frustration to last a lifetime, or if it was him, but everything and anything he did brought her to new heights of arousal.

It's him, her mind whispered. And she let that sink in, because whatever that realization meant for their future or their arrangement, in this moment, it was enough.

Sean nodded slowly, as if it was taking time for him to absorb the information. "Is there anywhere I can't touch? Anything you don't want?"

Good point. She hadn't thought of that. Hadn't considered that he might touch her somewhere, and she'd freak, and honestly, she didn't want to. Her ghosts had no place here in this precious time with Sean.

"Show me where he hurt you." His voice was a low, gravely sound. Like a rumble of thunder after the lightning.

"Um..." This night wasn't going how she'd thought it would.

"Show me where the scars are." He softly kissed her collarbone. He seemed to like it there.

"The scars?" That night had been brutal. There'd been so many bruises, big red and purple bruises, all over her body for days. But there wasn't a physical scar, not one that showed, at least. "They're on the inside," she murmured.

If he wanted to run screaming, now was his chance.

But Sean didn't run. He lifted her hand and turned it so

her palm was facing up, then kissed her gently on the pulse point of her left wrist. "Show me where, on the inside."

Emotion pricked her eyes, and she blinked it back. The warmth of his hand flowed into the veins of her wrist and spread through her entire body, until every bit of cold inside her was replaced by his heat.

Slowly she lifted their joined hands and moved them downward, over her belly, and lower, until her fingers brushed the softness between her legs.

"Here," she said, and his gaze moved to linger where their hands rested. "I have scars inside here." Horrible memories of how she'd been violated bled into the periphery of her brain, until there was an aching throb just under her skin. Memories of pain, and the terrifying sensation of burning, forceful stretching of flesh that wasn't ready and didn't want to be touched. The pain between her legs had lasted for days afterward. Every time she moved, it was a reminder of what happened.

Her humiliation should have stopped her from continuing, but for Ivy it was so freeing being able to finally show someone the map of her assault that she continued, moving their joined hands upward, and his fingers thread through hers, holding tightly. She stopped at her left breast, where her heart beat erratically behind it.

"And here."

She knew her heart would never be the same. It was broken, irrevocably so. Which was why he didn't deserve her, and why she couldn't even imagine having a normal relationship with anybody. Especially Sean. He'd be wasted on her. He deserved someone who could love him back with a whole heart.

Sean's eyes flickered in the candlelight. The way he was looking at the pale skin of her breast made her certain he saw right through her exterior to her heart beneath. Could he see the damage that was imprinted there? Did he understand now why she'd requested a no-strings arrangement?

Unable to stop now, she brought their joined hands up to her temple, spreading her fingers so his flattened over hers. This was the money spot of her brokenness. The scar that was so deep not even the counselor she saw for months after could do much to repair it.

"Here." She tapped the side of her head. "The worst scar is in here." Her tormented mind. It plagued her night and day.

Ethan had done a total mind fuck on her, and it was probably the worst damage he'd done that night. He controlled it still, because he'd never paid for what he did to her, and she knew he likely never would.

And there it was, the roadmap of her damage. Sean's to navigate, hers to own.

He leaned forward and kissed the temple she'd tapped, pulling her attention back to him. His lips lingered there a full minute before he lowered his head to kiss the skin above her heart. Again, he paused, lips pressed against every heartbeat. He moved lower again, and she tensed, knowing where he was headed. He was following the map, after all. And she wanted his mouth where he was taking it. Oh, did she ever. But she couldn't shake the intrusive thought that it would be wrong for him to put his mouth on something so desecrated. Here was the sucky thing about the mind body connection—it really stunted healing. It's why she always considered the scars in her mind to be the worst, because they held all the rest back. And even though she knew it, she couldn't change how they made her see herself. Defiled. Dirty. Unclean. Unworthy.

He picked up on her tension and sat back on his

haunches. "If you don't know what turns you on, and what turns you off, then we'll go over it. Every single inch, so I can learn your body, Ivy. And you can learn it too."

He settled at the opposite end from her. "If I do anything you don't like, say so. I understand English, so any form of *no*, *don't*, or *stop* will work. I'm also pretty good at reading facial expressions if you don't feel like talking, so I want to be clear you're not the one who has to learn how to communicate. It's on me to understand what you're telling me." He lifted her foot. "We'll start here," he told her before he brazenly sucked her toe into his mouth.

She shrieked and jerked, nearly kicking him in the face, and his chuckle resounded in the bedroom.

"An *off* then," he noted, before licking the underside of her foot's arch.

Ivy gasped, and he looked up at her, assessing the sound. He licked again, and she moaned.

"That one's an *on*. See how we're going to do this?" Slowly, mind-blowingly slowly, he worked his mouth over her feet and up her legs.

Ivy let her body react, melting when she liked something, like his caress on the underside of her knee, and making it clear when she didn't.

So far, though, Ivy's favorite parts were the sounds coming from Sean. His low growls and moans as he tasted and nibbled her flesh, like he truly enjoyed every part of her. He didn't seem to have any *offs*. He didn't avoid anything, appeared to have no shame either. There was no part of her he didn't taste, lick, or touch and, amazingly to Ivy, enjoy. No part of her he didn't relish or savor.

He nipped and kissed the soft skin of her thighs, putting his hand between them to nudge them wider so he could stroke his tongue along the inside. She heard her own moans as his day-old stubble scratched along the tender flesh of her inner thigh when he kissed her. She *loved* it. And told him so. Over and over.

Torturously, he avoided her center, even though, by that point, it was drenched and aching for him. Her body was so hot, her skin on fire from his slow torment. She was sure she wouldn't mind if he kissed her there now. Pretty sure, at least.

But he avoided it, instead moving up her stomach, over her breast, and spending time with each nipple in turn, until they were hard peaks, straining in his direction, begging for more. It was like there was an electric line between her nipples and her core. When one was stimulated, everything became electric.

Sean kissed every inch of her from hairline to earlobe to neck—oh God, her neck. Maybe that was her favorite. The thighs had been good but the neck—especially the spot right beneath her ear.

This was all reminding her of the childhood song where the bones all connected together to make one body. Maybe sexual stimulation was the same, all connected, because when his mouth touched her ear, desire shivered down her neck, then to her nipples. Her core was now aching so acutely she wondered if she might orgasm like this.

Then he loosely lifted her wrist, raising it above her head, and instinctively she tensed. Sean stopped immediately, his eyes finding hers. He held her there with his gaze, and she swallowed.

"Talk to me."

"I don't like—My hands need to be free," she managed.

Sean dipped to the side, tucked her into his chest, and kissed her deeply, his hands finding the spots she loved, and easing her into her relaxed state again.

After a while, he asked, "How does that feel?"

"Good." Once again, her brain was fuzzy with need.

"I promise I'll never restrain you. I want you to always be free to move and touch whatever and whenever you want. I like that you do. In fact, I love it. I don't want to trap you, Ivy. I want to worship you." His eyes shone with truth, then with humor. "And also, I wanted access."

"Access?" she asked, her arm still over her head, even though he'd let go. "To what?"

"To this." He ducked his head and flicked his tongue over her armpit, and she nearly came clean off the bed.

"Ohmigod!" she shrieked. "Off, off, off!" She struggled between squealing and laughing.

This man really needed some *offs* of his own. A rush of thoughts raced through her head. Was she even wearing deodorant? She resisted the urge to do the sniff test. Who licked armpits? It tickled. Did she like that? Nope. "That's a big *off*. Don't ever do that again."

He laughed. "Okay. But how about here?" He suckled the side swell of her breast, then the underside. And she melted.

"Sean." His name was a moan on her lips, and he replied with a rumbling hum of his own.

"I love when you say my name like that. All soft and sexy, like me licking you is better than chocolate."

"Don't get ahead of yourself, big guy," she murmured, but he was heading south again and then only one word rang through her head. "Please."

She was begging, even as her thighs fell open. When he put his lips on her, any worry or disgust she'd had was no more than a chalk outline in her brain. A shadow of something that should be there, but surprisingly wasn't anymore. The power of the armpit lick? After all, if the man could taste her there and not be repulsed, he'd probably enjoy her flavor anywhere.

Also, the ache of need was now becoming unbearable. If he didn't do something to relieve the pressure soon, she'd explode. And then there it was. His tongue running over her, parting her seam, and delving between. Raw, hungry groans emerged from him, like he was a starving man feasting, and something unclipped in Ivy's heart and floated away, just like that. She wasn't dirty or unclean. As Sean hungrily devoured her, she started to believe she might be...delicious.

Even more miraculous, her mind silenced, allowing her body to chase her release freely. Thighs clamped around his head, fingers dug into the comforter beside her in a death grip, guttural moans falling from her lips, only interrupted by his name, hips pressed upward, closer to his face. If she was embarrassing herself, there was no stopping it. She was completely out of control, with no way to get back into the driver's seat. Not that she even wanted to go there, because never in a hundred thousand million of her twenty-six years had she ever experienced this level of bliss.

No, good wasn't the right word. It didn't do justice to the current coursing through her body. *Alive.* She'd never been this alive.

"Sean, that's—Oh God, I'm going to—I can't—" And then she was. Crying out, because words were beyond her as she rocketed through the strongest sexual release she'd ever experienced. Aching in intensity, bordering on agony but not painful at all, only...electrifying. And it went on and on, wave after wave, like a tide rushing in and washing away everything on the shoreline. As she sobbed through her climax, she let it take away all of her inhibitions and self-doubt, until there was nothing left but a smooth surface. A fresh start.

Still shuddering when it was over, Ivy flopped back onto the mattress, staring at the ceiling as she tried to catch her breath. Only a few seconds passed before two hands gripped her ankles and tugged her down to the edge of the bed. She shrieked as her naked ass slid down the bed.

Looking up, she met Sean's heated, laughter-filled gaze. Standing at the foot of the bed, he grinned, like he knew exactly what he was doing. His hands resting on her ankles slid up her calves, sending all kinds of happy dances through her nerve endings. When he got to her knees, he spread them apart and made room for himself between. His erection, already covered in a condom, bobbed in her direction, long and thick, making her hot all over again.

She lifted herself to her elbows. "Your turn?" she asked, feeling bad that she'd come so hard, while not giving a single thought to his climax, even though this night was supposed to be all about him.

Sean gripped himself and drew nearer, all amusement replaced with a hunger that belied the feast he'd just had. "Our turn," he corrected in a low, husky voice that made all her insides melt.

"Look at me," he instructed, and she did.

She met his gaze as he stepped forward and slid into her, watching as desire darkened his eyes, reveling in how his jaw bunched in restraint as he slowly pushed in. The sheen of sweat on his dark skin glistened in the candlelight, his brow furrowed.

He looked magnificent, and Ivy didn't take her eyes off him for one second. Not until he was fully lodged inside her, so deeply embedded in her body she couldn't tell where she ended and he began. He was still standing at the foot of the bed, while she lay in front of him, knees up, hands gripping the bedsheets.

She lowered her gaze then, to the place where they were joined. His hips pressed firmly against her thighs, their bodies so tightly joined there was really nothing to see. There was only a sensation so intense she worried she might splinter apart.

Then he started moving, pulling back, and she was mesmerized as he plunged back into her, sending her backward with the force, until she gasped. He stopped immediately, and she shook her head frantically.

"Again!" she begged, fixated on their united bodies.

"Eyes up, sweetheart. I need to see you."

With effort, she lifted her gaze to him. "Please, Sean. Don't stop," she whispered, making sure not to break eye contact again.

Satisfied with whatever he saw in her eyes, he rocked forward, in and out, over and over, using his grip under her knees as leverage, his thighs hitting the base of the bed every time he came flush with her body.

Ivy switched between looking at Sean's face, his creased brow and intense focus, and between them. She couldn't help it. The sight of him emerging and disappearing inside her was the most erotic thing she'd ever seen. Going on instinct, she moved her fingers to the nub of flesh right above where they were linked, and rubbed. Sensation burst through her anew.

Was this her actual life? Having better sex than she could've ever imagined, with the hottest man in existence. It didn't feel real. And yet here she was, on the verge of a second orgasm.

"Jesus. You're so amazing. So beautiful. When I'm with

you—" His voice was rough and strained, no more than a rasp in the darkened room.

"What?" she panted, wanting to know what she did to him, if it was anything close to what he did with her.

"When I am with you, Ivy, I feel everything."

Definitely relatable. Never in a million years could she have guessed it could be like this with him. That he could make her feel this way. That he would know, so instinctively, what she would want and need, even on a night that was very specifically supposed to be about fulfilling his wants and needs.

Even the way he'd situated himself in front of her, and not on top of, meant everything to her. He'd taken a night that was supposed to be solely about his enjoyment and turned it into one of the most gratifying experiences of *her* life.

Emotion swamped her alongside the physical momentum, and she had the flash of realization that there was no way she could keep this casual. Casual was gone, replaced by something much stronger. Friendship wasn't an accurate enough word to describe what existed between them. Friends didn't fuck like they could read each other's minds, like they shared the same soul. In fact, they didn't fuck at all. They made love.

She would have panicked at that, but Sean had increased his tempo, and her fingers moved to match. And then the world exploded. Sean bared his teeth, his body stiffening, every muscle taut and straining right before he jerked inside her one last time. A grunt ripped from his throat, her name following suit like he was in the middle of a charismatic worship service, and it was enough to set her free again.

But this time, her heart tumbled over the edge along with her body.

CHAPTER NINETEEN

Sean blacked out. In the recesses of his fuzzed, blissed-out brain, he realized he was only like this after sex with Ivy. Completely spent, fully satisfied. Being with her filled every void, physical and emotional.

Now she curled up beside him, her palm coming to rest over his heart. Her sigh sounded so content he couldn't help the surge of pride that burst through him.

Slowly but surely, she was unraveling in the very best way. Unwinding whatever haunted her mind and contorted her heart, replacing it with something new. Which was fitting, because that was exactly what was happening inside of him. Something magical was growing between them, and he nearly laughed at how sentimental that sounded—if it weren't so true.

Leisurely, he moved to disentangle himself from her, kissed her lightly on the mouth, then went to the bathroom to dispose of the condom. When he came out, he found her getting dressed.

"You going somewhere?" he asked, his chest tightening

at the sight of her jerky movements as she pulled her pants up over her legs.

Ivy glanced at him, blowing her bangs away from her eyes. "Oh, yeah, you know, I thought I'd go back to my place, get some paperwork done before bed."

"It's late," he stated matter-of-factly, stepping closer to her and stilling her fingers as she fumbled with her shirt. What the fuck had happened between thirty seconds ago and now? "Ivy—"

Her body was trembling. She was obviously grappling for control. And he could relate. Things between them were so far beyond casual that it was laughable. Control was slipping out of both of their fingers, and running seemed instinctive. Run and protect yourself. But he didn't want to run. If this was fight or flight, he was fighting.

"Work can wait until the morning. Stay," he urged, lowering his head so he could meet her gaze. "Stay the night with me."

"I can't stay." She huffed, sounding appalled. "That goes against all the FWB rules. Friends With Benefits," she clarified, talking to him like he was dense, and maybe he was because the more she talked, the less he followed.

"There are rules?"

"Of course there are rules!" She ticked them off on her fingers. "No sleep overs. No dates. No gifts. No holidays like Valentine's Day. You know, that kind of thing."

He didn't know. He was lost. He put his hands on her shoulders and leveled her with a stare. "But we slept together last time."

Her chin dropped as she averted her gaze. "That was a slip. And it was before we set the rules. It shouldn't happen again."

"But what if I want to ask you on a date?" His palm

found the curve of her cheek, tilting her face up to his. "Like I was about to before you started throwing down rules like Cena throws down opponents."

She swallowed, and he grinned, satisfied that he caught her off guard for once. "You were about to ask me on a date?"

"Yeah." He kissed her lips because her nibbling on them was driving him crazy. "To the Fight for the Cure gala. I have to be in the corner with the guys when they fight, and I want a date so—" He backed her up until her legs touched the side of his bed and she sat down. Then he sank to one knee and her surprised gasp speared his heart. "Ivy Harrington, will you do me the great honor of going to the gala with me?"

He took a moment to fully enjoy the surprised look on her face. He had no idea why it was so shocking that he'd ask her to go with him. They normally would have gone together, and had gone to work related events together before. Then again, it had been weeks since things between them could be classified as normal. Normal had been tossed out the window when she'd cornered him in the hall and asked him to be her fuck buddy.

Well, he was happy to fuck, but he wasn't looking for a buddy. "Ivy?" he asked when she continued to stare at him like he'd spontaneously popped a second head.

"I have nothing to wear," she told him.

"Isn't that Hope's wheelhouse? Besides, you could wear jeans and a t-shirt for all I care. You look like a million bucks in everything."

When she blushed at his compliment, he got up and eased her up the mattress. Careful not to crowd her, or get on top of her, he lay beside her, and gently tugged her pants down her legs, bending to kiss her navel, which he had learned earlier she really loved.

Nibbling along her ribs, he murmured against her skin. "Mostly, I really want you there, in *my* corner." He kissed his way to her stomach. "Will you come?"

She sighed and arched against his lips as he trailed his way down her body.

"Is that a yes?"

"I guess there's always an exception to the rules," she said, her words catching as he continued southward.

"Is *that* a yes?" he asked again, before dipping his tongue into the soft flesh between her legs, smiling against her hot skin when she moaned.

"*Yes.*"

~

*I*vy *jerked against the bed, but she couldn't move. She was pinned, held down by a horrible weight. No matter how hard she struggled, she couldn't push it off.*

He was stronger. So much stronger. Between him and the mattress, she was trapped. Not only trapped, but completely, terrifyingly aware of what was about to happen. Tears streaked down her face as he told her what he planned to do, how he had friends waiting to take their turn. She choked on the saliva and mucus backing up in her throat. She had tried screaming, but he'd clamped his hand over her mouth, and it shifted when she did, covering her nose so she couldn't breathe. Her vision blurred, and she hoped, prayed that she'd pass out—or die.

Darkness crowded her, and for a split second she thought her prayers were answered. Then he was there again, heavy on top of her, breathing his hot, disgusting alcohol stench all over her.

His hand covering her mouth lifted as he reached down to

unzip his pants, and Ivy did the only thing she could. She sucked in a big breath and screamed.

"Ivy," a voice in the darkness murmured, low but so commanding she had no choice but to hear it, listen to it, and follow it out of the black. "You're with me, Sean. We're in my bed, in my apartment. It's just us. I've got you."

Following the sound of his voice out of her nightmare, she came fully awake. She was naked, but the sheets around her were soaked in sweat. Blinking furiously, she gulped huge breaths of air and crawled backward, pressing her back to the headboard, pulling her knees to her chest.

Sean sat beside her, his face a mask of concern, and the familiar shame crept over her.

"See why sleepovers are a bad idea?" she muttered, her heartbeat thundering in her chest, echoing through her voice, making it sound shaky.

Sean said nothing as he moved closer, the sheets pooled around his waist, exposing his phenomenal torso. If she weren't shaking so badly, she'd pause to appreciate every muscle, but going on past experience, recovering from a nightmare's adrenaline spike took time.

"How often do you have nightmares like this?" he asked, his voice gentle and warm.

The emotions roaring through her responded to it, settling slightly, as if his calm steadiness gave them the traction to slow down. She shrugged. "Not as often anymore. Maybe three or four times a week."

He frowned like that was a lot. He didn't know there'd been a time when she refused to sleep simply to avoid the nightmares that plagued her nightly—or even multiple times in one night.

"What do you do after you have them?"

He hadn't asked what she dreamed about, and she was

grateful for that. And because he wasn't pushing her, she gave him the truth. "I usually go for a run. I can never fall asleep afterward."

Sean quickly checked the phone on his night table. "Four in the morning," he murmured. "It's pretty early for a run. How about we go in a couple of hours?" His gaze swept over her, assessing, searching. "Is it okay if I touch you right now?" he asked carefully.

She almost cringed in embarrassment and frustration with herself. It had been years. How long did a person go before they didn't need to be asked if they could be touched after a nightmare? But Sean was looking at her like he didn't care. Like he'd ask forever, if that's what she needed. Normally after a nightmare she never wanted to be touched. She wanted to run until her lungs burned, and then have the hottest shower she could stand until every memory her nightmares triggered was cleaned off her body. But tonight, the need to punish her body wasn't screaming as loudly as normal. Tonight, being touched didn't feel as revolting as it had before. Tonight wasn't normal. And she wanted to lean into it.

So she nodded and said, "Yes, it's okay."

Gently, he drew her down to him, brushing her hair out of the way so her cheek lay flat against his chest. They lay there in the quiet, his fingers tracing a line up and down her arm.

"I can hear your heartbeat," Ivy whispered into the stillness.

His responding rumble vibrated against her cheek. "Count them."

The rhythmic thumping against her ear was hypnotic, and her own heart scrambled to match it. On an inhale, she closed her eyes—and counted while he steadily stroked her arm.

One...two...three...

Her head rose and fell with his breath.

Four...five...

The beats passed, until her hand and his heart were one unit, moving together in a continuous rhythm. As she focused, the rest of her tension deflated, and miraculously her breathing deepened as her body grew heavy.

As if he could tell, he said, "It's okay, Ivy. No more nightmares tonight. You can sleep, I've got you."

And with the pulse of his heart strumming its lullaby under her hand, she slept.

CHAPTER TWENTY

"Long dresses make me look even shorter than I am," Ivy protested. She and Hope were in a small boutique on NW 23rd Ave. It had been a week since Sean asked her to the gala, and she'd put off shopping as long as she could.

Hope loomed in front of her, with a long black mermaid-style dress dangling from her fingertips, and sighed in frustration. Not her first that day.

"You've already refused to try on the lace cocktail dress I suggested." Hope complained.

"Because I hate lace."

"Regardless, when are you going to trust that I know what I am doing? I've been to dozens of galas. Hundreds! I know what will work and what won't."

"Yes," Ivy agreed. "And you know what will work on your long, willowy, perfect body. Which is everything. But I'm five-foot-three and flat as a washboard with no bum to speak of and bulky arms. A long dress will drown any assets I do have, and by assets, I mean my calves. I have nice calves."

Hope rolled her eyes and shoved Ivy into the change-room with the dress. "You're average height according to the North American standard, and you have small but perky breasts, your arms are toned not bulky, and the only washboard on you are your abdominals. Ivy, really, you should hear yourself. You've earned the body you're in. Now try on this dress. Trust me, with gowns and height—or lack thereof —it's all about the silhouette."

True, she shouldn't be so self-critical. Enough people had come through the gym thinking it was a one-way street to self-love to last Ivy a lifetime. She'd worked years to hone a strong, lean body with fight skills to match, and it still hadn't healed what was wrong on her inside. So she was tired of everyone, especially the media, trying to sell people this idea that they'd find self-respect in the gym. *Love yourself, as you are, which is fabulous. Own it.* That was her message to everyone.

Except it was very different touting someone else's body positivity. It was a lot easier to be self-critical than admit that, yeah, she did have a pretty smoking bod, albeit a shortish one, and she'd worked damned hard to get it that way too.

Nevertheless, as she stared down the gown she'd hung on the hook, the shame and self-loathing she'd carried like an Albatross for three years reared its ugly head. Who was she kidding? Sean Thompson was going to be a big name the night of the gala. He had five fighters entered in the competition. It was his chance to promote his gym, his brand, and his skills as a trainer. He'd be doing as much schmoozing as supporting his fighters. This was a huge night for him and his business, and he needed someone strong, capable, and supportive by his side.

Not a broken, used, shadow of a girl who was playing desperately at being normal. But as Ivy reached for the adjectives that defined her for so long, she found they didn't fit as well as they used to. Since she and Sean had started their—whatever it was they were doing—her self-hatred had morphed into something different. Something worthwhile.

The transformation had been slow and painful, but it was there.

And to honor the metamorphosis inside her, she put the dress on and turned into someone she barely recognized. The silhouette hugged her hips and seemed to lengthen her legs before flaring at the bottom. The snug, low cut top made her breasts look a few sizes bigger than they were.

Staring in the mirror, she took her own breath away.

A loud bang on the door interrupted her self-admiration.

"Let me see it," Hope demanded.

When Ivy unlocked the door, Hope yanked it open and a proud grin broke across her face. "I won't even say I told you so. You look stunning. We'll pin your hair up to show off your neck and get you shoes that have a low vamp, so we can give your legs extra length. We'll throw in my Prada clutch and favorite Cartier necklace as a finishing touch, and Sean won't even know what hit him."

Ivy blinked. "I don't even know what a vamp is, but I think you've proved your point. You know what you're doing."

"Darn right I do." Hope smiled smugly before saying to the store clerk who was now hovering behind her. "We'll take it."

~

Ivy and Hope celebrated their shopping victory by stopping at a restaurant close to the boutique for dinner. Ivy ordered a glass of wine, because she'd earned it after what Hope put her through. When Hope ordered sparkling water, Ivy raised her eyebrows hopefully. "Anything I need to know?"

Hope smiled shyly. "No." She looked down at her hands that were folding and refolding the cloth napkin. "Well, maybe. It's too soon to tell, but..."

"But...?"

"Something feels different this time. My boobs are sore." She cupped said boobs in her hands and gave them a little squeeze. "Like tingly sore. I googled it, and apparently that's one of the early signs. But I have another few days yet before it's worth peeing on the stick to confirm."

Ivy watched her friend struggle to hide her smile, so she gave free rein to her own, hoping it would catch. "Hope, this is exciting news! So let's be excited!"

"I know, but..." Hope's smile wavered. "The disappointment of being wrong has been so hard. I hate going through it each month."

Empathy swamped Ivy's heart, and she reached across the table for her friend's hand. "All the more reason to channel your namesake and have a little hope." She squeezed Hope's hand. "If you're wrong, then we'll deal with that, together. But in the meantime, give yourself permission to be excited and hopeful."

Hope wiped away a tear that had escaped her lovely brown eyes. "You've changed," she said, her eyes glittering. "It's a good thing."

Ivy shook her head, releasing Hope's hand and settling back against her seat as their server arrived with their meals. A veggie burger and fries for Ivy, a chicken salad for Hope.

After the server left, Hope said, "I mean it, Ivy. You seem...lighter."

Ivy shrugged, even though she'd been thinking about similar things lately. In the last few weeks, she'd learned so much about herself. Things she didn't realize she'd needed to learn. Like even though she was terrified to let anyone in, she wanted to. And she was starting to feel safer with herself, more accepting of the feelings and emotions that she'd spent years, even before the attack, trying to tamp down. The inadequacy and loneliness, the hurt and betrayal. She'd discovered that the more she allowed herself to understand the things that burned her heart and mind, the more she could release them.

In doing so, she felt like a weight had been taken off of her shoulders. She knew who she had to thank for it, too. A tall, dark, muscular, big-hearted man who had the patience of a saint and the fingers of a god. Well, fingers and...

"I do feel more relaxed these days," she conceded, picking up her burger.

"The sexual glow looks good on you," Hope stated, then took a bite of her salad.

Ivy almost choked on her food.

"I guess," Hope said, as she munched on her salad, "the whole friends-with-benefits thing is doing what you wanted it to do."

"And then some." She cleared her throat. "Letting go with Sean these last few weeks has been like a...rebirth. I never knew sex could feel like that."

"Like a full body experience?" Hope asked.

Ivy nodded, because that was exactly what it was like.

When Sean was touching her, kissing her, filling her, she noticed it everywhere.

He'd helped her rediscover so much of herself. Her life, sanity, soul. And she didn't know how she'd ever repay him, but she knew she wanted to, so badly. She wanted to give him the second chance he'd given her.

Which is why she'd done something a couple of days ago that she hoped would show Sean how much she cared about him, while also giving him a chance to heal a part of himself. She might have overstepped a wee bit, but when the opportunity had presented itself she had taken it and now, for better or worse, the deed was done.

She shoved her fries around on her plate before taking a sip of her wine. Hope might be able to advise her wisely.

"So, I did something with the very best intentions, but I might have meddled the teensiest little bit."

"Oh no." Hope set her fork and folded her hands in front of her. "What did you do? Please tell me you didn't sign me up for the high-intensity cardio class I mentioned a while back, because it was merely a passing thought. I wasn't actually serious."

"No, nothing to do with you. It's about Sean. He's done a lot for me in the last few weeks, actually more like the last few years. He's trained me, built me up, supported me. He's been like my best friend."

"Hey!"

"You know what I mean." Ivy rolled her eyes. "You're more like a sister. Sean's been—" *Everything.* The word hovered on the tip of her tongue, shocking her how easily she'd been prepared to use it to describe what he now meant to her. Not exactly friends-with-benefits territory.

But that was a thought for another day. A totally separate problem from the one she'd created a few days ago.

"Sean's helped me to start healing, in so many ways. And I wanted to do something to help him too. And well, I know things have been strained with his brother, and I was in Sean's office when he wasn't there, and his phone rang, and I really didn't mean to answer it, but when I saw who it was, I did and—"

Something over Hope's shoulder caught Ivy's eye, halting her next words. Actually, not something, but someone. Someone who made her break out in a cold sweat.

It was only his profile, but she could swear it was him. He was sitting, leaning forward over a table, talking to a woman in harsh tones. The woman was cowering away from him, but he had a grip on her arm that Ivy knew would be bruising. His expression was fierce. Angry. So familiar.

"What is it?" Hope looked over her shoulder, following Ivy's gaze. "Oh my God," she whispered hoarsely. "That can't be him."

Ivy was only going by his profile and his actions and the thundering beat of her heart, but she was pretty sure it was him. *Ethan.* The man of her nightmares, asleep and awake.

She watched, part of her fixated on the present scene, part of her back in that dark frat room years ago. In the present, he lifted a hand as if to strike, and Ivy flinched as if she were the woman, and not several tables away. But he must have come to his senses and realized he was in a public place because he dropped his hand, fist clenched tight, before abruptly shoving back his chair and standing. He pulled the young woman up with him.

He threw money on the table, then dragged her toward the front door. The woman trailing behind on wobbly legs, glancing around frantically, fear in her eyes—fear Ivy recognized.

"I don't think it was him," Hope whispered. "I saw his face when he got up. I am pretty sure it wasn't him."

But Ivy was beyond listening. All she cared about was the look she saw in the woman's eyes. It was the terror of knowing that she was about to be hurt and humiliated by someone much stronger than her, and she wasn't strong enough to defend herself.

Ivy also hadn't been strong enough once. But she was strong enough now, and this time, she wouldn't cower and freeze. This time, she would have her vengeance.

CHAPTER TWENTY-ONE

Sean's phone rang as he sat in his office in the gym afterhours, going over last-minute prep work for his trainees. He almost didn't answer. He was one week out from fight night, and he was as nervous as his fighters. He wanted to make sure everything was in place, that they were all ready for the big event. But when he saw Hope's name flash on his screen, he swiped. She rarely called him, and the fact that she was calling and not texting set off his inner alarm bell.

"Hope, what's up?" he asked into the phone.

"Sean?" Her voice was high-pitched and breathy, like she was running.

"Hope? Are you okay? Where are you? What's wrong?"

"It's Ivy."

Sean jumped out of his seat so fast his chair squeaked in protest as it spun behind him. He grabbed his keys and sprinted for the door.

"What about Ivy? Hope, where are you?"

"Oh God, she's actually going after him. *Jesus*. I should've pounced on her."

"Hope!" Sean barked into the phone, dread now pooling in his gut. "Gone after who? Where *are* you?"

"We were at a restaurant." More huffing, and the sound of high heels clacking on cement.

He was halfway through his empty gym, but his legs might as well have been lead. They weren't moving him fast enough. Not nearly fast enough.

Hope kept talking in his ear. "Oh God, I don't see them. Where did they go? You have to come. I have no idea what she means to do. This guy doesn't even know her, but she thinks he's—She thinks—But he's not, Sean. At least I don't think so."

"Hope, you aren't making any sense. Slow down and tell me *exactly* where you are." He'd made it through the front door, barely remembering to lock and alarm it behind him. He raced to his army green Toyota Tacoma, his heart thundering in his ears as Hope finally gave him her exact location.

"Okay. I'm ten minutes away. I'm going to hang up so you can call Gabe. And the police. Call the police."

~

Seven minutes later, Sean screeched to a halt in front of the restaurant Hope had indicated. The sound of police sirens at his heels filled him with a sickening sense of déjà vu.

Get out of the car. Now. His brother's voice shouted in his head. A voice from another night. Another time.

He shoved it aside as he jumped out of his truck. Ivy needed him. He had to stay focused on that. He rushed to Hope, who was running to meet him.

"In the alley!" she cried breathlessly, terror lacing in her voice and face as she pointed down the street at an alley.

Sean darted past her, a fist gripping his gut. He turned the corner into the dark alley and saw a man twice Ivy's size gripping her by the neck, pushing her backward against the building as she struggled. He held her with enough force that she almost came up off her feet.

His heart leaped into his throat.

"You fucking bitch! Who do you think you are? This is none of your goddamn business." A woman came up beside him.

"Bradley, stop. Don't hurt her. Let's just go," she pleaded, her voice shaking, tears streaking down her cheeks.

With his free hand, Bradley gave the woman a rough shove.

Sean saw Ivy struggling to defend herself, but she couldn't get her breath, and it was slowing her reaction.

"Ivy!" he barked, schooling his voice to sound menacing —and not laced with the fear that was shooting through every vein in his body.

His shout drew the man's attention, as he'd hoped it would, giving Ivy the opportunity to get her feet under her. In one swift, clean motion, she kneed her attacker hard in the groin, and pride shot through Sean as he ran toward her. Bradley dropped his hands from her throat to cup his family jewels, a string of profanities bursting from his mouth. Ivy didn't relent, she reacted as Sean had trained her to react. Lifting a leg, she push kicked him right in the chest, making him stagger backward, giving her enough room to execute a perfect roundhouse kick that crumpled the bastard on the concrete just as Sean got to them.

He didn't hesitate, didn't waste a single second as he

gathered her into his arms and pulled her tightly to his body, breathing her in. The scent of honey and roses an instant comfort.

"You gave me a fucking heart attack. What were you thinking?" He muffled into her hair.

But there was no time to answer, because they were immediately swarmed by several police officers. The commotion and chaos of the next few seconds pulling them apart.

After Sean released her, Ivy made her way over to the woman hunched against the brick wall, and spoke to her in a low, firm voice. The woman nodded, then laid her head on Ivy's shoulder. Looking a little stunned at the reaction, Ivy gently wrapped her arms around the woman's shaking frame and hugged her.

It was then, as she held the sobbing woman in her arms, that Ivy lifted her gaze and locked eyes with him.

~

For a half an hour Ivy answered police questions, then sat beside the woman named Ali, at her request, as she made her statement. Sean hovered close by the whole time, like a bodyguard, watchful but stoic.

When she'd ascertained that Ali had a safe place to stay for the night and had given the officers all the information she could, she hugged Hope long and hard before reassuringly shoving her into Gabe's car and waving them off. Then, and only then, did she do what she had been dreading since she'd seen his silhouette in the mouth of the alley—she walked toward Sean where he'd been waiting by his car. Time to face the real music.

He maintained his deceptively calm facade, arms folded across his chest as he leaned a hip against the hood, but Ivy knew better. His eyes were lit with a swirl of emotions that ranged from anger to fear to relief. It was that last one she clung to as she approached him.

Her body was still shaking with residual emotion and adrenaline. All she wanted was ten minutes with a punching bag. Anything to relieve the remaining tension in her body before she had to calmly confront Sean. Obviously, he'd disapprove of her going after Bradley, and she could admit, in hindsight, following an angry, violent male into a dark backstreet wasn't the smartest thing she'd done recently. But she'd saved Ali from another assault, and she couldn't bring herself to regret it.

"Hey," she greeted, aiming for a casual voice that matched his stance.

His eyes glittered ominously in response. He pushed off the hood and opened the passenger side door. "Get in."

She briefly considered commenting on his tone, but if roles had been reversed, she'd have been mad too. And if she didn't say anything, she might get a silent ride home, with time to gather herself before she had to go a round with him. Enough time to stop her trembling.

He slammed the door the second she was seated and rounded the hood to his own side. The car ride was silent, but home wasn't their direction. A few minutes later he pulled up in front of Thompson Kickboxing. It was dark, the gym long closed, and only the outside lights illuminated the pathway in front of the building. The darkened windows loomed like glass giants in front of her.

"What are we doing here?" she asked quietly.

Sean looked at her a beat, gaze traveling over her body

in his *checking for injuries* way, then got out of the truck and walked to her side. He opened her door, held out his hand, which she accepted, and tugged her out of her seat.

No words were spoken as he linked their fingers and led her to the gym's entrance. His manner was easy as he turned the key in the lock, reset the alarm panel, and flipped on the lights, but tension radiated from him. Jaw set tight, he walked with her through the gym to the back, where the ring stood in the center. The overhead light shone down on it, making it look big and daunting.

He couldn't possibly mean—

He picked up a set of boxing gloves and tossed them at her. Oh God, he did mean. He wanted to get in the ring with her.

"Put them on."

Ivy stood mute, clutching the gloves to her chest. Earlier she'd thought she could use a good physical fight to release the tension built during her confrontation in the alley, but now, face to face with Sean, she was second-guessing herself.

Under the spotlight, a thin sheen of sweat made his darker skin glisten while his nostrils flared as he inhaled and exhaled. And suddenly she saw it, the livid anger burning in him.

Seeing his anger, immediately triggered her own, and like a dam breaking it flooded her. Not only anger over what happened at the restaurant and in the alley, but anger that was years old. In a tsunami of emotion, all of the rage, pain, and hate she'd been carrying crashed over her, and her knees nearly buckled under the weight.

For years she'd crammed it away. Set it apart from everything else in her life, but in that moment, standing in the ring, hugging boxing gloves to her chest, she was forced to confront all of it. And it stole her breath.

"I can't," she choked out, her throat tightening painfully, trapping her breath inside her.

Sean stepped closer, his face growing harder and more serious the nearer he drew. "Put. Them. On." He enunciated each word, biting them out through gritted teeth.

"You're angry," she whispered, unsure if his anger was a response to hers or the other way around.

She thought she might have seen a familiar softness flickered in his eyes, but it was gone in an instant. He pulled the gloves out of her hands, dark eyes never leaving hers, and though they were covered in a shroud of anger—his, hers—the eye contact was comforting. Centering.

In that strong, steady gaze, realization dawned. An understanding that this was the moment she'd been running from for the last three years. Her past had caught up with her. The monster was in that ring, and Sean was going to help her fight it.

"You're right, Ivy. I am angry," he said, tightening the first glove around her wrist. "I'm so fucking angry, you have no idea." He reached for her other hand and shoved the other glove into place. "But not as angry as you are. You've been angry since you arrived in Portland. It's been bubbling under the surface, just waiting for an opportunity to rage. Tonight, you wanted to lash out. You wanted to fight. You looked for it. Chased it." The words spit out of him as he lifted her through the ropes and into the ring. "And I'm here to tell you that if it's a fight you want, you do it in this ring, with me, and not with some crazy motherfucker who needs a shitload of anger management and could have killed you without a second thought."

Sean lithely hopped up into the ring and strapped on

training pads. Then he circled her, his long legs eating up the distance around the ring once. Twice.

"You do not put yourself in danger like that. Do you understand me? You want to fight someone, you want to hit something, you want to let it all out? You do it in here. With me. The end."

His gaze was watchful, his body moving constantly, muscles rippling with practiced control, but his eyes never left hers. "Come at me, sweetheart. I know you want to."

She shook her head, and tears prick the back of her eyes, the emotion from the night boiling up from her toes and surging through her body. He was right. She's full of anger. She's lived with it so long it felt like a body part. Always there, right under the surface, choking her.

So. Much. Fucking. Anger.

"I see it, Ivy. The rage. I've always seen it. It's time to let it out." He came within striking distance. "Here. Now. This is a safe place to let it out."

"I can't," she croaked. Oh God, what would it look like if she did what he asked? If she did what she really wanted to do? If she opened the tap on her anger and let it pour all over Sean, her safe space.

"You want to fight? Then you fight here. You want to get angry? You get angry here. Leave everything on this mat." Sean's voice was rising to a yell as he goaded her. The tendons in his neck straining with the force.

"I know what you're doing," she managed to get out through the lump in her throat.

"Do you want me to stop?" he growled, leveling her with a gaze that was dead serious.

He would. She knew he would stop with one word from her. But the edges of her anger were already lifting, peeling back like an old Band-Aid. And part of her wanted that bandage to come off, to reveal the wound beneath, expose it to the air.

Blinking back tears, she imagined what life would be like if she could do what he was asking. If she let go and purged all of her anger, how would she feel? What would be left if she released all the hurt, fury, and shame? Her anger had been her purpose for so long. It drove her to be stronger, to work harder, to get out of bed every morning. What would she be without it?

Could she let it go? Here, with him? In this space they'd created together, where he'd never let her fall?

"Ivy, do you want me to stop?" His voice was clear, deliberate, punctuating each syllable in his question.

Trust fall. It had never been about sex. Or intimacy. Or relationship. The thing she feared was the truth. The truth of what happened that night. How it made her feel like she was worthless, deserving of nothing. No joy, no passion, no happy ending. Like it had set her fate to one channel, where she was doomed to live half a life because everything she might have had for her future had been stripped of her in one fucking horrible hour.

But that wasn't the truth anymore. Maybe it never had been. It was time to confront the monster of her past.

Through blurry eyes, she shook her head. *No, don't stop. I want to fall into you.*

With a rough nod, Sean paced around her, eyes never leaving hers.

"You said someone hurt you," he gritted out. "Is that why you always have this anger inside you?" His words set off a fire in her belly, like acid burning.

Nausea churned as painful memories hovered at the edges of her brain.

"Did someone touch you when you didn't want them

to?" He barely got the words through his clenched teeth, but when they were spoken, they fired across the ring at her like daggers. "Did you think it was him tonight? Were you out to finally get your revenge?"

"I—" Staggering, she took a few steps back. Words choking her. Tears now so thick she could hardly see him.

But he didn't stop. He advanced, his blurry figure coming closer, moving in on her. She raised her fists in a defensive-ready position.

"You couldn't fight back, could you?" He kept advancing. "And you've spent every day since hating yourself for it. Haven't you?"

The bandage pulled, tore.

"*Haven't you!*" Sean yelled.

"*Yes!*" she screamed back as she threw a right jab. Her fist hit his training pad with a loud *thwack*.

"*Again!*" he shouted so loudly it vibrated through her, and his harsh, enraged voice unleashed something inside her.

She struck out again. Then again. Over and over, harder and harder. Sean held steady, absorbing her blows easily. She was so weak against him. Why was she still so weak? Her muscles strained with exertion. Her breath came in loud, harsh grunts, but she didn't stop. All the memories, all the fear, all the anger poured out of her through her fists.

Memories assaulted her. Bruising hands hurting her body. Horrible words lashing her ears. Pain burning her sensitive flesh.

This time, she didn't shove the memories to the back of her mind. This time, she let them come at her full force. The anger surging through her fueling her with a strength that finally gave her the ability to fight back with everything she had. Her fists pounded, her legs kicked, and all her movements merged in one fluid, ferocious attack.

Reality and memory became one.

"*Get off me!*" she screamed at Ethan's body looming over her. "I *hate* you." A guttural noise tore from her throat, like a foreign beast had inhabited her body all this time and had finally been set free.

She shoved against the man in front of her and did what she'd wished she'd done that dark night. She fought with all her strength. A scream of agony rose from the very depth of her soul and morphed into a primal roar.

Time suspended, and with her anger as her only compass, she wasn't sure where she was. Until her voice choked on a painfully hoarse sob, and her knees gave out. But she wasn't falling. She was finally being caught after years of endless, aimless free-falling. Familiar arms cradled her against the warm, solid strength she now associated with comfort and safety.

"I've got you, Ivy. I've got you, sweetheart." Sean's husky voice broke through the haze of memories.

The monsters fled, battered and bruised, as she slowly came back to awareness.

"It's okay. You're okay." Sean's hands soothingly stroked her hair.

She realized that her face was pressed against his tear-drenched shirt, and not caring one iota, she stayed that way, focusing all her energy on his heartbeat. She counted the beats like he'd taught her to do. She wasn't in that frat room anymore. She was with Sean.

More heartbeats.

More time passed.

More slow, even strokes up and down her back.

When she was ready, she leaned back so she could look

up into his dark eyes, and in them she saw a deep, penetrating emotion. She realized it hadn't been anger she'd seen in them before. It had been fear. She'd scared him when she went into that alley tonight.

"You back?" he asked, voice thick and rough.

Ivy nodded. She was back. And never wanted to be anywhere but surrounded by his warm embrace.

CHAPTER TWENTY-TWO

"I thought it was him." Ivy's voice sounded muffled against Sean's shirt, but he didn't ask her to repeat herself, and she was grateful for that.

Sitting on the floor of the ring, he held her on his lap, cocooned in his warmth.

"In the restaurant with Hope, I thought I saw Ethan." Her brain hurt. She hadn't cried that hard in years. "Sometimes I think I see him everywhere. On the street. At work. In stores. Since I saw Adam at Bowie's, it's been worse. It's like...I'm looking for them." She swallowed painfully, her throat parched and raw.

She was desperate for a drink of water, but she had to get the story out first. The urge to do so was stronger than her thirst. It was time for Sean to know.

"Ethan—He, he was the one who—three years ago, he —" God, why was it so hard to say? "He raped me."

"He raped you," Sean repeated, his voice tight. Hard.

When Ivy nodded against his shirt, his growl reverberated in his chest and against her ear. As always, the sound comforted her, and she went on.

"It was my last year of college. Hope and I were room-mates since the beginning, and even though we were polar opposites, we bonded over our mutual desire to excel at school. We spent our time in class, studying, or working part-time jobs to pay for everything our scholarships didn't cover. There wasn't time for partying. No living the college experience of most of our peers." Ivy inhaled deeply, taking in her surroundings. The scent of Sean's skin, warm, musky, and familiar. The sound of the gym fans buzzing overhead. The feel of Sean's body heat enveloping her.

"One night, after midterms in the final semester, Hope was convinced we needed a typical college experience before we graduated, so she convinced me to go to a party that her business school friends were throwing at their frat house. I figured why not, so we got dressed up, which was huge for me because back then I lived in leggings." She swallowed hard, remembering the feel of the silky skirt she'd chosen that night. The lace underwear she'd put on thinking ahead, in case she got lucky, she didn't want to be caught in laundry-day undies.

"At the party, I met one of Hope's business class peers, Ethan. He seemed nice and was interested in me. We danced and talked and had a couple of drinks." They had sat on the couch for a long time talking. He'd asked so many questions about her interest in physical therapy, praised her on the scholarship she'd won to get into. He told her about himself, his family, his brothers. He'd seemed so—normal. So kind. "When he asked if I wanted to go somewhere less noisy to talk, I didn't think much of it. I—"

And here came the shame. After time in therapy, she knew she had no reason to feel like she had done anything wrong or stupid, but still it crept through her as she admitted, "I wanted to go. I was attracted to him, and I wanted to go with him. So I went." Willingly, she'd followed him to her doom. "I wanted to find Hope first, to let her know not to wait for me, but Ethan said she was having fun and not to bother her. I should have looked for her."

"Not your fault," Sean murmured and drew her in closer.

When she'd tried to talk about this in therapy sessions, she'd required lots of personal space. But here, in the middle of a fighting ring, with him, she only wanted to lean in.

"Ethan brought me into a bedroom on the second floor, and inside I saw another person, Adam, the guy who showed up in Bowie's a few months ago. That's—That's when I knew."

"*Fuck.* Ivy." Sean leaned back the smallest bit and looked down at her, his brows furrowed in disbelief and anger.

Ivy nodded. "I tried to get away, but Ethan held me back. He sent Adam into the hallway to keep watch. Then he pinned me down on the bed while he—"

Years had passed, yet it still seemed so fresh. Like she'd been running a marathon, but never gaining on the finish line. Until now. Until Sean gave her a safe space and helped her to confront the thing that had held her back for far too long.

Everything about this was so different from any time she'd had to talk or think about it before, and she knew what that difference was.

With Sean, her trust fall partner, she was truly safe. She recognized now that it was a security he had cultivated slowly over time, and that the foundation he laid had been trust. And that had armed her with a strength she could have never built up in any gym.

"Hope found me before it could get any worse."

"How much fucking worse could it get, Ivy?" Sean's words pinched out between his clenched teeth.

"Well, Adam... He was outside. Waiting. For his turn." This time, when she swallowed, the lump in her throat throbbed painfully. She wouldn't have survived if Hope hadn't arrived when she did. She was sure of it.

"I should've killed that motherfucker when I had the chance."

"No. That's not who you are." She squeezed his hand, remembering his bloody knuckles the day after Adam had confronted her and Hope in Bowie's.

That day she'd wanted to offer some kind of explanation for what had happened. Then she'd seen his fists, raw and swollen. And she'd known she'd never have to explain anything to Sean. He always had her back, would always take care of her. Overcome with gratitude, she couldn't speak, so she'd lifted those bruised knuckles to her lips and kissed each one, hoping it was enough to convey her feelings.

"Anyway, Hope came in screeching and swearing and throwing anything she could get her hands on. She grabbed me and dragged me out of there, and that was it."

Sean turned her in his arms and held her with his gaze. "But that wasn't it, Ivy. That was only the beginning." He smoothed her sweaty bangs away from her face before asking softly, "Did you call the police? Press charges?"

And there it was. The million-dollar question everyone asked people like her.

"No." She tensed, preparing herself for a lecture, like the one she'd received from both Hope and Joel.

At the time, it felt like no one on the outside would understand her reasons for not telling the police or anyone who didn't absolutely have to know. And there were only a handful of people who did know.

In recent years, media coverage about the prevalence of sexual assault had increased. And many women, from the famous to the everyday, had taken to social media to share their experiences and to show how far their voices reached. Their courage was contagious, because when one stood up, others followed, until there was a fresh wave of determined voices telling the world they weren't going to take it anymore.

But behind those voices was the silent majority. And that was where Ivy remained firmly rooted. She'd wouldn't press charges or call out names on social media or anywhere else. And as hard as she tried never to think about it, she did often think about the other women who might have fallen victim to Ethan or Adam because she hadn't the guts to speak up. It sickened her, to think that her decision could have contributed to another woman's abuse.

That weight on her soul was horrible.

Yet the alternative—the rehashing, the victim blaming, the guilt, the shame, the humiliation of being accused of lying about something so horrific—she couldn't face it. So she'd run as far as she could from that night. But it had only chased her.

Lost in her litany of defensive thoughts, she was slow to realize that Sean hadn't reprimanded or questioned her decision or asked for details or explanations. He simply held her, and eventually she relaxed into his embrace.

"You're the strongest person I know," he murmured into her hair.

She cringed at that sentiment. It seemed misplaced, for all the reasons she'd listed in her head and more. She had to tell him.

"I came to Portland to run away." She'd opted to go with the abbreviated version.

"You came here to rebuild. Someone tried to break you and you picked up what you had left, came here and built yourself back up. Do you know how brave that is?" He caressed her face, skimming her jaw, his hand settling around the back of her neck. "You always impressed me with your endurance and determination. I knew something had happened, but—Ivy, you're an overcomer."

That undid her. She never thought of herself that way. She believed she was a coward for not pressing charges. Weak for not being able to fight her attackers off herself. She'd never seen herself as strong in this situation. But Sean made her want to believe it. Made her think that she could believe in herself.

"I want to go home," she told him.

And he nodded, carefully unfolding them from where they'd sat pretzeled together in the center of the ring. He lifted her, cradling her in his arms with great reverence, like she was precious.

He held her hand the whole drive home. After everything she'd told him, a burning need to never let her go again consumed him. Christ, who was he kidding? He'd had this burning need for months, maybe even years, but now, knowing the truth, the details of what had happened, knowing something he could never un-know, it compelled him more than ever to never let her out of his sight. His protective instincts were raging, and mixed up in it was a deep regret he hadn't been there when she'd needed him most.

Which was illogical, since they hadn't known each other back then. But the guilt remained. He couldn't take away her past, but he could make damned sure no harm ever came her way again. He'd give his last breath making sure of that.

He kept his hand at the small of her back as they walked up the steps to their apartments, took her keys from her trembling hands and opened her door for her. Her body shook as if she were in shock. The events of the night had taken a serious toll.

"Bed," he told her, shutting her door behind them. "I'll stay the night." He planned to stay every night from here on in, but he wasn't telling her that now. He didn't want to overwhelm her, even if she looked relieved when he'd said he'd stay.

"I need a shower first," she told him in a small voice.

Were her teeth chattering?

Pausing on her way to the bathroom, she turned toward him without making eye contact. "Whenever I talk about it, or even think about it too much, I feel—yucky. Like little bits of what he did are stuck all over me, and I need to scrub them off." She inhaled a shuddering breath. "What he left behind, it's ugly." She hunched into herself like she was trying to make herself smaller.

Fuck. This was so fucking hard. Her suffering, the kind he couldn't put a dent in, might be the thing that finally drove him mad.

He wanted to howl and rage. He wanted to stick those pigs on a stake and roast them alive. He wanted to worship her until she saw how clean and beautiful she was inside and out. But those were his desires, not hers.

So instead, he did what he'd been doing all night. He didn't say anything.

Maybe this could be a show, instead of tell, scenario. He

went to her, took her hand, which was freezing (double fuck) and led her to the bathroom where he turned on the water in the tub. When it was hot, he helped her undress.

She didn't raise her gaze as he pulled her shirt up her torso and the arms she lifted for him. With her creamy smooth skin revealed, he glided his hands over her shoulders and down her back to unclasp her bra. He gently guided the straps down until she was naked from the waste up.

Then he turned her toward the steam-fogged mirror. "Look up, Ivy."

Her eyes drifted upward and widened as she took in the image of her blurred figure in the mirror. Sean towered behind her. They were a striking contrast. His image was tall and dark and muscular. Hers was small and light and lean. In the dimly lit bathroom, reflected in the foggy mirror, she looked exquisitely exposed and a little shell-shocked.

"Beautiful," he said in a hoarse whisper against her ear, stating the word like the fact that it was. "Understand." It wasn't a question. He brushed his lips along the side of her neck, reveling in the shiver of pleasure that ran up her body. "You are beautiful."

This was the one thing he had on the past. He made her feel good, and he'd continue to make her feel good until she could remember nothing but the pleasure they brought each other.

When she was completely naked, he helped her into the shower. She hissed when the water hit her back.

"Too hot?"

"No, it's perfect." She crossed her arms over her breasts, hugging herself. "Are you coming in?"

"Do you want me to?" He wasn't sure what she'd want from him right now. This was all new to him. All he had was his gut, and his trust that she would tell him if he was doing something wrong.

Ivy nodded and made room for him. He undressed slowly, giving her lots of time to change her mind. The water poured over her head, pulling down her hair, making it cloak her face, hiding her from him.

When he got in the shower, her gaze lowered to their feet. How could he get her to stop that habit?

"Ivy." He nudged her chin up with his finger.

A hiccup escaped her as she tried to stifle a sob. Water droplets dripped off her eyelashes as she looked up at him.

"I—I went with him," she stammered through trembling lips. "That night, I was excited. I'd had more than a bit to drink, and I was feeling good, relaxed. He was nice to me. I remember—" She made a choking sound that cracked his heart in two. "I remember being relieved that I wore nice underwear. Lace. I went up to that room with him because I wanted to." Her shoulders slumped, and she covered her face with both hands, sobbing into them.

Wrapping his arms around her, he simply, helplessly held her, everything in his body aching, as if it was a sponge to her pain. Abdominal muscles cramped, lungs constricted, breath heaved. Her body convulsed against his, and he gladly absorbed the shocks, letting them rattle him like a storm.

When her sobbing slowed, he set her back against the tiled wall and dipped low so she was focused on him and not the memories in her head.

"Ivy, I need you to hear me right now." He swiped her wet hair away from her face and waited until she looked at him fully. "For a long time, you've been carrying all this, mostly by yourself. And I can only imagine how hard that's been. But the fact that you trusted me enough to share this means a lot. It means everything," he said sincerely. "And you need to know you're not alone. I'm here now, so I want you to listen to me. Listen and believe: What happened to you was not your fault. You did nothing wrong. Nothing you wore, drank, said, or did gave him the right to hurt you, or even fucking touch you. Ivy—" He kept her chin tipped up when she once again tried to find the floor with her gaze. "Nobody asks to be hurt. Nobody invites it in. Nobody. This was not your fault."

She blinked up at him. Water and tears were one. Sean hadn't considered killing anyone in a very long time. That violent part of his life was long over. But a bloodlust flowed through him now, and he knew he could, very easily, if he'd had the chance to get his hands on the men who'd done this to her.

As it stood, there was nothing he could do now but hold and love her. *Love.* The emotion hit him like a punch to the solar plexus.

He loved her. Had loved her almost from the moment they'd met. He saw it crystal clear now. And someone had *hurt* the woman he loved.

The beast inside him raged, but the man in the shower quietly held her.

CHAPTER TWENTY-THREE

Under the spray of the shower, with Sean holding her and looking intently into her eyes, every emotion and every feeling she'd ever suppressed rushed to the surface.

And she wasn't sorry, because the frontrunner of them all was love. She recognized it only because it was identical to the first time she realized what loving someone was truly like.

On her tenth birthday, her parents had left for another trip.

Her nana had found her crying on her bed. Instead of making a fuss about it, or even trying to comfort her, she'd pulled Ivy to her feet, drove her to the mall, and bought her the prettiest lavender colored dress Ivy had ever seen. When they got home, Nana had served a traditional English high tea. Wearing her new dress while sitting with her grandmother and sipping tea from fancy cups and eating dainty cucumber sandwiches, love had filled Ivy's heart to bursting.

That exact same feeling was flowing through her right now. A full-to-the-brim kind of love. It propelled Ivy into

Sean's arms, knocking him back. He caught his balance quickly, and her with it, wrapping his arms around her, holding her tightly to his chest.

People had told her it wasn't her fault before. Hope, Joel, her counselor. She knew it was true, but the back of her mind always niggled with *what-ifs*.

What if she'd paid more attention during the self-defense classes in high school? What if she hadn't gone to the party? What if she'd worn something different? What if she hadn't started talking to Ethan?

Those what-ifs had nearly killed her. She hadn't realized how deeply she'd needed to hear all of them destroyed by Sean's affirmations. No idea how much she'd needed *him*.

She had new what-ifs now.

What if the problem was never something she'd done? What if the problem was Ethan all along? The problem was how he'd never learned to be a man like Sean or Gabe or Joel or Carter, or any of the men she knew who would never have done what Ethan did.

Lifting up to her toes, she pressed a quick kiss to his mouth. "Thank you."

She wanted to say more. Wanted to tell him about her overstuffed heart, and all her feelings. But she'd been the one who insisted this thing between them stay casual. What an idiot she'd been, determined not to put any labels or pressures on their friends-with-benefits arrangement. Now she'd put herself into a situation where she couldn't drop the L word in the shower after an emotionally charged night. No matter how much her heart was screaming with it.

It would have to wait. Wait to see if she still had the over-stuffed-heart feeling in the morning. Wait to see whether, after all was said and done, he'd still look at her the way he was looking at her now. As if he'd burn down the whole world to keep her safe. She'd wait until the exact right time and say the words out loud. Words she hadn't spoken to anyone but her nana in decades. Maybe ever. Not even to Hope.

And for the first time, she was excited about it, because suddenly love didn't seem as scary as it once had.

Instead of saying what was bursting in her heart, she gave Sean the next biggest thing she could think of. Her trust.

She pressed her mouth to his again, savoring his lips.

"I want you, Sean," she murmured against his lips.

"Ivy, it's been a long night. We don't have to do this now. *You* don't have to do this now."

She shut him up with another kiss. No way was he going to ruin this moment. It *had* been a long night, one that left her simultaneously exhausted and full of energy. It was like Sean had pulled some kind of plug, and the weight of negative energy she'd carried for years had drained out of her, and in its place was a freedom that buoyed her back into the light.

Shutting off the water, she stepped out of the shower and pulled Sean with her.

"I want this," she reinforced, reaching for a towel, she wrapped it around her body. "I want you inside me. Over me. On top of me." She wasn't sure if he realized the significance of what she was asking.

He'd never been in the dominant position for their lovemaking. However, the look that blazed to life in his eyes told her he understood.

Before tonight, she'd thought that having Sean in any kind of dominant position during sex would trigger flashbacks and then a total panic attack. She hadn't wanted to try it because things were going well, and when things were going well, she wasn't one to screw them up on purpose.

But tonight had been more than a breakthrough. Tonight had been a rebirth. She hadn't purged the events of that night in its entirety. What happened would live as a part of her forever. There was going to have to be a lot more unpacking to do, and she knew it. But tonight, she had shared the worst of her fear and self-loathing and guilt and shame and he had held her and told her what she'd needed to hear. So yeah, this was most definitely what she wanted.

Ethan didn't own her sexual agency anymore. He had no power over it, and she refused to let him have any control over her.

More than that, though, it was the idea of Sean moving over her and inside her, his chest rubbing against her breasts while he made those sexy hot sounds he made during sex. It was the idea of Sean, her friend, her lover, her safe space, being the one to share this moment with. She wanted that, and she wanted it now. The thought of it turned her *on*.

Ivy dropped her towel and grabbed for him again, not wanting to wait. Walking backward toward her bedroom while she pulled him along by the hand, she savored his eyes burning into hers. He was probably assessing how serious she was, so she reassured him.

"I feel like I have this space inside me only you can fill. I know we've done this my way every time. I've led and told you what I was ready for and what I wasn't. But tonight, I don't want to think. I want to feel. I want to feel you. And I want to go with whatever *we* feel, together." When the backs of her knees hit the edge of her bed, she fell onto it with a giggle. God, she felt good. Free. Unafraid. Unashamed. For the first time in so, so long.

She extended her arms above her head, reveling in the way Sean's pupils dilated and darkened, his eyes becoming two dark orbs of unmistakable desire as she stretched out in front of him. That was not the way a friend looked at a friend. Fuck buddy or not.

The thrill of power shot up her spine and through her body. But he didn't move to join her.

"I want that, more than anything. Please," she added, not expecting this level of resistance from him.

The *please* must have done it because he bent over her in one fluid motion, capturing her lips in a hot, greedy kiss that made her lose the very last of her brain cells. She looped her arms around his neck and hung on as he devoured her, sweeping his tongue through her mouth, leaving no portion unloved.

His hands roamed her body, along the sensitive swells of her breasts, and between them, over her belly and lower. He pulled back on a sharp intake of breath when he touched the wetness between her legs. His eyes were almost shocked at how ready he found her.

"Mmm," she purred, her eyes drifting shut as his fingers rubbed and circled.

"Do you have any idea what it does to me, feeling how wet you get when I touch you?"

His mouth descended on her jaw before it traveled up to her ear. When he licked the sensitive underside of her earlobe, she moaned.

"Eyes." His voice rumbled into her ear, and the sound, so deep and low, shot more heat toward her core. "If I'm going to do this, Ivy, I'm going to need those eyes."

She opened them slowly and found him staring at her.

A glorious smile broke across his face.

"Stunning," he said, and kissed her, slowly and thoroughly. "Keep them open. I want you looking at me. I want you knowing who you're with. I want those eyes burning into mine when you come all over me. Understood?"

She nodded at him fiercely, her desperation so palpable it was like another person in the room. But those panting sounds that were filling the room, they were definitely coming from her.

When Sean started to move off her, she nearly cried.

"Just grabbing a condom, sweetheart."

"Right," she said, but didn't let him go. She held his forearms as he hovered over her. Had she given a single thought to protection? No. She had not. Her mind had one track, and it was headed to Orgasmville, do not pass Go.

Ivy had never imagined a day she'd be able to let go so completely with a man. Then again, she'd never imagined she could feel like this. So perfectly safe that all consideration to anything beyond his next touch went out the window.

She wanted to celebrate it.

When she didn't let go of him, Sean readjusted his position over her, bracing on his elbows on either side of her head. She had prepared herself for some kind of unease having him cover her like this, but none came. There was only warmth, need, and impatient desire.

"I could never take advantage of you," he stared at her intently. "And I've never done this without a condom. Never even considered it."

"Would you consider it now?" The words were out before she even knew she was thinking them. But as soon as she said them, she knew she wanted this experience with him.

But maybe she was on that page alone, because above her, Sean just blinked.

Worrying about his silence, she reminded him hesitantly, "I'm on the pill."

Had she overstepped? Was it too soon to take such a big leap? Maybe he wasn't ready? Then a terrible thought formed. What if the condom was more to protect him than her? What if he was worried that she had something, because of what happened?

Dirty, the devil whispered. Vicious feelings of shame and self-doubt attacked, replacing the warmth she'd been feeling with the cold chill of panic.

"Never mind, you don't—"

Sean cut her off with a kiss, hungry and demanding, and immediately her panic eased.

"Ivy." He kissed her, sucking at her lower lip. "You kill me, you know that? Every time," he muttered, almost to himself, before bending his head to her breasts, drawing in a nipple, pulling and rolling it with his tongue, inviting pleasure to shoot through her. After a few moments of the blissful torture, he lifted his head again, his eyes burning with sincerity. "Your *trust* fucking kills me." He placed a gentle kiss on her forehead, her nose, then her mouth before returning his gaze to hers. He looked solemn. Devoted. "There's no one on the planet I'd consider this with but you."

Dipping his head, he began a slow worship of her body, pausing at all the places he now knew drove her wild. Everywhere he touched sent tremors of sensation shooting through her until her body was like a live wire.

When his tongue flicked over the very center of her, she cried out his name. Her hips bucked up off the bed, and he stilled them by holding them in place as he lapped and sucked on her sensitive flesh. Her hands clawed wildly at the covers of her bed, fistfuls of fabric giving her a false sense of purchase. But there was nothing to tether her, and when he added the firm strokes of his fingers inside her, she nearly came right off the mattress altogether.

The pent-up emotional energy from the past hours poured out of her, her body shuddering with the force of her release. Pleasure and relief rolled over her in waves until eventually, the tsunami subsided, leaving her limp and weightless. But despite having had the orgasm to end all orgasms, Ivy had renewed intent for one thing.

She wanted him buried inside her, while she ran her hands over the hard, sculpted muscles of his back. And she wanted it. Right. Now.

Greedily, Ivy pulled at his shoulders until he was over her. "More," she begged, wriggling into position beneath him. "Now, Sean. Let me feel you. All of you, over all of me."

There was a grunt. Then he spread her legs wider than he ever had before to make room for himself between them. His face was pulled tight, like it was taking every last ounce of his willpower to hold on to his restraint. His passion fed hers, and she reveled in the erotic scene unfolding: Sean, huge and powerful, moving between her legs, gripping his massive, straining erection in his hands as he positioned himself at her entrance, giving it one firm stroke from base to tip.

He flicked his gaze to hers. "Eyes stay on me, Ivy," he commanded, his voice rough and deep.

She nodded, though she couldn't have averted her eyes even if she'd wanted to. The pull between them was that strong, that invisible string pulled so taut it was unbreakable. And then, in one long thrust, he entered her, simultaneously falling over her, his massive chest covering hers.

Solid and heavy. Warm and responsive. Even as his body pumped rhythmically against her, the force of his thrusts pushing her up the mattress, there was no roughness. No unease, no fear. There was no room for it in her mind.

Not when every part of her was bursting with fulfillment and, oh, so much love. Love for this man who had held her tenderly. This man whose relentless patience had led her to this moment where, for the first time in years, the stirrings of true healing rippled inside her. This man who'd given her the hope that one day, with work and him at her side, enough time might pass that she could have the future she dreamed of. A future free of her haunted past.

Floating on gratitude, love, and passion, her body built to another tipping point.

Sean's grunts of pleasure fell hot and rough against her ear, and she could tell by the way all his muscles were growing tenser around her that he was as close as she was. When he lifted his head, his eyes burned into hers.

"Look at me, Ivy," he growled, hovering over her. "You're about to make me come, sweetheart, and I need you looking at me when I do."

His words, his deep voice, the pressure he was creating where their bodies were joined, set off a domino effect of release in her body. Ivy wrapped her legs tightly around his torso so that this time she'd be tethered to something. To him.

His name detonated off her lips. Desperate but ready.

He increased his tempo in response, reaching between them, spreading her more intimately, and pressing his fingers against her. It was like a trigger going off. Her hoarse cries of release filled the room. The effort of keeping her eyes open through the blinding passion caused tears to stream down her cheeks. His name fell like a litany from her mouth. Over and over.

Around the roaring in her head and the endless flames

of climax engulfing her body, Sean went still above her, a final groan escaping him, and then a rush of moisture. His. Hers. Melding together, becoming one.

Long moments they lay together, still joined. Breathless.

"Ivy." He said her voice almost like a question. Like he was as stunned as she was by what had happened.

"I know." She panted. "Do people really have sex like this?" She didn't realize she'd said her question out loud until Sean spoke into the quiet room.

"I sure as hell never have. Not like that." He was half on her, half on the mattress beside her, so his full weight wasn't crushing her. More amazingly, he was still lodged deeply inside her, and from what she could feel, still hard. "I don't know what to say."

"Say nothing," she murmured, the heaviness of exhaustion and satisfaction pulling her into another state of consciousness. "Talk later. Sleeping time now."

She let her eyes drift shut. Time passed. Could have been minutes, could have been an entire ice age. All she knew, or rather felt, some unidentifiable time later, was her body being readjusted on her bed, then the soft down of her comforter coming over her shoulders, wrapping her in warmth, and the solid wall of Sean's body wrapping up behind her, pulling her in so that she was fully cocooned.

And in that safe bubble of sexual gratification, love, and trust, she fell into a deep, blissful sleep, with the thought of her past, or what was yet to come nowhere on her radar.

～

Sean lay on Ivy's bed, one arm behind his head, the other stretched out, which Ivy had taken as an invitation to use as a pillow. He'd lost feeling in it about an hour ago, and he'd made no attempt to move it. He didn't want to do a single thing that might disrupt this moment.

It was long past midnight, and he was lying awake, processing the information he'd just learned. Stories like Ivy's were all too familiar.

He'd grown up in a family of love, and his parents did their best with what they'd had. But the neighborhood they'd lived in had normalized violence. Domestic abuse, gang wars, sexual assault, the list went on.

Desensitized was too harsh a word to describe how he'd come to cope with his surroundings, but it was safe to say there wasn't much that phased him.

Tonight had, though. Tonight had phased him right into insomnia. Ivy's words were on repeat in his head. Her voice, her story, her memories playing out like a film in his brain. Every scene unfolding in his imagination as vividly as she'd told it.

He wanted to hunt those motherfuckers down so justice could be served. And not wishy-washy police justice, where a rich offender could pay off a judge or a ferocious lawyer could discredit a survivor in court.

No. The only justice he craved was the street type from his past. Jordan. Jordan would know what to do.

Thoughts of his brother led to thoughts about the phone calls he'd been avoiding. The short, to-the-point messages saved on his voicemail. Messages about a newfound freedom and Jordan wanting to spend some of that freedom visiting Sean.

Now more than ever, Sean realized what a bad idea that would be. He'd like to believe that Jordan had reformed, and maybe he had. From all accounts, it sounded like big brother was trying his damnedest to get back on the right track. But Jordan had run with some seriously violent gangs back home. Gangs that Sean had made the mistake of tangling with himself before he'd come to Portland. Not trusting his brother, and avoiding him on top of that, caused a pitch fork of guilt to stab at his stomach.

He wanted to give his brother the benefit of the doubt, but now that he had Ivy, now that he *knew* everything Ivy had gone through and was still going through emotionally and psychologically, there was no way in hell he could risk allowing even a whiff of violence back into her life.

And Jordan was more than a whiff. He was a full-on arctic airflow. Where he went, trouble followed. Every damn time. Sean couldn't take a chance like that with Ivy. She was too precious.

There was no decision, really. He'd abandon his brother again. And fuck, that felt horrible.

Holding Ivy like this, he was overcome with emotion. How many times had she fallen asleep on his shoulder or lap during their Netflix nights? How many times had she wandered over to his apartment with an excuse to see him? She'd run out of cream for her coffee. She needed a chocolate fix and hid her stash at his place so she wouldn't binge eat it. She wanted to know his class schedule for the next day, even though she could damn well check it online instead of coming to him.

It wasn't only her being drawn to him. He'd moved across the hall from her for a reason, damnit. The primal part of him had to be close to her, had to be within arm's reach if she needed anything, if she needed him.

Precious. She was so fucking precious. He couldn't let her be hurt in any way. Never again.

He wrapped his free arm around her. He couldn't lose her, and he wouldn't be a threat to her either.

Jordan would understand.

CHAPTER TWENTY-FOUR

Ivy sat on a Swiss ball in her office rolling her hips one way, then the other, looking over her last file of the day. It was Friday afternoon. Fight night. Gala night.

She'd said goodbye to her last client and was closing her clinic early so she could go home and beautify for the evening. And by beautify she meant Hope was coming over armed to the teeth with her make-up case and hair irons.

Dolling herself up so she met the standard of acceptable date material had suddenly become important to her. Tonight was a big night for Sean, and she wanted to be there for him in the way he'd been there for her so many times in the last few years. She wanted to act and look the part.

Caring about superficial things like hair and makeup wasn't her typical personality. Her parents had abandoned her to chase the glamorous, jet-setting lifestyle, so she'd been turned off at an early age. But Sean had never abandoned her. He'd been one of the most steadfast people in her life. From the first moment, he'd given her whatever she needed, however she needed it. And tonight, she wanted to give back to him.

Almost a full week had passed since the night she'd revealed everything to him. And instead of being left vulnerable and raw, she was filled with a renewed sense of empowerment. Her story was hers to tell, and she'd told the one person she'd grown to love and trust despite all the odds. If the bond between them had been connected by an invisible string before, it had fused now, into something stronger, more durable.

At least *she* thought so. Sean had acted mentally preoccupied all week. Which made sense, considering the upcoming fight, and the tense final days training his fighters. This was the night that the training, the stress, the hours, the effort, all came down to a few minutes in the ring. She understood focus. So she'd tried not to overthink his slight aloofness.

Besides, he wasn't ignoring or avoiding her. The opposite, in fact. He'd been intensely protective the last week, had gone with her on her early morning runs, made sure she had a safe way of getting to work and waited for her when she had a late client so he could take her home himself. When she'd made the tongue-in-cheek suggestion that he add her to the Find Friends App on his phone, he'd immediately done just that—then took hers and done the same, so she'd know where he was if she needed him.

He came down to the clinic several times a day and pulled her into the private room she used for massage, pressed her against the wall and kissed her until neither of them could breathe. He brought her lunch and stayed at her apartment exclusively. They hadn't spent a night apart since she'd told him her story, as if her telling him gave him permission to finally unravel all of his protective instinct onto her.

Was it weird that his protectiveness didn't feel overbearing? For all the shit she'd given the gym ladies for their fawning over the firefighters, she wasn't even mildly embarrassed to admit she liked this watchful side of Sean. It made her feel safe, cared for, secure—both in her physical safety and her emotional well-being. And he filled the role so naturally, like he'd always wanted to treat her this way.

But he always had. Now he wasn't being discreet about it. Now he was showing her and everyone how well he could take care of her. And, with all due respect to the feminists she admired in her time, she was here for it. Because she'd never been cherished like this.

If she knew one thing, it was that she had a lot of trust issues to work through, but knowing she could work through them with Sean at her side gave her a sense of safety. And, whether he wanted to admit it or not, Sean still had a lot of healing to do, too. Healing that wouldn't happen until he'd resolved things with his brother. And Ivy was determined to help the brothers move beyond their past, the same way Sean had helped Ivy move on from hers.

Smiling as she got up from the Swiss ball, she went to her office and put away the file. She grabbed her bag and headed out the door, eager to get the evening going. Sean deserved a happy ending too, and tonight, after the gala, he would find it.

~

Fight for the Cure was a full-scale black-tie event, complete with a roped off red carpet and cameras flashing when guests arrived.

Totally out of her comfort zone, Ivy stayed in Joel's shadow at all times, who—by contrast—appeared totally at ease, sipping his champagne and taking in the crowd while appearing hotter than sin in his tux.

"How do you stomach these things?" she asked as she had a taste of her own sparkling wine. "I feel like I'm at a souped-up version of one of Hope's formal Oscar house parties, but the chairs are less comfortable than her couch."

Joel chuckled and downed the rest of his drink. "When you grow up like Hope and I did, you get used to it. The upper echelon love nothing more than an excuse to spend a fortune on an outfit and dig out the family jewels. Though that said..." Joel's gaze assessed her, and he smiled. "The family jewels look stunning on you this evening, Ivy."

She lifted her hand to the monstrosity of a diamond necklace that Hope had insisted she borrow. Hope had enjoyed using Ivy as her real-life dress-up doll, but she had to admit the end result was impressive. Tonight, she could have passed as a princess. "Well, technically, they're your family jewels. But thank you."

"The fights are about to begin." Joel dropped his hand to the small of her back. "Let's find our seats, shall we?"

Ivy followed him to their row. He'd been her date thus far in the evening, and she hadn't seen Sean since he'd left the apartment to meet his fighters at the venue early. Tingly sensations fluttered in her lower body when she remembered the sight of Sean emerging from the bedroom dressed to the nines in a black three-piece suit.

She might literally have drooled at how good he looked. She had definitely tried to jump him right then and there, but he'd laughed, bent low to give her an all-consuming kiss, then murmured in his deep sexy voice, "Later. We'll do anything you want."

The words had been a sharp reality check, and nerves

replaced the sexual tension, because she knew what was happening later. And it wasn't what Sean expected.

After he'd left, she'd been preened and pampered into perfection by Hope, so Sean had yet to see her fully decked out in her gala wear.

"Did I miss anything?" Hope asked as she and Gabe took their seats beside Ivy and Joel.

"No, they haven't started yet. Where were you? You left twenty minutes ago to get a drink." Ivy asked with a smile.

Hope blushed and glanced at Gabe, seated close beside her, his fingers laced with hers, his gaze on the fighters and coaches prepping in their corners of the ring.

"Gabe looked so dang hot, I couldn't wait for later to—" Hope lowered her voice to a whisper. "It's these pregnancy hormones. They make me horny as heck. I literally dragged him into the most private bathroom at the end of the hall, locked the door, and had my wicked way with him. I couldn't help myself. I was going to burst!"

Ivy didn't bother holding back her snort of laughter. A few days ago, Hope had peed on the stick and confirmed her pregnancy. Since then, both Hope and Gabe had been walking around giddy as kids on Christmas morning. Ivy couldn't have been happier. Her friend deserved this, as did Gabe, and she couldn't think of two people more worthy of being entrusted with more children.

The lights dimmed, and the MC officially opened the evening, announcing the first fight. After that, there was only high-voltage energy in the room, and everybody got caught up in the electric excitement in the air.

Fighters of different levels and weight classes went head-to-head. The Fighting Five did so well that Ivy had a hard time telling them apart from the selected pro-fighters making an appearance at the charity event.

The crowd was wild, cheering for their favorites. The lights and music embellished the magical evening. But Ivy's attention rarely diverted from Sean. When he had a fighter in the ring, he stood alongside the ropes, hovering close to their corner.

He watched his fighter's every move with his quiet hawk-eyed focus, occasionally shouting an instruction. At the break, he'd jump between the ropes and crouch low to speak to his fighter, probably offering further support, instruction, and encouragement. Watching him was more riveting than the fight.

Hours later, after winners were declared, and the shouts and cheers from the crowd had faded, people started to get up from their seats to move to the dinner portion of the evening.

"Those were some great fights. Sean's really going to draw attention to his gym, seeing as all his fighters made it to the finals in their weight classes," Joel said as he stood up beside her. His hands were in his pockets, jacket open, silk bow tie catching the light, and he looked every inch the prominent business man he was. "Not to mention that final win. People will be asking where the fighter trained and whom with. It'll be good for business. Just watch."

"Is business all you ever think about?" Ivy asked, because the last thing she was thinking of was business. Her heart was beating wildly in her chest with the anticipation of seeing Sean shortly. "There's more to life than what's good for business. You know that, right?"

Joel lived and breathed work. As far as she knew, there was no girlfriend or partner in his life. Did the man even take vacations?

She was surprised when Joel's gray eyes darkened and

then distanced, like she'd lost him to a memory she wasn't privy to.

After an awkward beat of silence, he finally refocused on her and said, "Yeah, I'll stick with what I'm good at—building my father's empire and making a shitload of money in property development for the generations of Morgans to come." His tone was sardonic in a way she'd never heard before, and it piqued her interest.

"Do you ever plan on producing some of those generations to come?" It was a forward question, one she'd normally never ask, but her curiosity had let that one slip out before she could think better of it.

His eyes darkened again. Maybe she overstepped. She opened her mouth to apologize, but he cut her off.

"My sister is working on that," he muttered. "My legacy will be the work I pour into the company. I'll leave it to her and Gabe to provide offspring that can inherit it all. Ruby already shows a decent mind for business with her lemonade stands and dog walking flyers," he added, referring to Gabe's young daughter. "She'd make a hell of a CEO one day."

"Joel, it's okay to put business aside once in a while and take time for you. Build something outside of properties and apartment towers. Something for you. Maybe even *someone* for you. There's no reason you can't have a partner and children of your own. If that's what you want."

Joel stared at her, an odd mixture of pain and resignation in his eyes. And she knew she was missing a big puzzle piece in the life of Joel Morgan.

"One thing I learned is that buildings and apartment towers can't hurt me, but love sure as hell can." Then he seemed to very purposefully soften his gaze, and said to her, "But if anything could tempt me to try for love again, it's seeing how you've transformed since you accepted Sean as your *someone*. It brings me a lot of peace seeing you so happy and in love after everything you've been through."

Ivy was going to ask him what he meant by him trying for love *again*, but his mention of her being in love tripped her up.

"Oh, we aren't—I mean, I'm not. We aren't even a thing —really," she was sounding ridiculous even to herself. "We're just kind of seeing where it's going. No pressure. You know, casual."

Joel considered her a moment, then tilted his head back and let out a raucous laugh. "Casual. Right. 'Cause the way he's looking at you right now has *no pressure* written all over it? Ivy, before you lecture me on love, you might want to stop denying what's clearly laid out in front of you."

Taking her gently by the shoulders, Joel turned her so she could have his view of the ring.

Sure enough, Sean was standing where he'd been most of the evening. One of the other trainers was talking to him, but Sean was staring over the man's shoulder, his gaze fixed on her. Even from a distance, his eyes burned with passion. And something else. Something definitely, 100 percent, not casual.

CHAPTER TWENTY-FIVE

The invisible thread between them tugged and tugged until Ivy was moving toward Sean without much conscious thought, like she was being reeled in. Except he was headed in her direction as if drawn by the same pull. By the time she'd reached the main arena, he'd met her halfway.

Lord have mercy, the man looked lethal in a black suit. Professional and powerful. Self-assured and in control. So, unlike she'd ever seen him and yet so fully himself, it was beautiful. He suited this image, just as he suited his athletic gear. His confidence made it so he was always in his comfort zone.

She didn't even have a moment to greet him before Sean wrapped his hand around her nape and brought his mouth down on hers for a ferocious and crushing kiss. He inhaled her, and she let him, because she wanted to soak it all up. The taste of him, the smell of his heated skin, the sound of the low groan that rumbled from his throat, the softness of his lips as they fused with hers in a kiss that stole her breath and the last of her brain cells at the same time.

When he finally pulled away, she was gasping. For air, for sanity, for more.

"You are stunning," he said in a thick, gravelly voice.

As heat crept to her cheeks at the compliment, she lifted a hand to smooth a piece of her hair. "It's all Hope."

"No. It's all you, Ivy. Trust me." He pressed her palm to his mouth. "I spent every second I wasn't focused on the ring looking for you in the crowd, and once I found you, you were all I saw. I've never been so damn jealous of Joel in all my life. It should have been me who brought you here, sat with you, wined and dined you."

"Joel brought me here, but you'll be with me the rest of the night." Ivy reached up on tiptoes and nipped at his lips. "You can wine and dine me now." She nodded in the direction of the reception area where dinner was being served.

"Damn straight. It bothered me, knowing everyone must have thought you were his." He pulled her in so that every hard line of his body pressed against hers. His head dipped, and his breath feathered hotly against her cheek. "I want them to know you're mine, Ivy."

He sounded so intense, looked even more so with his dark, demanding eyes, and her last whiff of feminism must have gone the way of her brain cells because, by God, she *liked* it. She wanted to be his. More than that, she wanted him to be hers. She wanted to officially put an end to her stupid friend-with-benefits crap and call a thing a thing. She wanted—

"From now on, we're a couple. Not fuck friends. Not a casual fling. Not lovers having a meaningless affair," he said decisively, as if he gave zero shits that they were in a room filled with people who could easily overhear his heartfelt declarations. "From now on, there will be strings attached, Ivy. Commitments, expectations, labels."

"Labels?" Her voice was a high-pitched squeak. She didn't know how else to respond.

He'd said all the things she'd wanted in her head and heart, and it seemed so surreal. So unlike anything she ever believed she could have.

"Yeah, labels. Like boyfriend and girlfriend. Like partners. Like you're mine and I'm yours, and every damn person we pass on the street is going to know it because I like PDA, and I'm going to PDA all over you, until you feel me like a tattoo on your heart." He lay his hand over hers. "Like I feel you on mine."

She was pretty sure she was ruining Hope's carefully curated look by opening and closing her mouth like a guppy, but she couldn't help it. She was feeling all the feelings, but no words were forming coherently on her lips.

Sean grinned and pulled her up on her toes until she was almost eye level with him. He kissed her gently, then held her gaze.

"Blink once if you're with me. Twice if you're not," he whispered, a smile playing at his lips, because dammit, the man knew her. Knew when she was speechless and not capable of stringing words together.

And she loved it. Loved that he knew her so well. Loved that he'd poured years of patience, blood, sweat, and time into getting to this moment with her. Loved that his pursuit had been so intentional. That he never gave up.

So of course she blinked. One long, slow blink so there'd be no mistaking it for anything else. Because she was with him. All the way with him. To the end.

~

For the rest of the evening, Sean grinned like an idiot. He was on top of the world. His fighters had done well, better than well. They'd performed like champions in the ring the same way they did every day on the job, and he was damn proud.

He knew his dad would be proud too. And that knowledge hugged his heart in a way he hadn't known he needed.

All night, people had been asking him about his gym, his training packages, and his availability. One pro who'd fought the exhibition fight had approached him, and after a nice chat, they'd set up a time to check out Thompson Kickboxing as a new potential training venue.

But that wasn't the cherry on the ice cream. No, his cherry had been sitting in the crowd, dressed hot enough to kill a man, with her gaze fixed on him. Her presence centered him, leveled out his anxiety, and calmed his nerves.

He hadn't let Ivy leave his side since he'd kissed her earlier and demanded she be his girlfriend. What she didn't know was that he'd almost slipped up and said the word that was really on his mind, but he caught himself at the last minute. He'd learned during his years with her that he had to go slow.

Time. It would all work out in time. He was happy to go slow, to savor her. After everything they'd been through together, that felt right. Their trust had been a slow growth, like a forest that needed deep roots before it could thrive. From the early days, he knew building trust would be essential for her, but what he hadn't realized was how essential it would be for him.

His tricky past would inevitably cross over into his equally tricky present, and he needed to trust Ivy to go at his pace while he tried to figure out what to do about his brother.

Avoiding Jordan long-term wasn't an option. If the last weeks had taught him anything, it was that having the people who mattered most around you was important. Jordan mattered. He was complicated, but he mattered.

He wasn't going to risk Ivy being hurt or triggered in any way, so working out how Jordan could fit into their life was going to take some time. But he'd do it, because he was long past due to sort his shit out. And he was looking forward to moving on, hopefully with his brother and his love by his side.

Speaking of love, he'd have to find a way to tell her without freaking her out. He mentally added it to the growing list of heart-to-hearts he had to have.

But not now. He wanted to indulge in one night of simply enjoying her. Watching her across the table, he understood he was damn blessed to be the lucky bastard who'd take her home tonight, peel off her dress, and worship her body. The one who'd wake up with her in tangled sheets and watch the sunrise as they ran along the waterfront.

It had been a long night, and they were both ready to go home. Every time their gazes collided, she flushed and squirmed a little in her seat, making him wonder if she was clenching those pretty little thighs together under the table.

The stroke of her shoe glided up his calf, just as his thoughts took a turn towards Hornyville. Of course the friction beelined straight to his cock.

She casually lifted her wineglass to her lips, smiling around the rim.

Oh fuck, two could play this game.

He reached down under the table casually, as if maybe

he dropped something, but caught her ankle instead, bringing it up to rest on his knee. Ivy's eyes widened like two pale moons rising, and her mouth formed a little surprised O. Sean held her gaze, the corner of his mouth lifting.

Ivy's chest rose and fell as her breathing picked up. She was aroused and unsure what to do about it. His fingers traveled up her Achilles and toward her calf.

Now? She mouthed the word, then pointed a finger downward toward the floor. *Here?* Her eyes heated as the wheels in her head started turning, and he could practically see the thoughts playing through her mind.

What were the chances she'd be into finding a quiet corner where they could—? No way. She couldn't be ready for that. But the tip of her tongue that darted out and wet her lips told him differently. His brain let loose and he imagined taking her by the hand and leading her to a quiet alcove. But could he trust what he thought he saw playing out in the reflection of her eyes? Maybe he'd ask her.

Sean pushed back from his seat, relishing in her silent intake of air through parted lips. He moved toward her, taking his time as he read her gaze for anything that resembled uncertainty or fear. To his immense relief, he saw nothing but heat and need.

Finally, he came up behind her chair and placed his hands on the satin covered back. Her spine straightened as she leaned back slightly against him.

He bent low to whisper in her ear. "Do you want to fuck?"

Her gasp was loud enough for him to hear this time. He'd shocked her, and she liked it. He was slowly testing new waters. He'd learned her body so well. He knew what she liked and didn't like physically. Now he wanted to extend his research to other things she might like when it came to the dance of sex. Like words. Demands. Risky locations—like a hotel ballroom.

"Ivy, do you want to fuck?"

There were people all around them, adding to the thrill of the moment.

Ivy tilted her face slightly, so the corner of her mouth brushed his.

"Yes," she whispered, so quietly it was no more than a breath off her lips.

"Get up." He tugged at her seat, pulling it out, and she rose to meet him. His eyes burned into hers. If she had a fantasy tonight, he was going to deliver.

~

It didn't take Sean long to find a private alcove outside the ballroom. The second floor of the hotel was a maze of large ballrooms and banquet halls. Many had been repurposed for tonight's large-scale, multi-event evening. He led her down one of the hallways, away from all the crowds, then turned into a corner tucked behind a mahogany stairwell. There they were completely hidden from view.

The velvet carpet was a rich swirl of deep reds and golds. The cream walls, with gold-tinted sidings, added to the sensual feel and heightened her anticipation for the up-against-a-wall sex she was about to have. *Hoped* she was about to have.

Sean pressed her back against the wall, covering her. And even though they were about to PDA in a very big way, she was safe and protected.

Bending down, he took her mouth on a hot, wet ride that stole her breath and had her moaning softly in under five seconds.

"You're so beautiful. So fucking gorgeous I can hardly stand it." He yanked her dress up her legs in hard, determined tugs. "The way you look at me. It makes me feel like I'm the only man that exists."

"You are," she panted, as his fingers found the satin edge of her panties. "To me, you are."

On a satisfied growl, he dragged her panties down, cool air hitting her skin as the fabric left her body.

He'd never been this rough with her. Never this impassioned. Every movement was a step closer to his end goal of taking her up against the wall. And she was on board with it, fully present in his pursuit. He was headed in the same direction as her, and as long as they were going in the same direction, wanting the same thing, she realized it didn't matter what he was doing. Everything he did turned her on because they were in it together. They both held the power. Together.

The clink of his belt buckle opening dropped her attention to his crotch.

"Sean," she whispered as he freed himself.

Every time she saw him, there was a moment of awe. He was so big it made no sense that he could fit into her. But he did. He fit perfectly, every time. Knowing the heights he could take her to made her body ache with anticipation.

"I'm going to go hard, Ivy. And fast. Are you with me?" He hoisted her up in one fluid movement, pinning her to the wall with his hips as he positioned himself to enter her.

Ivy nodded frantically, delirious with need, desperate for wanting.

"Say it."

"Yes. I'm with you. All the way with you."

"Eyes," he demanded, and she obeyed him, her gaze locking on his.

In one powerful thrust, he lodged himself fully inside her. They gasped in unison, their breath stolen by the blissful friction their joining created. His pace increased, his pelvis rubbing her sensitive flesh.

It was crazy. They weren't even undressed. There was a party happening not far from where they were. It was exciting. And the thrill only fueled her desire.

Sean's tempo increased, and he dropped his face into the crook of her neck, grunting softly, murmuring almost unintelligibly. She only caught the words like *everything*, *soul*, and *perfect*. But more than his words, Ivy *felt* what he was trying to say. And soon she was quaking around him, her body combusting in an explosion of sensations and total fulfillment.

When he thickened inside her, preparing to meet her in her climax, he began to thrust madly, until he went rigid, pressing his forehead into hers as he let go. And her own body responded, drawing out his release. It completed her satisfaction—knowing she'd brought him his own.

After a long moment, he withdrew, slowly setting her back on her feet. "Good thing you're wearing a long dress, because you're going to feel me dripping down your thighs the rest of the night, sweet girl."

That was it. She was toast. If this was Sean unfiltered, she wasn't going back to the other version. After he'd rebuckled his belt, he glanced over his shoulder, then bent, using her underwear to gently clean the worst of the mess from inside of her thighs.

The way he talked to her, rough and dirty, then touched her like she was his most cherished gift—if her heart hadn't been lost to him already, the last ten minutes would have done it.

"I'm going to take you home and shower you. Then we

need to talk about some things. After that, we're going to do this again, but slow and sweet. All night long. As many times as we can."

His words made her insides dissolve into complete goo. It didn't seem real. After all that happened, all she'd been through, she'd found him. Everything in her life—it had all led her to him.

The euphoria of the evening left her dazed as she said her goodbyes, ignoring Hope's knowing smile and Joel's smirk. Gabe clapped Sean on the shoulder and murmured something that had both men chuckling. Sean's hand rode low on her back the whole time. He never broke the connection. Not as they collected their coats from the coat check, not as they exited the hotel, and not the whole car ride home.

By the time they pulled up in front of their apartment, Ivy was primed and ready to go another eight rounds or so. She had nothing on her mind but Sean until they climbed the steps to their apartments and she saw a man sitting in the hall by Sean's door.

She'd forgotten the surprise she'd organized to be waiting for him at home. She hadn't remembered to give the man a warning or a heads up like she'd planned. She'd been so full of Sean, of the evening they'd shared and the antici-pation for what he'd promised was yet to come, that she'd forgotten about Jordan.

When eerily familiar dark-brown eyes lifted at their arrival, homing in on Sean, then shifting to her, then back to Sean, Ivy's nerves replaced her desire. And when Sean froze like a statue beside her, dread replaced that too.

CHAPTER TWENTY-SIX

I t was like an apparition. Totally surreal and impossible. And yet...there was his brother, sitting in the hall in front of his door, eyes wary, apprehension etched in his brow.

Relief and confusion hit like one-two punches to his chest. Then, belatedly, panic, because he'd been caught completely off guard, and Ivy was with him. Carefully, he took a step forward, so she was slightly behind him.

Jordan's eyes narrowed as he caught the movement, and he slowly got to his feet, hands raised out on either side of his shoulders, a universal sign of surrender.

"Sean," his brother said in acknowledgement.

They were a similar height and build. But where Sean had honed his physique in a gym, Jordan had hardened his in prison. For seven years, Jordan's brain and body had been the only weapons he'd had to protect himself in a place where men were kept caged behind bars. And as a result, Jordan looked harder, fiercer than he should have at thirty-five. With his heavily inked arms, scar marring his left eyebrow, and hair cropped short to the scalp, he looked so much harsher than Sean remembered him.

Then again, they hadn't seen each other since the night the police hauled Jordan away. So it had been a while.

"What are you doing here?" Sean demanded, sounding colder than he intended. An inexplicable feeling thrummed through him. On the one hand, his brother was here, safe and in one piece. There was so much relief. On the other hand, guilt barreled through his chest. His past was standing right in front of him, silent and waiting. While his future fidgeted nervously beside him, as if she finally sensed the sudden and massive shift in the tectonic plates of his life.

Ivy didn't know. And Jordan didn't know that she didn't know.

Because he'd been dishonest with both of them.

"I invited him," Ivy said, stepping forward.

Shock sucked all the air out of his lungs, making his jaw slacken.

"I was in your office a few weeks ago dropping off a file. Your phone was on your desk. A text came in while I was standing there." Ivy set her fists on her hips when he narrowed his eyes. "Oh, come on, Sean. It's not like I was purposefully snooping. I was standing there, and your phone lit up. It was right after we'd had that conversation about your brother."

He remembered. It had been one of their most intimate moments. Ivy curled on his lap as he bared his soul to her. Most of his soul. Not all. He'd planned on baring the rest tonight.

"I knew you were struggling with what to do, so—" She paused, looking abashed. Then she quickly straightened her spine, lifting her chin defiantly. "I'll never be able to repay what you've done for me over the last three years. I wanted to help you find the peace you've helped me find. So I scribbled down his number and got in touch with him, because I didn't think you'd do it yourself."

Shock gave way to betrayal, which quickly slid into anger. "Ivy, did it ever occur to you that I didn't want to see him?"

She nodded. "It was impulsive, and I overstepped. But he's your brother. All the family you have left. You can't cut him off. You didn't want to! Don't try to deny it now because you're angry," she added decisively, pointing at him. "You wanted to reconnect. You just didn't know how."

Dammit, he hated that she'd seen his weaknesses so clearly. Hated that she now saw the part of him he hadn't wanted her to see until he was ready.

"So you took it upon yourself to take the leap for me?" he asked, incredulous. "So you brought him to Portland, not even asking if there was a legitimate reason I might not want him here?"

Ivy held her ground, feet planted, eyes locked on his. The crystal blue cut into his soul like a knife. "Is there a legitimate reason?"

"He's a criminal!" Sean exploded. "An ex-gangster! Hell, he could still be in that world. Do you have any idea what kind of people he ran with?" He'd never shouted at her before, but some situations required yelling, and her repeatedly putting herself in harm's way was one of those legitimate reasons. "You, of all people, should know what men who think they're above the law can do. Did you ever once think he could be a danger to you? That I didn't want him here because I was trying to protect you?"

She took a shocked step away from him and closer to

Jordan. His two worlds had collided in front of his face, and he was so *fucking* unprepared.

Jordan scowled, his eyes hard and...hurt. "Is this the part where we pretend I did time because of something *I* did?"

Nausea roiled in Sean's gut as everything about that night, almost a decade ago, flashed through his mind.

Ivy's head swiveled between them. "What does that mean?" she asked, her face tilted toward Sean, but her gaze locked on Jordan. "Sean?"

Fuck. How had this night spiraled so quickly.

"You know what?" Jordan grabbed his backpack from the floor. "I shouldn't have come. But thanks for reaching out to me, Ivy. It meant a lot that you did, even though this was a mistake."

"No, wait!" Ivy grabbed Jordan's arm as he tried to pass. "Sean, say something. You can't let him go."

I wanted to help you find some of the peace you've helped me find. But he wouldn't call what was poisoning his soul peace. And it would be so much easier if Jordan left.

The woman he loved looked up at him, wide-eyed and pleading. His brother watched him, waiting for him to say something. But what was there to say?

The truth.

"Forget this shit," Jordan muttered as he carefully removed Ivy's hand from his arm then headed toward the stairs.

Fuck.

"It was me," Sean admitted before he could overthink it. Those three words were like releasing a trigger, and the shot echoed throughout the hallway.

"Yeah, it *was* you!" Jordan whirled on him, jabbing his finger at Sean's heart. "It was you who thought you could risk everything and take that goddamn cocaine across town in a fuckin' stolen car. You who thought it was a smart idea to put your whole fuckin' future on the line and take away the last thing Mom had that was good in her life."

"There was no other choice!" Sean shouted back.

Jordan met him in his rage, advancing until they were chest to chest.

"There's always a fucking choice," Jordan growled.

"W-wait, what?" Ivy's voice broke through Sean's tension. "Are you saying...what I think you're saying?"

"That I went to prison for seven fucking years to save my brother's ass? Yes, that is exactly what we're both saying." Jordan's words were a blade, cutting through every part of the neat life Sean had built for himself in Portland. Then Jordan stepped away, putting distance between them. "But that was the whole point, brother. I did it so you could have all of this." He spread his arms wide. "So excuse me for thinking that after everything, you'd be a little more receptive to a visit."

"Oh my God," Ivy whispered.

Sean finally looked at Ivy. Her hand covered her mouth, like it was her turn to feel nauseous, and he couldn't blame her.

"Ivy—" He reached for her, but she stepped away, not stopping until she'd backed into her apartment door.

Fumbling for the doorknob, she stammered, "I just need —I need to not be here right now. I need to think. You should—You should talk to your brother." And she was gone.

Before he even had a chance to take his next breath, she was gone.

"You're a goddamn fool," Jordan said from behind him. And even though it was his brother's voice, he heard their mother talking.

"You don't know what the hell you're talking about," Sean muttered, still staring at Ivy's apartment door.

"I don't need to know what I'm talking about. I know what just went down. And what I saw was you being a damned fool."

Sean let out a harsh expulsion of breath before stalking over to unlock his own apartment door. He opened the door wide and gestured for his brother to go inside.

Jordan glowered at him, then headed for the stairs.

"Where the hell are you going?" Sean demanded, patience running thin, a pulsing throb kicking up behind his left eyeball.

Jordan paused at the stairwell. "Look, I shouldn't have come. You've been avoiding me for years, so I am not sure what made me think coming here was a good idea. But I wanted to see you. You're my brother. We've been through a lot, and I wanted to believe that we could have some kind of relationship again. Ivy made it sound possible. But I can see now that isn't going to happen, so there's no point in me hanging around."

The throb behind Sean's eye turned into a full-on pounding in his head. "I was caught off guard. Just—" Sean rubbed his palm against his eye. "Just come inside, and we'll talk."

A scowl etched Jordan's already hard features. "No thanks, brother. I heard you loud and clear: you don't want to see me."

When Jordan tried to leave again, Sean shot forward, grabbed his brother's shoulder, and jerked him back. The muscles beneath his fingers bunched reflexively, preparing to react. But his brother's control was greater than his, because Jordan didn't move let alone strike.

For several beats, Sean stared at him. Guilt, relief, anger, joy, grief. It all hit at once. "I do want you here." His voice sounded like it was being scraped over a cheese grater. "I wasn't prepared for that...confrontation." He gestured vaguely around the hallway.

Jordan took his time studying Sean until he found whatever he needed to see and sighed. "Go apologize to the lady first." He had their mother's tone going on again.

Hell. Sean rubbed the spot between his eyes.

Ivy's expression when she'd realized the truth was cemented into his head. Her shock and utter devastation made him feel like shit. Shittier than he'd already been feeling. He frantically tried to compartmentalize everything that was threatening to overwhelm him.

Ivy's departure put her in the "will deal with later" pile. He knew where she was and that she was safe. She'd told him she needed time and so did he. Right now, everything was too raw and emotionally charged.

So yeah, that was going into the "deal with later" pile.

Whereas his prodigal brother was in the "needs urgent attention" pile because he appeared most likely to take off if unsupervised.

And Sean was fairly certain whatever came next with Jordan was going to require all of his undivided attention. There was a decade's worth of neglected history to work through. They could've probably used a good therapist and a bottle of Jack to help move things along as well. Unfortunately, none of which were presently inside his apartment.

"I'll talk to Ivy a bit later. We tend to be more rational when we don't have steam coming out of our ears." He sighed when Jordan made no move from the stairwell to his apartment. "Are you coming in, or do I have to throw you over my shoulder?"

A quarter smile cracked his brother's face. "No way you

could lift me, man," he muttered but made his way back toward the apartment. "But promise me you'll talk to her soon. You said some shit you shouldn't have said, and she's been nothing but sweet to me. Sweeter than anyone's been in a long time. I could tell, even from her texts, that she's got it bad for you, that she's a keeper. You fuck this up and I might have to go and pick up the pieces."

Sean tensed as his brother strode by him and through the door. The image of his brother holding Ivy while he comforted her set his teeth on edge. Again.

"I said I'll talk to her, and I will," Sean grumbled.

Jordan nodded, dropped his bag in the middle of Sean's living room, and did a slow 360, taking the apartment in. Then he moved to stare out the corner window overlooking the street. It was dark out, but the city was still lit up by office buildings, streetlamps, and other apartments.

"You've come a long way from the old neighborhood, brother," Jordan commented quietly.

Guilt took another enormous bite out of Sean's gut as he crossed to the sofa and sank down on it. He had so much he had wanted to say to his brother, and yet there was nothing he could say that could make up for the years Jordan had lost in prison. No way he could take away the criminal record that should have been his.

"Why didn't you return my calls when I got out?" Jordan asked, his back still to Sean as he stared at the street below. "I asked you to call me back and you never did. I wanted to know if you'd come see me. Visit the cemetery with me. You know…" He turned finally, eyes sad, face drawn. "I never got to see Mom buried, so I never got a chance to say goodbye. When I got out, I thought we'd go pay respects together. Why didn't you call me back?"

Sean blew out a breath. Stripped of all defenses, there was nothing left but the truth. "Shame."

Silence screamed between them until Jordan spoke, his voice was gruff with emotion. "When I got out, I did everything I could to set my life right. I did my parole, volunteered in the community, took night classes, and got a job. I stayed away from old trouble. You think I don't know that Mom died disappointed in me? That I wasn't ashamed of myself too? I did all I could to right my wrongs, but you never gave me a chance to show you I changed." Jordan's tone was laced with self-deprecation.

The pressure building inside Sean since he'd seen his brother sitting outside his apartment burst. He sprang to his feet.

"I was ashamed of *me*," he shouted, jabbing his finger into his own chest. "I was ashamed that you were caged in a cell because of *me*, while I was starting over in another city. It was me who should have gone to prison." He walked across his living room, stopped at a photograph of his parents that he had sitting on a shelf. "I buried Mom, packed my bags, and left. While you did *my* time. How was I supposed to face you?" He faced his brother. "What was I supposed to do? Come back and give you a slap on the back as thanks? I didn't know what to say," He yelled, throwing his hands in the air. Then he sighed, his anger suddenly spent. "So I said nothing. I did nothing, and I avoided you because seeing you would mean I'd have to face my greatest failure. And yes, that made me feel shame, goddammit."

The room was so quiet he could only hear the pounding of his heart. He'd finally gotten off his chest his biggest regret and his brother only stared at him.

When Jordan finally spoke, all he said was, "That's not the way I see it, brother."

CHAPTER TWENTY-SEVEN

There were only a few times when Sean couldn't name his emotions. Most of those times had included Ivy, like when he stood in the alley and watched her take down a man twice her size. Or when he watched her sleep so peacefully in the curve of his body, as if she hadn't experienced a trauma most people couldn't even imagine.

In those instances, Sean could have been shown a pictograph of every emoji in existence and not been able to pick the one that best described the chaos of feelings inside him. Not being able to pinpoint what he was dealing with made it harder to control.

He stood stock-still in the middle of his living room, every muscle in his body taut, with *that* chaos pulsing through him. His headache was so intense it was now more of a full body throb. The night his brother had taken the blame for him was a core memory, every detail etched forever into his brain.

Toward the end of their mother's illness, everything was acutely awful. Neither Sean's income from his part-time jobs, nor the cash Jordan brought in from time to time covered the costs. Insurance wasn't part of their reality.

As their mother deteriorated, Sean took fewer shifts so he could stay home and care for her, while Jordan disappeared for longer and longer stretches of time. No one talked about the wads of bills Jordan casually tossed onto the kitchen counter every week or so. They were just grateful that whatever Jordan did resulted in the cash they desperately needed.

To this day, Sean resented the helplessness that made him approach the contacts who set up the quick-cash jobs. A thing he thought he'd never do. And all for what? His mom had died ten days later.

But he hadn't known that when he'd used his brother's street cred to land a shipment drop in another neighborhood. His promised cut would've paid for at least another round of medication.

It should've been simple. He had to pick up a car loaded with the goods and drive it into another part of town where he was to wait until a third party arrived to take the car and goods away.

He knew the goods were contraband and that the car was stolen. But he took the job anyway, because he'd believed he had no other choice.

There's always a choice. His brother's earlier words interrupted the memory. But if there had been another choice, he didn't know what it would have been.

What he hadn't anticipated was Jordan catching up with him as he got into the car. Jordan had been livid. He'd told Sean to go home. Instead, Sean had driven off, with his brother in the passenger seat, in a car full of cocaine.

Near the drop off location sirens had sounded behind them. Sean remembered it like it was yesterday.

Blue and red lights in his rearview. Sweat trickling down his neck. Heart pounding. The image of his mom, lying in bed at home, zoning in and out of consciousness. His brother yelling in his ear.

When Sean turned into an alley, Jordan had shoved Sean out of the still moving car, jumped into the driver's seat, and driven off in a screech of tires. He'd never forget the sound. Could still smell the burn of rubber. Taste the gas fumes. Felt the ache in his shoulder where he'd landed on the concrete behind a dumpster.

The police caught up with Jordan in the next alley. When Sean had caught up, he'd stood in the shadows, watching like a coward as the police officers pinned his brother to the ground.

He'd watched, stunned, as they read Jordan his rights, then shoved him into their vehicle. He'd abandoned his brother to the wolves. Betrayed him by not moving a single inch.

Long after the police had taken Jordan away, he'd stood in that shadowed alley, his body shaking and cold. His stomach clenched so painfully, he'd vomited beside a dumpster. Knowing that his whole life had changed. And not just his, but Jordan's as well.

He'd thought about running to the station and turning himself in. But the image of his mother, dying in her bed, plagued him. And he'd made the fucking choice to let his brother go. Alone.

He'd been a coward that night and every night after.

Eventually, he'd gone home, burned his clothes in a trash can, and sat beside his mother for the rest of the night. He didn't tell her what happened. It hadn't mattered much, anyway. She'd been delirious on pain meds and slept most of the time. She passed away shortly after Jordan's arrest. He'd remembered feeling a gut-wrenching regret with the simultaneous relief of knowing she died ignorant of the fact that her eldest son was going to prison—for a crime her youngest, her pride and fucking joy, had participated in.

But his lowest point came after his mother's death. When he'd made the decision that would change the course of everything.

A month after his mom took her last breath on a gasp, he'd climbed off a Greyhound in Portland, with a couple of hundred dollars in his pocket, and a vow to never look back. He worked multiple jobs at gyms and took night courses. With a hell of a lot of hard work mixed with good timing and connections, he'd ended up where he was now. The owner of Thompson Kickboxing and a trainer with a growing reputation for success.

But the thought of his brother sitting in jail—with God-knows-what happening to him while he served time that should have been his—haunted him day and night. Their last day together replayed constantly in his mind, but no matter how many times he spun it in his head, his shame and guilt kept him from figuring out his next step.

Then he met Ivy.

Ivy, who—like him—had come to Portland with nothing but a desire to rebuild. Ivy with her haunted eyes and fierce determination to become a stronger, more resilient version of herself. Ivy, who became his friend, business partner of sorts, and now lover. Ivy, who changed his whole world and made everything in it better. Ivy, who taught him what strength and courage truly was.

Ivy, who deserved a man who could provide her with unrestrained safety and security. And he couldn't do that, not when his past now stood a few feet from him, reminding him that the thing she needed to be protected from the most was...him.

"Is that what this is about?" Jordan's question cut through his self-loathing like a red-hot knife. His tone sounded so dumbfounded that Sean's back went up defensively.

"Yes!" he exploded. "I can't go back and hand myself over to the police. I can't give you back the years you lost in prison. I can't make it right, and I have no idea where we go from here."

Jordan's eyes softened, taking some of the hardness from his features. "Sean, when I found out you'd taken that job, I fuckin' lost it. Jesus himself couldn't have kept me from coming after you." He ran his hand over his scalp, a gesture that was so familiar. "And you know what? If that job hadn't gone to you, it would've gone to me. And the night would've ended exactly the same way. I thank God that I got you out of a situation you should've never been in. But, man, I tell you I would've run that deal, regardless. And if I hadn't been caught that night, I would've kept running those drops and my luck would've ended, eventually."

"That night, you came after me—"

Jordan cut him off with a sharp shake of his head. "You had no business in that world. You were the one who was going to make something of himself. Seeing you get in a stolen car full of drugs, I never panicked like that before."

For the life of him, Sean had no idea what to say. This whole conversation was so surreal.

Jordan crossed to where Sean had hung his punching bag, and gave it a push, catching it on its return. "What I never understood was what you were thinking. You were smart enough for college. You tried to keep peace in the neighborhood. Why would you suddenly do a drug deal?"

"Mom." He'd have done anything to make her better. But no amount of money, legal or illegally procured, could have saved her.

"She would've had my ass if she knew I'd let you get wrapped up in anything I was involved in."

They both let out a half-hearted chuckle, because, hell, it was true.

Jordan sighed heavily. "It wasn't your fault."

It was amazing how five words would change an entire perspective. "I thought you would have never been there that night if it hadn't been for me."

"You thought wrong." Jordan shoved his hands deep into his jean pockets.

"Yeah, well, it doesn't change the fact that I was planning to do something illegal. Something I would have followed through with if you hadn't showed. Something I was never held accountable for," Sean said grimly. "There was no punishment for me. I watched you being taken away, while I walked off a free man."

Jordan rocked back on his heels, pursing his lips as he weighed the silence. "You sure about that, brother? Because from where I'm standing, I'd say you've punished yourself plenty."

Sean's gaze narrowed as it met his brother's.

"Do you think you fooled anyone out there?" Jordan pointed at the door and the hallway behind it. "All that shit about protecting her from your dangerous big brother. Yeah, I heard you."

Sean hung his head, shame devouring him as his words came back to kick his ass.

"But you're not worried about protecting her from me. You're worried about protecting her from *you*. Because you've spent a shit ton of years in a prison of your own making, letting the devil tell you that you're something you're not. You're not *me*, Sean. You're this guy—" Jordan gestured to the room around them, a room full of evidence of years of hard work and determination. "You're the guy who used his brains to find a way *out* and made something of himself. That's who you are."

Moisture pricked at Sean's eyes, hot and stinging.

"And okay, you weren't all wrong getting mad in the hallway. I'd keep me away from the girlfriend if I were you, too. I get it. I know it. I fucked with my future, but I wasn't going to let you fuck with yours." Jordan walked up to Sean, and clapped him on the shoulder, holding his hand there. "I'm still your big brother. It was my job to protect you. Not the other way around. I shoved you out of that car because I wanted you to get away. The only thing that got me through doing my time was knowing you were free to live your life the way you were meant to." He dropped his hand back to his side.

Sean swallowed past the lump in his throat, trying to get a grip on the storm inside him. "I owe you my life, but I have no idea where to start making it up to you. No idea how the fuck I was supposed to give you back the years you lost in prison for me."

"You don't owe me anything." Jordan shuffled from one foot to the other, his gaze darting to Sean's, then back to the floor. "But I am going to ask you for something, anyway."

"Anything," Sean said without hesitation.

"I want another chance. I'm not that deadbeat from the old neighborhood anymore. Prison—" A shadow dropping over Jordan's eyes as his throat worked. "I'm never going back there. I want a real future. And I want you to be part of it."

Sean moved before Jordan finished speaking. He didn't

care if it weirded Jordan out. Didn't care if they hadn't touched each other in almost a decade. He wrapped his arms around the only family he had left and held tight. "You're my brother. No way I'm making a future without you. Fuck, I'm sorry I wasn't there for you sooner."

Jordan thumped him on the back, almost knocking the wind out of him and reminding Sean how strong his brother was. As far as hugs went, it was awkward as hell, but he relished it. He had his brother here in one piece. His big brother who'd protected him and saved his life. There was nothing more in life he could ask for. Except—

"Ivy."

"Yeah," Jordan agreed, breaking their hug. "You fucked up with her big time."

It was eerie that even though they hadn't had any kind of relationship in a decade, his brother could still read his mind.

"You should go grovel," Jordan advised.

Ivy deserved more than groveling. She deserved everything. He had to come up with something, and fast, before he found himself in her rearview forever.

CHAPTER TWENTY-EIGHT

I vy had been sitting in her nana's rocking chair for a full day and a half, staring out the bay window in the sunroom, drinking copious amounts of Earl Grey tea, and eating more fresh baked scones than she had any right to consume.

She'd come here to give Sean and his brother space to talk things out. And also because she'd needed a hot minute to sort through her own emotions after everything that had happened in the hallway.

Once she'd made the decision to go, it hadn't taken long to make a few phone calls, set up a locum for her clinic, pack a bag and drive the three hours north to her nana's house in Bellevue, Washington. Space had seemed appropriate when everything was still fresh and raw.

But maybe distance did make the heart grow fonder, because now that she was here all she'd done was rock in the damn chair and long for Sean. The heartache was unbearable.

And the view outside the bay window matched her mood. In the spring, Nana's yard was lush with color from the rhododendrons, azaleas, and hydrangeas, but now, in autumn, it was devoid of brightness. On a day like today, when the incessant rain made the gloom even darker, only the auburn tinted bushes brought life to the world outside.

The dreariness seeped into her core. Confusion, regret, frustration, it was all hitting her. She had so many questions for Sean, and she was trying her damnedest not to jump to conclusions. Had he lied to her about everything all this time? Why hadn't he told her the truth about his past? Didn't he trust her? What really happened the night Jordan got arrested?

Her dizzying cycle of unhappy thoughts were interrupted by the squeaking sounds of the tea cart coming down the hallway. Seconds later, her nana appeared with another serving of steaming tea.

Nana hadn't asked much about Ivy's unscheduled visit. She'd simply proceeded to make pot after pot of tea, and waited until Ivy was ready to talk. Which is what she'd done all of Ivy's life.

Most of the time, it didn't take long before Ivy was blubbering all her despair over a perfectly brewed cup of Earl Grey and a homemade cinnamon sugared scone. But this time, she hadn't done much talking. And it wasn't fair to blow out as quickly as she'd blown in, without a word as to why.

With a sigh of resignation, Ivy recognized that she owed her nana an explanation for her sudden, unexpected visit. "I'm sorry, Nana. Come on, I'll help you with this."

She got up to take over pushing the cart into the living room, before returning to her place in the rocker.

Nana took a seat on the Victorian chaise beside her. She was in her early 80s but had better posture than a ballerina in her 20s. She sat ramrod straight, hands folded neatly on her lap. The cart sat neatly beside her, the steam from the teapot rising between them.

"I know I haven't said much about why I'm here," Ivy began. "And I know I have spent the better part of that time sitting in here, thinking."

"In my experience, thinking too much only leads to sleepless nights and indigestion." Nana picked up the pot and poured tea into the delicate English Rose teacup at her side. When she was done, she lifted the cup by its saucer and, with a remarkably steady hand, passed it to Ivy.

Holding the porcelain filled Ivy with an immediate sense of calm. Drinking tea with Nana had become synonymous with comfort.

"I blame myself, you know," Nana said, before Ivy continued with her explanation.

Ivy's eyebrows shot up. "For what?"

"For you having parents who didn't know how to love you in the way you deserved."

Abruptly tears filled Ivy's eyes. Not what she was expecting. "Nana—"

"No." Nana set her teacup and saucer on the table in front of her, straightened her shoulders more than they already had been, and faced Ivy. "It's true. I raised your father to be independent and self-sufficient. I refused to coddle him, but I fear, in doing so, I inadvertently gave him the belief that children were a necessary contribution to the world, and not the joyous gift of endless love that they truly are."

All this was spoken without betraying a single emotion while Ivy sat in her rocker, silent tears streaming down her face.

"You see," Nana went on, "your parents believed that the mere fact that they loved you was enough. That they didn't need to show you or shower you in it. They believed that building a relationship with you wasn't important."

"Nana, no," Ivy whispered, tasting the tang of her salty tears as she spoke.

"Yes," her grandmother returned. "Your father knew no better because I never educated him on the joy it would bring everyone if he expressed his love." She took another sip of her tea. "I was a product of my generation. A young mother, widowed early, in a country not her own. I found myself playing the role of mother and provider, all at once. When I was raising your father, I didn't understand how beautifully love and relationships went together. In fact, I didn't learn that," she paused, taking a steadying breath, "until you."

Ivy couldn't help the muffled sob that escaped her. She'd never heard her nana speak about something so personal. She always had the British stoicism perfected.

"I hope, my dear, that I did not make the same mistake with you. In my second chance as guardian, I hope I conveyed the bouquet that love is. That it goes beyond mere feeling and can encapsulate the richness of friendship, intimacy, and encounter. Any number of beautiful things are evoked by love. It isn't enough to feel it. You have to live it to truly thrive."

And there it was. The Nana laser vision. Somehow she knew, with her nana intuition, that Ivy was here because of a matter of the heart.

"I screwed up." Ivy sniffled into one of the pretty paper napkins from the tea tray.

"I gathered that, child. Why don't you indulge me with the specifics?" Nana reached over and patted Ivy's hand.

"I risked my heart on someone who was a friend. Well, the truth is, he was always more than that. He was my champion, my protector, the person who was always there. Even when I didn't know it. I thought—" Ivy took a breath. Was it okay to talk to your grandma about sex? Where on the scale of awkward to totally normal did that fall? "I thought we could be friends, and then be...closer than friends, but without having to be in a relationship. I thought that's what I wanted."

"Let me guess? You realized that being casual lovers wasn't possible when you are actually in love?"

"Nana!" Ivy gasped. What did Nana know about casual lovers?

"My dear, I had my share of affairs before I met and married your grandfather. I am well accustomed to the realities of a casual liaison. And I can assure you, they are doomed from the start when true feelings are involved. Which I assume they are in your case with your beau. Am I correct?"

Ivy nodded.

"How, then, did you come to *screw it up*?"

"Sean is so much more than a friend. It should have been obvious from the start, but I was too blind to see it." Blind and terrified. "He saved me from a dark time. He was patient, and he drew me back into the light. I owed him for what he'd done and wanted to show the same kindness. I wanted to repay him, so I—" She sighed, regret lacing her voice. "I encouraged his estranged brother to come to Portland, because I thought if they could reconcile and find peace, then Sean would have the same sense of healing he gave me."

There was a long silence in which her grandmother simply watched her.

"How very presumptuous of you," Nana finally said.

"I just wanted to give back."

"No, you wanted to assuage your own guilt for all he did for you." Nana set her teacup down with a clunk. "You couldn't imagine that someone would not only love you, but that they'd want to show that love without expecting anything in return, so you took it upon yourself to level the playing field. Until you realized it wasn't a game."

Geez. Nana with the truth.

"You're right," Ivy moaned.

"Of course I am, dear."

"I'm a horrible person."

"No, you're not. Like I said, I blame myself for not raising your father better, and for not amending my errors while raising you." Her tone was so matter of fact, while she sat primly on her chaise, that no one but Ivy would have seen the subtle lines of hurt around her eyes.

Tell her. Ivy's conscience whispered to her from her soul. *Tell her the truth. Don't let her blame herself.*

"You loved me before anyone else did. You taught me all about love. It wasn't you, it was—" Pause. Swallow. Breathe. "Back in college—" The staccato beat of her heart echoed in her throat as she tried to get the words out. "There were men who...hurt me."

Nana clasped Ivy's hands tightly in her own, her grip surprisingly strong given her age. "I know, darling. I know."

Ivy tried to see through the tears blurring her vision. "You do?"

Nana nodded. "You came home for Christmas that year, but it wasn't you. There was a light missing from your eyes, like the fire inside you had been put out. And the woman in me knew."

"How could you know?" Ivy gasped as a grim realization dawned.

To her horror, Nana nodded.

"In my generation, no one spoke about it. If anything, one just assumed it would happen eventually. A supposed gentleman swatting your behind at work. A classmate making unwanted advances at a dance. Boys making lewd comments as you hurried past them, heading home from school. A date taking liberties simply because you'd allowed a kiss. And worse. Much worse. I have seen many women with the look you wore when you came home for the holiday that year."

Ivy could hardly keep up with what she was hearing. The statistics were there, a simple Google search away. And yet, hearing it from her elderly grandmother...

"What did you do?" she queasily asked. "How did you move on?"

Nana shrugged her slim shoulders. "I simply immersed myself in the business of my life and pushed it to the farthest recesses of my mind. What else was there for me to do? There were no clinics or therapists to assist you. Families did not address such matters. It is why—" She gulped a breath, showing the first real sign that this conversation was taking an emotional toll. "It is why I did not say anything to you when you came home that holiday. I did not know what to say. Did not know how I could help. I heard you crying in your room and could do nothing but stand outside the door while tears rolled down my own face. Another way I failed you."

"No!" Ivy exclaimed. "Nana, no. It wasn't your responsibility to help me."

"Dear girl, but it was," Nana murmured. "And that is the strength of this new generation. We all carry the responsibility of helping each other. This is no longer a dirty little secret. It is no longer something you have to hide in shame. It was my only solace, knowing that there were those with far more experience than I who could help you and support you. I hoped if you could not reach out to me, you would have reached for others who had the grace and experience to support you."

"I went to see a counselor right after for a bit," Ivy admitted. "And I had Hope, who listened whenever I needed to talk. But I didn't *want* to talk about it. I...couldn't. I just wanted to forget and move one. Feel normal." She swallowed but it did nothing to rid the lump in her throat. "I never did though. I always felt so weak. So broken. Then later there was Sean. He taught me how to defend myself, helped me get strong." She shook her head. "No, he helped me *feel* strong. He was gentle and patient and he *loved* me."

Nana cleared her throat, then briskly wiped tears from her eyes with her napkin. She pulled herself up straight again and looked Ivy straight in the eye. "Well then, if he is half the man you proclaim him to be, I imagine he loves you *still*. You must simply pull yourself together and apologize to him."

Ivy whipped her head up, panicked. "Do you think it's too late?"

Nana stood and placed her teacup and saucer on the tea tray. Then she collected Ivy's cup.

"I am not saying any such thing. Although it would certainly be his prerogative if he decided he wasn't going to while-away his life waiting for you to stop moping about." She pushed the tea cart toward the kitchen. "But I'll tell you this, Ivy Felicity Harrington. If you think that you get to live this life again, you have been sorely misinformed."

And with that, Ivy was left alone in the sunroom, the cart's squeaky wheels echoing in her grandmother's wake.

Enough was enough. She had to get back and make things right.

Bringing Jordan to Portland without telling Sean had been a huge misjudgment. She'd thought Sean and Jordan would have an awkward man hug and then a conversation. But, geez, had she been wrong.

It had been horrible seeing a part of Sean she didn't recognize, but after her rocking chair musings she understood it. Shock and panic made people act differently. He was trying to protect his past. To keep it locked down like she'd done with hers. He didn't want her to see the ugly parts of him.

They'd worked through that on her end. But the difference was, Sean had gone slowly with her. He'd made sure all her fail-safes were in place before he confronted her truths with her.

She hadn't given him the same courtesy. Ugh. Her whole body cringed when she thought of how she'd blindsided him. *Hurt* him.

Urgency filled her as she bolted out of the rocking chair, and down the hall to her room to pack. What had she been doing here? Wasting time, that's what. She needed to get back to Portland, and she needed to get back now. She'd come up with an apology speech on her drive back.

CHAPTER TWENTY-NINE

Pacing the small office in the back of Gabe's bar was the only thing keeping Sean's sanity intact. From the chair behind the desk, Gabe's gaze tracked him in total silence. If this was a therapy session, it wasn't working.

He hadn't heard from Ivy in a day and a half. Which he was prepared to admit was 110 percent his own fault. But she'd just up and fucking left, without so much as a Post-It note of explanation. He'd learned from Erica that a locum was covering Ivy's patients, but not a single fucking person knew where she'd gone. Or at least no one was telling him.

He'd called Hope, who'd assured him in clipped tones that Ivy was in a safe place and needed some space.

Fuck space. Space was what had gotten them into this mess. Emotional space, mental space, physical space. The more they put between them, the worse off they were. He needed to find her, immediately.

"Dude, I had new floors put in a couple months ago. You break it, you buy it, you know that, right?" Gabe reclined in his fancy leather chair, beer in hand.

Sean wanted to smack that beer out of his friend's hand and wipe that knowing look off his face.

"I'm not going to damage your goddamn floors." He clenched his molars harder than was probably dentist recommended.

Gabe set down his beer and raised his palms. "Look, I've been where you are. Literally, like exactly where you are, pacing this room like a caged animal. No idea where my woman was at, thinking that all hell was going to rain down on me—again."

Sean closed eyes and pinched the bridge of his nose. "I really, really need to know where she is."

He'd tried calling, texting, emailing, but stopped short of sending a carrier pigeon. He'd gotten nothing but a big fat silence that screamed, *Stay the fuck out of my life, you asshole.*

Gabe's footsteps came around the desk. Then a firm grip clasped his shoulder.

"No one said this shit was easy."

When Gabe didn't elaborate, Sean sighed loudly and opened his eyes to the ceiling. "The being dumped shit?" Because if this was what this was, it might kill him.

"The love shit," Gabe replied. "It's hard as fuck, but damn, it's worth it."

If there was ever a time to finally admit out loud that he loved Ivy, this would have been it, but his brother burst through the door with a force that sent it crashing against the wall.

"Dude, door!" Gabe choked out, as Sean demanded, "Jordan, what happened?"

Jordan grinned like he'd just won the ultimate prize. "I think I know how to find her."

~

Ivy pulled her suitcase out from under the wrought-iron bed her nana hadn't changed since Ivy's youth. The frilly and faded pastel-blue duvet set was so outdated that a vintage store probably wouldn't want it, but it was still the most comfortable bed she'd ever slept in. She set her suitcase on the mattress and started packing.

And by packing she meant tossing clothes and toiletries into her bag at willy-nilly. Time was of the essence. She'd wasted too much of it already when she could have been home talking to Sean. Apologize, explain, and hope that he could forgive her, that was her priority now.

"I'm going to miss you, dear," Nana mused from the bedroom doorway.

Ivy stuffed the last of her clothes into her suitcase, zipped it closed and faced her grandmother, the first person who'd shown her love. Even though she was still spry, sharp as a whip, and in phenomenally good health considering her eighty-plus years, Beatrix Harrington's age showed around her eyes. Not the fine laugh lines she'd acquired over the years, but a tiredness that hadn't been there before.

"I'll miss you too." She rushed forward to envelope her sweet, sassy, and too-British-for-her-own-good grandmother in her arms. "I'll come visit more often," she promised.

Nana let out a loud snort. "You're a busy, hardworking, young career woman. I have no expectation that you should cater to your ancient grandmother when you could be out courting that beau of yours."

Ivy smiled. "I love you, Nana. And, courting or not, I'm going to visit you more often," she said decisively and meant it. And next time, she'd bring Sean. If they managed to undo all the damage they'd done. *Ugh*, she couldn't even stomach the alternative.

Just as they stepped back from their embrace, the doorbell rang.

Nana perked up like she was a six-month-old puppy. "Oh, I'm sure that's the new delivery man!" she exclaimed with a youthful giddiness that Ivy wasn't used to. She gave Ivy a wink. "I told him to ring my bell instead of leaving the box at my door because I'm expecting a parcel of utmost importance. Very high priority."

"What are you expecting?" Ivy asked suspiciously. Ever since she'd taught her nana how to order online, she'd been on a mission to order every kitchen gadget known to man.

"Just a book," Nana announced with glee. "But I like the look of him. Fine muscles on that one."

"Nana!" Ivy gasped.

"Oh, don't be such a fuddy-duddy. One's never too old to appreciate the design of a fine male form." And on that note, Nana made her way down the hall.

Ivy couldn't help but chuckle in astonishment as she listened to her grandmother unlatch the lock and open the front door. Her nana was one of a kind.

When she grew up, she wanted to be exactly like her. And now, knowing more about what she had overcome, Ivy was even more inspired and in awe of her grandmother's strength in the face of all life had thrown at her.

"Ivy, dear!" Nana called from the front door, in her weird, high-pitched, teen-like voice. "This delivery seems to be for you."

Ivy dropped her chin to her chest. If Nana had ordered her another set of tea towels (because *one can never have too many, you know*) she was going to have enough to open a gift shop.

She picked up her suitcase and carried it down the hall

toward the front door. "Nana, I have more tea towels than—"

The sight before her made her heart jump into her throat, and her limbs go numb. She dropped her suitcase on the floor. Standing in the entrance, taking up the entire doorway and dwarfing her nana almost into extinction, stood Sean. All broad, brooding, and contrite six-foot-plus of him, holding the biggest bouquet of pink roses she had ever seen.

And suddenly, "Oh" was the only sound she could make.

CHAPTER THIRTY

Down the length of the hallway, the dark eyes that she'd missed centered her heart and steadied her. He didn't say anything, just locked his eyes on her and stared. And their string reconnected, like a lock snapping back into place.

Between them, her nana cleared her throat. "Well, dear, perhaps you'd like to invite our guest in." She glanced up at Sean. "Would you like a cup of tea?"

He looked down at Nana, and blinked, as if realizing she was still there. "Oh, no thank you. I'm good. But I'm hoping I can talk to Ivy." His gaze met hers again. "If that's okay with her."

"Well, of course it is. Heavens, why wouldn't it be?" Nana stepped aside to let him enter, before she slipped into the living room.

"Uh..." She was trying to get a grip and find her voice, really she was, but seeing Sean in her nana's foyer was so unexpected, like a scene out of *The Greatest Showman* and the headline read, *A battle of forces. The World's Strongest Man and the Tiniest Grandmother take the world by storm.*

Finally, she got her feet moving down the hallway toward him. "How did you know I was here?"

"Jordan figured it out," he told her, his voice the sexy rumble that she missed so much.

"Jordan?" How would he know she even had a grand-mother, never mind that she'd be here visiting her?

"He went to your clinic looking for you, found Hope helping with administrative stuff, and explained to her what happened. Luckily she listened to him, cause she sure as hell didn't give me the time of day." He huffed out a laugh. "My long-lost brother got your location out of her when I couldn't."

"Sounds like Hope," Ivy murmured.

Knowing Hope, she'd probably been in Jordan's pres-ence for less than three minutes before her sentimental heart rolled over to make room for him. She always had a soft spot for a tortured teddy bear hero.

"*Ivy.*" When he said her name with a quiet desperation, it was a full body experience. His eyes were tormented. "Please, can we talk?"

The sound of scraping along the hardwood made her turn to look. Nana was dragging Ivy's favorite rocking chair closer to the velvet settee. Ivy knew that her nana would have sooner died than drag anything across the floor, so Ivy could only assume she was trying to tell her something—or to say something.

"Would you like to come in?" Ivy asked Sean, gesturing toward the sitting room.

Sean let out a puff of air, as if a great weight had been lifted off him. "Yes. Yes, I would really like to come in."

Ivy nodded, proceeded him into the sitting room, and sat down on the rocking chair that was now within touching distance of the sofa, where Sean took a seat.

"I'll take these." Nana relieved Sean of the bouquet of roses. She made a show of sniffing them deeply. "My, aren't they lovely? The prettiest roses I have ever seen. Aren't they, Ivy?" She didn't wait for a reply as she took the bouquet out of the room.

"They're beautiful, Sean. Thank you, but you didn't need to bring me flowers." She fidgeted with the hem of her shirt.

He looked massive on the delicate piece of furniture, and Ivy nearly laughed at the sight of her big, bad Sean perched on her grandmother's dainty English settee.

"I would have brought the whole damn shop if I could have." He swallowed, looking oddly nervous, which made no sense since she was the one who needed to apologize. And she'd waited long enough to do it already.

"I'm so sorry, Sean." Saying the words had the same effect as finishing a long run. Centering and cleansing. And she'd waited far too long to get them out. "I should have never invited your brother back into your life without consulting you first."

But why did he look so shocked?

"You know, I am capable of apologizing when I've screwed up."

"Now that you mention it, I think that's the first time I've heard the words *I'm sorry* come out of your mouth." He chuckled, a soothing baritone. "But that's not why I'm surprised. You have nothing to apologize for. I need to thank you for what you did." The tip of his finger tilted her chin up until she met his gaze. "You were right. Without you, I wouldn't have made the first move with my brother. At least not for a long time, and by the time I did get my head out of my ass, it might have been too late to salvage any kind of relationship."

The creaky wheels of Nana's tea cart interrupted the moment, and Ivy rolled her eyes. Here came the Earl Grey.

"I know you said you didn't want a cup, but I thought—of course, you'd need one after your long drive." Nana stopped the cart beside them. "Ivy will pour for you." She walked to the front door and got the shoehorn off its hanger.

Nana was the only person Ivy knew who used a shoehorn.

She straightened from slipping her shoes on. "I'll be outside if you need me."

Ivy frowned. "Why?"

"To make my acquaintance with your friends waiting outside in their vehicle."

"What?" Ivy jumped up to look out the bay window.

Sure enough, Sean's car was parked in the driveway, with Jordan in the front passenger seat, and in the back was—

"Is that Hope?"

"And Gabe," Sean admitted. "Erica, Wendy, and Christine wanted to come too, but there wasn't room." He gave a helpless shrug. "Ivy, I screwed up too. Big time. I saw my brother in our hallway, and I panicked. I got scared, and I yelled at you, because I didn't want any part of my past to touch you. But also, because I didn't want you to find out like that."

Finding it hard to stand still when all she wanted to do was crawl onto his lap, Ivy started fidgeting again.

"You should never have to hide your past," she said. "I don't want that for you. Nothing from before will change how I feel about you." Her brow creased. "Did my past change how you feel about me?"

"God no. It makes me admire you even more. But my history isn't like yours. You overcame, I—" His gaze darted to the side. "My brother went to prison because of something I did. That's not anything to admire. It's a reason for you to get the hell away from me. Which you did, and had every right to do, except—I can't let you go. I just can't let you go."

CHAPTER THIRTY-ONE

After that, everything came out fast. It was like Ivy's silence drew all his secrets into existence. He spared no details.

Ivy sat in her rocking chair, knees tucked under her chin, her eyes revealing nothing. His pounding heart was like the metronome of his story. Less than two days ago, she'd looked at him like he was her hero, and now—he couldn't have guessed if his life depended on it. But he kept talking.

"I watched from a distance as the police shoved my brother to the ground and handcuffed him. Then I fucking ignored him for years while he served time." Her blank expression brought his frustration to a peak. "I saw him sitting in our hallway and I—" They were back to square one, and Ivy still hadn't moved a single muscle.

The silence was agitating enough that he had to get up. "I saw him sitting there and I thought, this is it, this is where I lose you."

Before he could say another word, she grabbed his hand. Using the grip, she launched herself out of her chair and into his arms. Her momentum and his surprise made him fall back on to the tiny couch he'd just gotten up from.

As he sat there trying to catch his breath, her scent enveloped him, roses and honey, and even though he knew he shouldn't, he put his arms around her and breathed her in.

"I'm so sorry," she murmured. "I'm so sorry I forced you to face all of that when you weren't ready. I'm sorry you and Jordan had to go through it in the first place. I'm sorry you thought for one second you could *ever* lose me. I'm sorry. I'm sorry."

Was his t-shirt getting wet? Shit, he'd made her cry. His heart twisted as he added that to his list of transgressions.

"Don't cry, baby," he whispered against her hair. "And don't apologize. Not ever." When her crying didn't let up, his stomach sank. "I wanted so badly to be the man you thought I was."

She pulled back. "The man I thought you were?" Confusion creased her brow.

"You started looking at me like I was some kind of savior. It killed me a little more every day, because I knew I wasn't half the man you thought I was. Then when you trusted me with what happened to you, I knew I had to tell you the truth before we could have the relationship I wanted. I was going to tell you the night of the gala, but then Jordan was there. I lost it and fucked things up again."

"No." She shook her head vehemently. "I should have consulted you before making a decision like that behind your back. I regret that I didn't tell you, but," she eyed him cheekily, "I don't regret the outcome, because you and your brother are working things out, and that's all I wanted." Leaning forward, she brushed her nose against his. "If you think that what you told me makes me think differently of you, then you're crazy."

She said it so nonchalantly, he choked back a laugh. "I'm crazy?"

"Yes, you are. You were never meant to be perfect. I never thought you were, ever."

"I'm not sure if you're trying to make me feel better or worse, but—"

Ivy threw back her head and laughed, and the sound warmed him from the soul outward. "Better! Trust me. I don't want perfect. I want trustworthy, and strong, and loyal. I want someone I know will never let me down if he can help it. I want you." She smoothed her palms over his face, then locked her fingers behind his neck. So close her breath was warm against his chin.

Closing his eyes and resting his forehead against hers, he murmured, "I let my brother down." That singular fact would always haunt him.

"You let him protect you. He'd have been let down if you'd gotten yourself arrested for doing something totally out of character." Ivy inhaled a deep breath. "Sean, look at me."

He lifted his head, and the eyes that had become the center of his whole world burned into his.

She looked him dead in the eye, her crystal-blues glistening. "You are, and always have been, exactly the man I thought you were. And *I love you*." Her breath caught on the last three words, like she wanted to stop them, but they slipped out of her mouth, anyway. Pressing her lips together, she held her breath and stared at him.

"I love you too." His words didn't hesitate. "So much." His voice cracked for the second time, but he couldn't muster the willpower to care. This woman unmanned him, and he didn't give a damn.

She was his best friend, his hero, his inspiration. She made him laugh and cry at the same time. He worried about her relentlessly and trusted her wholeheartedly. If he could only have one thing for the rest of his life, he'd pick her. Every time.

Needing to taste her more than his next breath, he crushed his lips against hers and drank her in, filling himself with her grace, her love, and her faith. How she had an abundance of all of it after what she'd survived he had no idea, but he was going to drink from her cup, because she sustained him. "You make me better," he murmured between kisses. "All the way better."

She pulled away. "We make each other better," she amended, then leaned in again, pressing her lips gently against his. "Don't let me go, okay?"

He chuckled because if she was being serious, she was the crazy one. "Not in this lifetime, sweetheart. Then he added, "and not the next one either."

Then he wrapped arms around her, and held her, until the front door opened and Nana brought everyone in for tea.

EPILOGUE

The sun had already risen by the time Ivy and Sean set out for their morning run together. It shone brightly over the Willamette River and despite the winter temperature, it warmed Ivy's cheeks as she ran.

There were only two more weeks until Christmas, and the trees along the river trail were strung with festive lights, reminding Ivy that they still had to put some on the tree they'd wrestled home the night before. Their home, because Sean had fully moved into her apartment shortly after they'd returned from Nana's. Even his punching bag hung from the corner where Hope's easel had once stood. The apartment was now a perfect blend of them both. Gym equipment and a vase of roses on the coffee table. Physio mats and running shoes. The purple heart pillow rested on their couch, while Sean's big TV took up most of one wall. It was home.

And for now, the apartment across the hall sat empty.

As she ran alongside Sean, Ivy reflected on the season of change she was in. She'd started seeing a counselor to help process the things that still needed working through. Sean had even attended a few sessions with her, and while those were heavy, emotional hours, they were the best therapy she'd ever had.

Jordan had returned to Chicago to tie things up before moving permanently to Portland to work at Sean's gym and attend community college.

Nana had plans to stay with them over Christmas which had motivated Sean to reno the second bedroom into a guest room befitting English nobility—which Nana fancied herself to be.

And for the first time in three years Ivy was truly excited about her future. It no longer loomed in front of her, like a mountain waiting to be climbed. It was now a highly antici-pated journey onward.

As the crisp winter air rushed in and out of her lungs while they ran, she relished in a true sense of reclaiming her life. In the last couple of weeks, she'd truly given herself permission to feel joy and delight, and *that* was her ultimate freedom. Every minute, she put more distance from the terrible day that had haunted her for far too long.

Wanting to savor the moment she was experiencing, Ivy slowed to a stop by her favorite spot overlooking the Steel Bridge. Of the many bridges that crossed the river, this one was her favorite. Unique in its vertical-lift and double-deck structure, the bridge had stood since 1912, weathering many storms, carrying countless travelers back and forth. Reliable and sturdy.

Walking to the guardrail she leaned against it and inhaled the fresh morning air as Sean came up behind her. Strong arms looped around her waist, drawing her back against solid muscle. Reliable and sturdy. She curled into him, humming her pleasure when his chin came to rest on the top of her head. When he held her like this, cocooned in his strength, she felt completely protected.

"I can't believe he's dead." She spoke into the open air, her gaze tracking the ribbon of cars crossing the bridge.

Sean's arms pulled tighter.

After the incident in the alley, Ivy decided that after three years, she was done shoulder checking. Done worrying about where *he* was and if she would see *him* again. Done living in fear that she'd be blindsided like she had been that night at the bar with Adam. She was tired of seeing ghosts everywhere she went. Of wondering if he knew where she was.

So one evening, after Thai takeout and half a tub of Ben and Jerry's, she'd opened her laptop and asked Sean to sit beside her on the couch. With his arm around her shoulders, holding her close, she Googled Ethan's name.

It seemed like something she should have done ages ago, but the stranglehold of her fear had often prevented her from doing the simplest things. Like type a name into a search engine. As if Ethan could climb through the screen and grab her. As if he could check her search history and track her down. As if he even remembered her.

But it turned out, none of those thoughts mattered, because the first thing that popped up when she hit the Enter button was Ethan's obituary.

The news landed with a dull thud. On the one hand, she'd been robbed of the closure she was finally ready for. On the other, she was relieved that no matter what her recovery looked like down the road, she never had to be afraid of *him* again. It was over. The stuff of her nightmares was gone. And there was a respite in that. A different kind of closure.

After a bit more digging, she'd come across a short

article in a local paper where the incident had occurred. Apparently, Ethan had gotten behind the wheel drunk and driven into a building. The article outlined the accident in clipped professional tones, noting that no one else had been involved, the driver had been killed on impact, and the property damage caused by the collision had been minimal considering the speed involved.

In the span of a few short paragraphs, Ivy's whole outlook shifted.

"Burning in the hell of his own making, I like to imagine," Sean said.

"Do you think he regretted what he did?" It was a question with no answer, and even if there was, it changed nothing.

"Ivy—"

"Never mind, forget it. That was a dumb thing to ask." And yet, tears burned in her eyes and blurred her vision.

Sean turned her in his arms, tipping her gaze up with a jerk of his chin. "It's not dumb." He dipped to kiss her nose, holding her eyes as he did it. "And I think that he probably did have regret, in the way anyone who breaks something beautiful and precious would." He brushed away the tear that had trailed down her cheek. "But regret hits differently for everyone. Some people lean into it and do their penance, whatever that might look like. Others turn away from it. Find excuses for it. Do whatever it takes to help them sleep at night. Drink till they're stupid, then drive their car into a concrete building."

A stretch of silence hung between them, before Sean said, "Would it make a difference? Knowing if he regretted it?"

She thought about that as she pressed her cheek against his chest and breathed in the comforting scent of him. "Nah.

What made the difference all came from me. From inside me. I'm free of that bastard now. After everything he put me through, I still found this great life. I have a career I am proud of, friends who love and support me. I feel safe and trust myself again. I'm not scared anymore, Sean. I learned how to love my body again, and how to let it feel love. He's God's problem now. Or the Devil's. I have my vengeance. And it's right here."

Emotion, intense and undefinable, swelled in her chest and threatened to erupt. But in front of her, Sean tipped back his head and laughed. It was a loud belly laugh that filled the air around them.

Smiling at his infectious howl, she stood there confused. Then he lifted her by the waist, twirling her around before crushing her to his chest in a hug that stole her breath.

"I love you, Ivy Harrington. More than anything. You set yourself free and you took me with you."

Love. For herself, for him, for the new life they were starting.

Ivy hugged Sean back with all her might as she said, "We set each other free."

They sealed her declaration with a kiss. Then, with the sun shining brightly over Portland, they jogged back down the river, heading home to build their life together.

Thank you for reading *Finding Freedom!* Keep reading to see how writing a book review can mean the world to an indie author like me!

DEAR READER

I hope you enjoyed Ivy and Sean's story. If you did, please consider posting a review and telling all of your friends who like heartfelt, contemporary romance with plenty of steam.

Review wherever you purchased *Finding Freedom* or on Goodreads, BookBub, or social media.

Leaving a positive review is a quick and easy way to support an indie author and they mean so much to us. Every time I read a positive review from a reader it fills up my whole bucket.

Don't be a stranger! Let's keep in touch. For exclusive updates and content, join my newsletter at ValentinaBurns.com

Valentina

ABOUT THE AUTHOR

Valentina Burns is a contemporary romance author living on Vancouver Island with her husband, two children, and a multitude of pets. When she was fifteen, she picked up her very first romance novel at her high school fall fair, and has been devouring the genre ever since. She's long dreamed of writing her own romance books and is inspired by stories with strong female protagonists and their swoon-worthy, well-muscled heroes. She loves to create believable and relatable characters that readers can connect with. Drawing upon her own life experiences, Valentina writes books that are genuine, emotional, and entertaining, with more than a little heat served on the side.

For exclusive updates and content, join Valentina's newsletter at ValentinaBurns.com

Where to find Valentina:

amazon.com/Valentina-Burns/e/B0C3Y7JN3J

goodreads.com/valentinaburns

bookbub.com/authors/valentina-burns

instagram.com/valentinaburnswrites

facebook.com/valentinaburnswrites

tiktok.com/@valentinaburnswrites

x.com/ValentinaBurns_

ACKNOWLEDGEMENTS

Thank you for reading *Finding Freedom!* This story was not easy to write, probably because it is very close to my heart. I poured a lot of myself into writing this book, not always sure how it would land with readers, and I was left feeling quite exposed and vulnerable by the end of it. I mention in the Author's Note that *Finding Freedom* is not meant to be a depiction of everyone's experience, but it is the story I needed to tell. And tell it I did, but it took an entire village, as well as the surrounding countryside, to make it happen.

To my family, the most incredible support system, I don't know how I got so lucky to have you in my life. Your enthusiasm and pride mean everything, and carried me through many hard days of self-doubt and set-backs. I love you all so much.

To Lindsay and Kate, for being the very first ones to read these pages. You always read anything I give you—in its rawest, most unedited state—and I love you for it.

Jackie, the world's more incredible friend/beta-reader/proofreader. I will never ever publish a book without your eyes on it. Ever. Your feedback is invaluable, your friendship even more so.

Emma, who reviewed this book for its sensitive content. Thank you for bringing your experience, expertise, and heart to this story. You helped me shape it into something truly beautiful and touching, and it is better because of you.

Erin, for coming through at the eleventh hour and proofreading. The Book Club Beauties–you gals saved me during this writing process, in more ways than one. I'm so glad we started our little group.

Supper Club Moms!! Ladies, you critique my content while sipping cocktails at the bar. You are the best friends a girl could ask for.

Of course, Jane, because these characters would not have a single ounce of fashion sense if not for you. Nor would I.

And all my indie author friends and champions, thank you for putting up with me: Joelle, Luna, Kay, MJ, Nomi, Marae, Kiira, Anna, Jillian, and Liz. It is so special to me to have this community of women who know, love, and write the same things I do. I stand on your shoulders.

Thank you especially to my editor, Jacqui, for digging deep and pulling out the very best of this story. Being able to work with you is magic. I am so grateful.

And to the Bookstagram and BookTok communities, online friends, readers, and reviewers. You have made my every dream come true. Your kindness, enthusiasm, and support helped make me be brave enough to share this story of my heart. Thank you for always loving my characters and begging for more. Thank you for leaving reviews and making incredible posts that are so inspired and creative. Thank you for filling my bucket and for encouraging me to continue down this path.

And Matt. Always Matt. The one love of my life. You took this shaky heart and made it steady. It beats to match yours now. I love you forever.

Finally, to the women I cannot name on page. You inspire me. Your bravery, determination, grit, and tenacity overwhelm me. I wish you knew how much you've changed me. Now let's change the world, for our daughters, and for the future.

xo Valentina